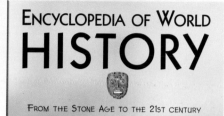

ENCYCLOPEDIA OF WORLD
HISTORY

FROM THE STONE AGE TO THE 21ST CENTURY

ENCYCLOPEDIA OF WORLD
HISTORY

FROM THE STONE AGE TO THE 21ST CENTURY

p

This is a Parragon Publishing Book
This edition published in 2005

Parragon Publishing
Queen Street House
4 Queen Street
Bath BA1 1HE, UK

Copyright © Parragon 2003

This edition was created by
Starry Dog Books

Consultant Editors
Brian Williams, Brenda Williams

Authors
Anita Ganeri, Hazel Mary Martell, Brian Williams

Illustrators
Martin Camm, Richard Hook, Rob Jakeway, John James, Shane Marsh, Roger Payne, Mark Peppé,
Eric Rowe, Peter Sarson, Roger Smith, Ross Watton, Michael Welply and Michael White

British Library Cataloguing-in-Publication Data

A catalogue record for this book is available from the British Library

ISBN 1-40545-896-8

Printed in Indonesia

Contents

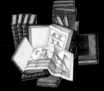

8

Discovering the Past

WHAT IS HISTORY? In its broadest sense, history is the story of people – the study of our past. Some historians look at important events, such as wars, revolutions, and governments, while others are interested in ordinary people's lives. Henry Ford, the American car manufacturer, once said "History is bunk," but most people would disagree. Our lives today are shaped by decisions and actions made decades, centuries, or even thousands of years ago. By understanding the past, we may be able to gain a more balanced view of the present.

Alabaster canopic jars from the tomb of an ancient Egyptian. We can find out a lot about ancient peoples from their religious beliefs. The Egyptians believed in life after death, and filled their tombs with things they thought they would need in the afterlife.

THE BASIC AIMS of history are to record and explain our past. Historians study a range of written and oral (spoken) evidence. Combined with archeology (the study of things people have left behind them, such as buildings and objects), historians interpret the facts to build up a picture of the past.

The first people to study history seriously were the ancient Greeks. In the 5th century BC, the Greek historian Herodotus (known as "the Father of History") set out to write a true and systematic record of the wars between the Greeks and the Persians. He hoped to preserve the memory of past events and show how two peoples came into conflict with one another.

A cuneiform writing tablet. Cuneiform was the first system of writing. The oldest tablets date from about 5,000 years ago. Ancient written records like this are the raw materials of history. Before writing, history was passed on by word of mouth.

↑ A historian studying the life of a medieval knight would look at the buildings of the time, such as this Crusader castle in Syria.

▶ Navigational instruments like this one were used in the 15th century by explorers in search of new lands. Throughout history, new inventions have changed the world and increased our knowledge.

The scientific study of archeology only began in the 18th century. Archeologists today investigate even the tiniest fragments left behind by our ancestors to help create a more complete picture of the past.

Interpreting the evidence is the most fascinating part of a historian's or archeologist's job. Historians, however, must always be aware of bias or prejudice in the things that they read or write. Bias means being influenced by a particular point of view, while prejudice means "judging before" – before you have all the facts. Historians themselves are influenced by the times they live in. Modern historians try to avoid applying the values and beliefs of the present to their interpretations of the past.

History is not just concerned with the distant past. It is the story of our lives – what is news today will be history tomorrow. Change can be sudden and dramatic, and long-held ideas may be overturned.

◀ Pictures can tell us much about life in the past, showing us people's homes, clothes, jobs, and food. This painting was done for the Duc du Berry (1340–1416).

▶ This carved ivory mask was worn as an ornament by the oba, or king, of Benin – a powerful African empire from the 14th to the 17th centuries. The wealth and sophistication of Benin was expressed in its art.

10

Historical Evidence

BEFORE historians can interpret the past, they must first establish the facts about the events they are studying. Historians look for evidence by researching many documents and records, called historical sources.

PRIMARY SOURCES are accounts written by people involved in the events, and include government and legal papers, wills, maps, business agreements, letters, and diaries. Historians read a wide range of texts, not just actual

▶ Julius Caesar (c. 101–44 BC) was a great general and dictator of Rome. He wrote an account of his conquest of Gaul (France). History is sometimes written by those who take a major part in it.

accounts of past events, but also works such as prayer books, which show the interests and beliefs of people in the past. Historians also look for evidence from government census records, and birth, death, and marriage registers. Possibly the most famous census ever carried out was the Domesday Book, compiled in 1086 by order of William the Conqueror, king of England. This was the first thorough survey of part of the British Isles, detailing who owned the land, who lived there and how much it was worth. No survey of the British Isles was conducted again until 1801.

▶ Viking rune stones tell stories from Viking history, recalling battles and heroic deeds.

▼ The Domesday Book was a nationwide survey of England (except for the far north). It was written in two large volumes. People had to answer questions under oath about their land and its value.

Historians also look for secondary sources – these are studies of primary sources made at a later date. Secondary sources include such documents as newspaper reports, or the books of previous historians. Newspapers provide many different opinions about an event, giving historians a valuable overview of what happened.

Texts are not always written in books or on paper. Over the centuries, people

☑ Leonardo da Vinci (1452–1519) was a pioneer inventor and artist, whose ideas were way ahead of his time. He drew detailed designs of a flying machine, from which a life-sized model was made and flown in 2002.

have written on clay, bone, silk, metal, stone, and wood. Even cultures that never developed a system of writing invented their own ways of keeping records. The Incas of Peru, for example, had a very advanced civilization, yet never developed writing. They recorded information using knotted lengths of string, called *quipus*.

Oral history is often a vital source of information, too. For thousands of years people have passed on their history by word of mouth, from generation to generation, in stories, songs, and poems. Today, historians make films and tape recordings as a record of events.

COPERNICANVM
Systema
TIVS CREATI
THESI
CANA IN
EXHIBITVM

↥ Nicolaus Copernicus (1473–1543) was the first person to suggest that the Earth went around the Sun. This is an illustration of his idea. Illustrations and maps like this can show us how much people knew about the world.

▶ Diaries provide invaluable eye-witness accounts of everyday life. Anne Frank's diary is a vivid account of life for Jews in Nazi-occupied Europe during World War II.

Archeological Evidence

ARCHEOLOGY is the study of the physical remains of the past – everything from a priceless statue to a garbage tip. It can tell us about societies that existed before written records were made.

▶ In 1922, Howard Carter (on the left) opened Tutankhamen's tomb in Egypt. The discovery of the tomb caused a sensation in archeology. It was filled with fabulous 3,500-year-old treasures!

IN THE PAST, some archeologists were little more than treasure-seekers. Today they use scientific methods to analyze their finds, preserve them, and build a picture of the past. Archeologists study artifacts (objects), features (buildings), and ecofacts (seeds or animal bones). Artifacts such as pottery, glass, and metal survive well, although often broken into many fragments. Objects made of organic materials, such as wood, leather, and fabric, usually rot, but can survive in the sea, rivers, bogs, desertlike areas, and freezing conditions.

▶ Paintings like this one, made by prehistoric hunters about 17,000 years ago, show what kind of animals people hunted for food.

By studying the remains of human skeletons, experts can tell how tall people were, what age they lived to and what diseases they suffered from. Burials often reveal a lot about the social structure of a society, as well as its beliefs. Remains such as animal bones and shells can tell us about people's diets, while seeds, pollen, and insect remains can build up a picture of their environment.

◀ Stonehenge in England was built from about 2800 BC to 2000 BC. No one is sure exactly what this stone circle was used for, but it may have been a giant Sun calendar.

When archeologists discover a site they want to examine, they set up an excavation, or dig. Most archeologists today work on rescue digs, attempting to record a site before it is destroyed, often by modern construction. Other sites for digs are identified by looking at maps, documents, or air photographs, which can reveal traces of buildings or fields that cannot be seen from the ground.

▶ A vast army of terracotta soldiers, armed with real weapons, was discovered guarding the tomb of China's first emperor, Shi Huangdi, who died in 210 BC.

At a dig, archeologists carefully remove layers of soil and record even the smallest evidence of past human activity. Many sites have had different inhabitants at different times. Usually, the top layers of soil reveal the most recent occupants.

The specific date of an object may be found by examining historical records or by comparing it with other similar finds whose date is known. Radiocarbon dating is a scientific technique used to help date objects. All living things contain some radioactive carbon, or C14. After a living thing dies, C14 decays (its atoms break down) at a known rate. If the amount of C14 in an organic find is known, its age can be estimated. This technique is used to date objects between about 40,000 years ago and AD 1500.

◤ This body of a woman was found preserved in a peat bog. She was buried in Denmark in AD 95. The peat prevented her flesh from rotting away, unlike most dead bodies.

▶ An archeological dig in Peru. The position and location of objects found in a dig can provide important clues as to their age and use. Every find must be carefully recorded.

The Ancient World

FROM PREHISTORIC TIMES TO AD 500

THE VAST PERIOD of time from 2.5 million years ago to AD 500 saw the appearance of the first human beings and the creation of the first civilizations. Our earliest ancestors appeared in Africa some 2.5 million years ago, having evolved from man-apes who came down from the trees and learned to walk upright on two legs.

OVER THOUSANDS OF YEARS, people learned how to make fire to keep themselves warm and to cook their food, how to hunt, and how to make tools. The first-ever metal tools and weapons were made in the Near East about 7,000 years ago.

Throughout the world, early people lived by hunting animals and gathering wild fruit, roots, and nuts to eat. By 10,000 years ago, however, an extraordinary change was taking place. People learned how to grow their own crops on patches of land and to raise their own animals for food. For the first

c. 2.5–2 million years BC	c. 40,000 BC	c. 10,000 BC	c. 8000 BC	c. 3500 BC	c. 2580 BC	c. 2500 BC	c. 1850 BC
Homo habilis appears in Africa. They are the first people to make tools.	Our direct ancestors, Homo sapiens, appear in many parts of the world.	The last Ice Age comes to an end.	Farming begins and the first towns are built in the Near East.	The Sumerians of Mesopotamia invent writing and the wheel.	The Great Pyramid at Giza, Egypt, is built.	The Indus civilization in ancient India is at its height.	Abraham leads his people from Ur to Canaan.

time in history, people began to build permanent homes, followed by towns and cities.

By about 5000 BC, the world's first civilizations began to emerge along the banks of rivers where the land was extremely rich for farming. The Sumerians, Assyrians, and Babylonians built magnificent cities and temples on the fertile plains between the Tigris and Euphrates rivers. The ancient Egyptians flourished along the river Nile. By about 500 BC, important civilizations had also appeared in India, China, Persia, and in North and South America.

The great age of ancient Greece and Rome is known as the Classical period. These two mighty civilizations played a major role in shaping the modern world. From Greece came discoveries in politics, philosophy, and science. These were spread farther afield by the Greek conqueror Alexander the Great, and by the Romans, who were great admirers of Greek culture and knowledge.

The Romans added achievements of their own and, by the 1st century AD, ruled over the most powerful empire ever seen. But by AD 500 their empire had fallen. The Middle Ages had begun.

1600–1100 BC	753 BC	c. 605–562 BC	269–232 BC	221 BC	27 BC–AD 14	AD 286	AD 476
Mycenaeans dominate mainland Greece.	Traditional date for the founding of Rome.	Reign of King Nebuchadnezzar II, who rebuilds the city of Babylon.	Reign of Emperor Ashoka Maurya in India.	Shi Huangdi unites China; he is its first emperor.	Augustus rules as the first Roman emperor.	The Roman empire is divided into west and east.	The last western emperor of Rome is deposed.

The First Humans

THERE HAS BEEN life on Earth for some 300 million years, but the first humanlike creatures appeared about 7 million years ago. These "man-apes" came down from the trees in which they, like other primates, lived. They walked on two legs and used tools.

This map shows the location of important fossil remains of early hominids and humans. *Homo erectus* was the first great colonizer, spreading out of Africa. Scientists still argue whether *Homo sapiens* first appeared in Africa or developed in other parts of the world.

THE TOUMAI SKULL found in Chad, in Africa, in 2002 may be a clue to the oldest hominid or humanlike creature known. Some scientists think it is 7 million years old. The fossil record then jumps to about 4 million years ago, when the Australopithecines lived in Africa. The most complete skeleton of an

A set of Australopithecine footprints was found by Mary Leakey in 1978, preserved in volcanic ash at Laetoli, Kenya. It showed that early hominids walked upright on two legs.

Australopithecus

Homo habilis

c. 4 million years ago
Australopithecus (meaning "southern ape") appear in Africa. They walk upright on two legs instead of on all fours.

c. 2.5–1.5 million years ago
Homo habilis ("handy man") appear in Africa. They are the first people to make and use tools.

c. 1.5 million years ago
Homo erectus ("upright man") appear in Africa. They are the first people to spread out of Africa.

c. 120,000 years ago
The Neanderthals, a sub-species of *Homo sapiens* ("wise man"), appear in Africa, Asia, and Europe. They are the first humans to bury their dead.

ustralopithecus was found in thiopia in 1974. The individual, icknamed "Lucy," died about million years ago, aged about 40. he was as tall as a 10-year-old.

The first true human beings, nown as *Homo habilis* (Latin for "handy an"), appeared about 2.5 million years go. They had bigger brains and made

FIRE
People first made fire by striking two flints together. It gave them protection from wild animals, allowed them to cook food, and provided heat and light.

tools from sticks and stones. A million years later another species, *Homo erectus* ("upright man") had appeared and gradually spread out of Africa into Europe and Asia. These early humans made better tools (for hunting), built shelters, and also used fire.

Many scientists believe that modern humans, *Homo sapiens* ("wise man"), evolved from these hominids. Two species lived side by side: Neanderthal people and modern people. By about 20,000 years ago the Neanderthals had died out, and modern humans, *Homo sapiens sapiens*, had spread to all of the continents.

omo erectus

Homo sapiens neanderthalensis

Homo sapiens sapiens

◄ As early people evolved, they gradually became less like apes and more like humans. They developed larger brains, and bodies designed for walking upright, with longer legs than arms. Standing upright left their hands free for using tools and weapons.

35,000 years ago
mo sapiens sapiens modern humans") living in many rts of the world, cluding Australia.

c. 30,000 years ago
The Neanderthals die out as modern humans appear in Asia and Europe.

c. 20,000 years ago
Modern humans have crossed from Asia into the Americas.

Making Tools

THE FIRST KNOWN tools were made by *Homo habilis* more than 2 million years ago. These were very simple tools made from pebbles. Gradually tools became more advanced. People soon discovered that flint was one of the best tool-making materials. Not only was it very hard, but it could also be chipped into many different shapes and sizes.

Stone lamp Flint cutter Flint fire lighter

Antler spearhead

Stone Age tools included lamps, cutters, and spearheads. For 98 percent of the time that people have lived on Earth, their tools have been made from stone, bone, wood, ivory, and antler.

USING A PEBBLE as a hammer, early people shaped flints into sharp-edged hand axes, knives, scrapers, and choppers. When blunt, the edges were resharpened with more chipping. Hand axes are among the oldest-known tools, with some dating from about 2 million years ago. They were used for cutting plants, meat, and skins.

Hand axe

Stone Age people used flint blades to skin animals and scrape them clean. The hides were used for making clothes, tents, and bags. Pieces were sewn together using needles made of antler or bone.

Flint scraper

Flint, bone, and antler were also used for making weapons. Bows and arrows were first used about 15,000 years ago. About 7,000 years ago, people in the Near East learned how to make metal tools from copper. By 3000 BC they were using a stronger alloy of copper – the Bronze Age had begun.

c. 2 million–12,000 years ago
The Old Stone (Paleolithic) Age. First stone tools made.

From 12,000 years ago
The Middle Stone (Mesolithic) Age. Greater variety of stone tools made.

From 10,000 years ago
The New Stone (Neolithic) Age. Stone sickles and hoes.

c. 7,000 years ago
The Copper Age begins in the Near East. First metal tools.

5,500 years ago
The Bronze Age begins in the Near East. Copper is first used in Europe.

3,000 years ago
The Iron Age begins in Europe. (Iron is used from c. 700 BC in the Near East and Africa.)

Cave Art

THE EARLIEST works of art were created some 40,000 years ago. During the last Ice Age, early artists painted pictures of the animals they hunted – bulls, reindeer, and buffalo – on the walls of the caves they sheltered in.

An almost life-sized painting of a buffalo decorates the ceiling of the Altamira caves in Spain. It is about 14,000 years old.

PAINTS WERE MADE from minerals such as clay, lime, and charcoal, ground into a powder and mixed with water or animal fat. They were applied with brushes made of fur, feathers, moss, or frayed twigs. The paintings were not done simply for decoration. They may have had a religious or magical meaning. Perhaps the painters thought they could bring good luck in the hunt.

Cave paintings have been found in Europe, Africa, Asia, and Australia. Europe's most famous paintings cover the walls of the Altamira caves (Spain) and Lascaux caves (France).

Painted between 17,000 and 12,000 years ago, they include buffalo, mammoths, horses, reindeer, and four huge white bulls. The Lascaux caves were rediscovered in 1940 by four schoolboys, out looking for their dog. The caves are now closed to the public, but full-sized copies of the prehistoric masterpieces have been made for people to see.

STONE SCULPTURE

This sandstone figure from Austria is one of the oldest sculptures found. It was made about 24,000 years ago. Called the Venus of Willendorf, it stands 4 inches (10.5 cm) high. Several similar statues have been found in Europe. They may represent mother goddesses, carved to bring good luck.

A buffalo carved from antler about 29,000 years ago. Its detail shows that the artist must have closely observed real buffalo.

c. 40,000 years ago	c. 29,000 years ago	c. 26,000 years ago	c. 24,000 years ago	c. 17,000–12,000 years ago
Rock engravings in Australia – may be the oldest art found.	Mammoth hunters make clay figures of people.	Cave paintings made in Namibia, Africa.	Venus of Willendorf is carved in Austria.	Animals are painted on cave walls at Lascaux, France.

Life in the Ice Age

DURING long periods of the Earth's history, large areas of land have been covered by ice. As temperatures fell, sheets of ice up to 650 feet (200 m) thick spread across land and sea. The last of these ice ages had a dramatic effect on human and animal life.

THE EARLIEST ICE AGE occurred some 2,300 million years ago. Geological evidence shows that succeeding ice ages lasted from between 20 and 50 million years. As the climate cooled, glaciers formed at the North and South poles. The ice advanced and retreated in waves, known as glaciations.

Men hunted mammoths in groups. They would either corner one of the huge beasts up against a cliff or trap it in a pit dug across its migration route. Then they killed it with spears and stones, and removed the skin, tusks and meat.

c. 2 million years ago
The Quaternary ice age begins. It consists of 17 glacials (cold periods) separated by 17 interglacials (warmer periods).

c. 24,000 years ago
The Ice Age enters its latest glacial. Ice covers about a third of the Earth. Sea levels fall by over 300 feet (90 m).

c. 22,000 years ago
Hunter-gatherers cross from Asia into North America via the Bering Strait "land bridge."

c. 18,000 years ago
The last Ice Age reaches its coldest point. People living at Mezhirich in the Ukraine build huts from mammoth bones and tusks.

HOW ANIMALS ADAPTED

This baby mammoth was found, perfectly preserved, in the frozen ground of Siberia, Russia. Animals had to adapt to survive the Ice Age. Some, such as the mammoth and the woolly rhinoceros, grew larger, because a bigger body is better at conserving heat.

The most recent Ice Age entered its coldest period about 22,000 years ago, when ice sheets covered much of North America and northern Eurasia. As the seas froze, the sea level fell by over 300 feet (90 m) in places, exposing "bridges" of land between land masses. The Bering Strait between Siberia and Alaska became dry land, allowing animals such as mammoths and deer to move between Asia and North America. After them came human hunters, the first humans to colonize North America. Camels and horses, moved from the Americas into Asia. When the climate warmed, the ice melted, sea levels rose, and this and other land bridges disappeared.

Conditions were extremely harsh for the people who lived near the ice sheets. Woolly mammoths were a valuable source of meat, skin (for clothes), and bones (for weapons and carvings). Men hunted in groups, driving the mammoths up against cliffs so they could close in for the kill. They attacked with sharp spears made of flint and wood, and large stones. One mammoth provided enough meat to last many months. Leftovers were stored in holes dug in the frozen ground. Bones and tusks made a framework for huts, which were covered with hides and turf.

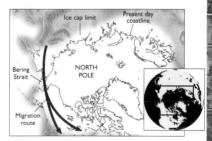

This map shows the extent of the ice cover in the Northern Hemisphere during the last Ice Age. "Land bridges" exposed by the drop in sea level allowed people and animals to migrate between Asia and North America.

14,000 years ago	c. 12,000 years ago	c. 8,000 years ago
The Bering Strait floods over again as the ice melts and sea levels rise.	In Europe, glaciers retreat and the Ice Age ends.	Rising sea level separates Britain from the continent of Europe.

The First Farmers

FOR MOST of human history, people found food by hunting wild animals and gathering berries, nuts, and roots. They lived as nomads, following the herds of animals they hunted. Then, about 10,000 years ago, a huge change took place. People learned how to grow crops and rear animals for food.

INSTEAD OF HAVING to roam farther and farther afield to find food to eat, people found they could grow enough for their families on a small plot of land. This meant that they had to settle in one place all year round and build permanent homes. These people were the first farmers. Their farming settlements grew to become the first villages, which in turn grew to become the first towns.

☑ On farms in Europe in about 3000 BC, people made clay pots, which they fired in kilns and used for storing grain and water. They used stone axes to fell trees and clear land, and stone sickles to harvest crops. They also spun wool and wove it into cloth on looms (far left).

c. 10,500 BC	c. 8000 BC	c. 7000 BC	c. 6500 BC
The first clay pots are made in Japan.	Farming begins in the Near East in an area known as the Fertile Crescent, and in Southeast Asia. Sheep are domesticated in Iraq.	Farming develops in Central and South America. Clay pots for storing grain and water are made in the Near East and Africa.	The oldest-known textiles are woven at Çatal Hüyük in Turkey.

DESERT ROCK ART

Cave paintings in Algeria dating from 10,000 years ago show people hunting giraffe, hippos, and elephant. Later paintings show farmers tending herds of cattle. After about 3000 BC, when the Sahara's climate became drier, the rock art shows desert animals, such as camels.

The first farms developed in the Near East and Europe in a region known as the Fertile Crescent (shaded area). Farming spread throughout Europe and western Asia, but it developed independently in the rest of Asia and in the Americas.

Plants and animals that are grown or raised by people are known as "domesticated." The first domesticated plants and animals were developed from those found in the wild. Wheat and barley, which had grown wild in parts of the Near East for thousands of years, were two of the first crops to be domesticated. People collected seeds from these wild plants and sowed them in ground dug over with deer antlers. (Plows were not invented until about 6,000 years ago.) The next year, the crop was harvested and the grain ground into flour to make bread, which was baked on hot stones. Farmers also learned how to tame wild sheep, goats, and pigs and breed them, so they no longer had to go hunting for their meat.

6000 BC	c. 5000 BC	c. 4400 BC	c. 4000 BC
eer, made om grain, is rewed in the ear East.	Farming is adopted in China and Egypt and spreads to Europe. It also begins in India, along the Indus and Ganges river valleys.	Horses are domesticated in eastern Europe and used for riding for the first time.	The first plows, made of sharp, forked sticks, are used in the Near East. The earliest plow marks discovered were in Mesopotamia.

The First Towns

ONCE people began to farm and to settle in permanent villages, the world's population grew rapidly. Towns grew up with a more complex way of life. More houses were built, services such as roads, drainage systems, and shops were established, and trade between towns flourished.

LITTLE IS known about the first towns. But the ruins of two ancient towns – Jericho in Jordan and Çatal Hüyük in Turkey – have given archeologists a fascinating glimpse into the past.

Jericho dates from about 8000 BC, and is one of the oldest towns to have been excavated. It was built near a natural spring used by farmers to water their fields. Wheat and barley were grown, and sheep and goats raised. Jericho stood on an important trade route and quickly grew wealthy. Among the goods traded were obsidian (a volcanic, glassy rock), shells, and semi-precious stones. Massive stone walls, some 9 feet (3 m) thick, kept out enemies. A lookout was kept from a 30-feet (9-m) tall circular watchtower. Inside the walls were small, circular houses made of mud bricks. At one time up to 2,000 people lived there. Jericho's

⬆ People have lived in the town of Jericho continuously since about 8000 BC. In the 8th century AD, the Arabic ruler Caliph Hisham ibn Abd al-Malik started to build a palace there, for use as a royal hunting lodge. Hisham's Palace was never completed, but its ruins (above) are still standing.

walls were destroyed many times,
but not by invading enemies. They were
toppled by a series of earthquakes.

Çatal Hüyük was built on a fertile river
plain. Its people grew wheat, barley, and
vegetables. Cattle-breeding was also
important. The town controlled the trade
in obsidian, used for making tools and
weapons. By 6500 BC, some 5,000 people
lived there. They lived in rectangular

> This skull of a young
woman was found in
Jericho. It may have been
used in religious rituals of
ancestor worship.

The town of
Çatal Hüyük in about
6000 BC. Rooms were
painted with vultures and
headless men, and contained
plaster bulls' heads and
statuettes of mother goddesses.
The men shown dressed as vultures (in the
center) are priests. It is thought that the dead
were put on platforms for vultures to pick clean.

houses, interconnected with no outside
doors. People entered through holes in
the roofs, reached by ladders. If the town
was attacked, the ladders were drawn
up, leaving no obvious means of entry.

c. 9000 BC
A shrine stands
on the site of
ancient Jericho
in the Near East.

c. 8000 BC
Jericho, built on the west bank of the
river Jordan, thrives – some 2,000
people live there. The first bricks are
made by Jericho's people.

c. 7000 BC
Jericho is destroyed by
an earthquake (the town
is later rebuilt). Çatal
Hüyük is founded.

c. 6500 BC
Some 5,000 people live in Çatal
Hüyük. Linen, made from flax,
is woven into cloth for clothes –
the oldest known textiles.

Mesopotamia and Sumer

ONE OF THE world's earliest civilizations grew up on the fertile plains between the rivers Tigris and Euphrates, in what is now Iraq. The area became known as Mesopotamia, "the land between the two rivers." About 5000 BC, the Sumerians settled in southern Mesopotamia.

◀ Writing was invented in Sumer in about 3500 BC, as a way of keeping temple records and merchants' accounts. This clay tablet shows the cuneiform ("wedge shaped") symbols used to represent words.

◢ A great ziggurat, or stepped temple, was built in the city of Ur by King Ur-Nammu in about 2100 BC.

Shrine to the Moon god Nanna at the very to[p]

◀ The Sumerians made splendid jewelry from gold and silver inlaid with semi-precious stones. Craft workers also made furniture, wine cups, and musical instruments. Such treasures were found in the Royal Tombs at Ur when they were excavated.

As earlier mud-brick temples fell into ruin, new temples were built on top, raising the platform higher and higher

c. 5000 BC	c. 4000 BC	c. 3500 BC	c. 2900–2400 BC
Early Sumerians begin to farm in Ubaid, southern Mesopotamia (Iraq).	The start of the Uruk Period. The Sumerians learn how to smelt metal. They use sailing boats on the Tigris and Euphrates rivers.	The Sumerians invent writing and the wheel. They discover how to make bronze from copper and tin.	The Early Dynastic Period. Kings are established in the main Sumerian cities.

THE FERTILE LAND of Mesopotamia was ideal for growing crops. Farmers soon learned how to build irrigation canals to bring water from the rivers to their fields. As more food was grown, the population increased, and by about 3500 BC some villages had grown into thriving towns. The towns of Ur and Uruk grew to become cities, and then independent city-states.

The cities were ruled by Councils of Elders, who appointed *lugals* (generals) to lead the armies in times of war. As wars between rival cities became more frequent, the lugals' powers grew, and from about 2900 BC the lugals were kings, ruling for life.

In the center of each city stood a temple to the city's patron god or goddess. The Sumerians believed the gods controlled every aspect

The Sumerians may have built reed houses similar to those of the Marsh Arabs, who live on the banks of the river Tigris in southern Iraq.

of nature and everyday life. It was vital to keep the gods happy with daily offerings, or they might send wars, floods, or disease to punish the people.

The Sumerians were expert at math. They had two systems of counting. One was decimal, like the system we use today; the other used units of 60 (the Sumerians were the first people to divide an hour into 60 minutes). They also devised a calendar, a complex legal system, and used the wheel for pot-making and on carts. But their most important invention was writing.

GILGAMESH

The most famous of the Sumerians' many myths and legends is the epic of King Gilgamesh and his quest to find the secret of eternal life. He learns that a plant that gives immortality grows at the bottom of the sea, but the plant is stolen by a snake before he can use it.

c. 2400–2100 BC	c. 2300 BC	c. 2100 BC	c. 2000 BC
Sumer is conquered by the Akkadians, then by the Gutians.	The Sumerian city of Agade dominates the region.	The city of Ur reaches the height of its power under King Ur-Nammu.	The epic of Gilgamesh is first written down. The city of Ur is destroyed by the Elamites. Sumerian civilization comes to an end.

Ancient Egypt

WITHOUT the life-giving waters of the river Nile, ancient Egypt would have been a barren desert, too dry for farming. The river gave the ancient Egyptians drinking water, as well as water for irrigation. It also deposited rich soil along its banks each year when it flooded.

ALONG THE Nile's banks, farmers grew wheat and barley (for bread and beer), flax (for linen), and fruit and vegetables. They also raised cattle, sheep, and goats. So vital was the river that the Greek historian Herodotus described ancient Egypt as the "gift of the Nile."

Boats were the main form of transportation, used for fishing, hunting, and carrying cargo and passengers. When a pharaoh died, his body was taken by barge to his tomb.

Queen Nefertiti was the chief wife of King Akhenaten, who ruled Egypt from about 1364–1347 BC Akhenaten and Nefertiti ha six daughters, one of whom married King Tutankhamen.

The first villages of ancient Egypt appeared some 7,000 years ago. In time these small settlements increased and two kingdoms were created – Lower Egypt in the Nile delta and Upper Egypt along the river valley. In about 3100 BC, King Menes, the ruler of Upper Egypt, united the two kingdoms and built his capital at Memphis. He established the first dynasty (line of kings) of ancient Egypt.

Farmers at work in Egypt. The farmers' year was split into three parts: the Inundation (July to November) when the Nile flooded, the Growing Season (December to March), and Harvest (March to July). When the flood made farmwork impossible, farmers were sent to work on the royal buildings.

c. 5000–3100 BC	c. 4000 BC	c. 3200 BC	c. 3100 BC	c. 3100–2686
Predynastic Period in Egypt. Several cultures appear along the Nile valley.	Boats on the Nile use sails for the first time.	Early hieroglyphs are used in Egypt.	King Menes unites Lower and Upper Egypt.	Archaic Period (Dynasties 1 and 2).

PYRAMID CONSTRUCTION

No one knows exactly how the pyramids were built. It is thought that stone blocks, some as heavy as cars, were pulled to the site on wooden sleds dragged by teams of workers, then hauled up a series of spiral mud and brick ramps into place. Layer by layer the pyramid grew. Finally, the capstone at the top was added and the whole structure covered in white limestone casing blocks. Then the ramps were dismantled.

The king was the most powerful person in ancient Egypt. He was worshiped as the god Horus. From about 2554 BC, the king was given the title "pharaoh," from the Egyptian words "per a," meaning "great house." Two officials, called viziers, helped him govern and collect taxes. Officials also ran the major state departments – the Treasury, the Royal Works (which supervised the building of pyramids and tombs), the Granaries, Cattle, and Foreign Affairs. Every aspect of Egyptian life was under the pharaoh's control.

2686–50 BC	c. 2589–2566 BC	c. 2580 BC	c. 2246–2150 BC	c. 2150–2040 BC	c. 2040–1640 BC	c. 1640–1552 BC
Old Kingdom (Dynasties 3 to 6). The first of the pyramids are built.	Reign of King Khufu (Dynasty 4).	The Sphinx and Great Pyramid at Giza (a tomb for King Khufu) are built.	Reign of King Pepi II (Dynasty 6), the longest reign in history.	First Intermediate Period (Dynasties 7 to 10).	Middle Kingdom (Dynasties 11 to 13). King Mentuhotep II reunites Egypt and restores order.	Second Intermediate Period (Dynasties 14 to 17). The Hyksos people from Asia overrun Egypt.

Life and Death in Egypt

THE ancient Egyptians believed in life after death. They buried their dead in tombs filled with items for use in the afterlife. These tombs, with their paintings and treasures, tell us much about these remarkable people.

The walls of tombs were covered with paintings of gods and goddesses. Shown here are, on the left, Osiris, the god of the dead and Atum, the Sun god, on the right.

THE EGYPTIANS BELIEVED that for a person's soul to prosper in the next world, the body had to be preserved. This is why they made mummies. Dead bodies were embalmed and dried, then wrapped in linen strips and placed in coffins. The finest tombs were those of the kings. Some were buried in pyramids, but later rulers of Egypt were laid to rest in rock tombs, in the Valley of the Kings. Most tombs were ransacked

Hieroglyphics was the system of picture-writing used in ancient Egypt. Each picture, or hieroglyph, stood for an idea or a sound. Hieroglyphs were written on walls as well as on sheets of papyrus. People trained to write them were called scribes.

The Great Temple at Abu Simbel was built by King Ramses II. Four gigantic seated statues of the king guard the entrance.

When a body was mummified, the dead person's liver, lungs, stomach, and intestines were removed, wrapped, and stored in containers called canopic jars. The head-shaped lids represented protective gods.

c. 1552–1085 BC
The New Kingdom in Egypt (Dynasties 18 to 20).

c. 1479–1425 BC
Reign of King Tuthmosis III. The Egyptian empire is at the height of its power.

c. 1364–1347 B
Reign of King Akhenaten.

robbers, but one survived largely intact. It was
scovered and opened in 1922 by British
cheologist Howard Carter. The tomb
longed to the boy-king
tankhamen, and inside were
celess treasures of a vanished world.

Egypt's greatness lasted for over
00 years. The Egyptians were
lled in math and astronomy,
d drew up a calendar of 365
ys. They had a system of
ture-writing called
eroglyphics. Their doctors
ere the best in the world. They
ilt pyramids and temples bigger
an any structures seen before,
d traded overseas in large
ps. It is not surprising that
en peoples who later
nquered Egypt, such as the
mans, stood in awe of the
yptians' achievements.

Tutankhamen's gold death
sk covered the face of the
d king. His body lay wrapped
inen inside a nest of three
fins, encased in a stone
cophagus and protected by
r wooden shrines.

| 347–1337 BC gn of King ankhamen. | c. 1289–1224 BC Reign of King Ramses II. | c. 1085–664 BC Third Intermediate Period (Dynasties 21 to 25). | c. 664–332 BC The Late Period (Dynasties 26 to 30). c.525–404 BC The Persians rule as Dynasty 27. | 332 BC Alexander the Great takes control of Egypt. Founds Alexandria (331 BC). | 323–30 BC Rule by the Ptolemies until Cleopatra kills herself in 30 BC. Egypt then becomes a province of the Roman empire. |

Indus Valley

ABOUT 3000 BC a great civilization grew up along the river Indus in the Indian subcontinent (in what is now Pakistan). It is known as the Indus Valley civilization. About 2500 BC it reached the height of its power.

The area covered by the Indus Valley civilization (in what is now Pakistan) and its main cities

THE INDUS VALLEY civilization was larger than either Sumer or ancient Egypt. Its two great cities were Harappa and Mohenjo Daro, each with a population of some 40,000 people.

The civilization had a highly organized system of trade. Merchants traded grain and other agricultural produce, grown on the fertile river plains. Artifacts and jewelry were also traded for precious metals and cloth. From about 2000 BC, however, this mighty civilization began to decline, possibly because terrible floods destroyed the crops, or because the river Indus changed course and the fertile farmland dried up. Another theory is that over-grazing left the land too dry and poor to support crops.

This stone statue, found among the ruins of Mohenjo Daro, may be of a priest or king.

The streets of Mohenjo Daro were laid out in a grid and had a drainage system for the houses. Important buildings included the hilltop citadel and the Great Bath, used for religious ritual.

c. 3000 BC
Farming settlements grow up along the river Indus.

c. 2500 BC
The Indus Valley civilization is at its height.

c. 1500 BC
The region is taken over by the Aryans – Indo-Europeans from western Asia. Their religious beliefs mix with those of the Indus cities to form the basis of the religion of Hinduism.

Megalithic Europe

FROM about 4500 BC people in Europe began building monuments such as stone circles, using massive standing stones called megaliths. They also erected dolmens – two upright stones topped by a horizontal one – as tombs.

> This clay mother-goddess figure was found at the Hypogeum, a megalithic underground monument on the island of Malta.

STONE CIRCLES were laid out carefully, according to strict mathematical rules, but no one is sure what they were used for. They may have been used for studying the Sun, Moon, and stars, or they may have been temples, where religious ceremonies were held. Experts think that sacrifices, both human and animal, may have taken place inside these intriguing circles of stone.

Megalithic builders also constructed stone monuments over the graves of their dead. Often these were long, passagelike chambers lined with megaliths and buried under a mound of soil, a structure known as a barrow.

One tomb contained over 40 skeletons, possibly several generations of the same family. The bodies were not put immediately into the grave, but were exposed until most of the flesh had rotted away. Offerings of food and drink, pots and tools were left at the tomb entrance for the dead to use in the next world.

> Stonehenge in England was built in three stages from about 2800 BC. Some of the stones align with the Sun on Midsummer's Day; others with the phases of the Moon.

c. 4500 BC	c. 4000 BC	c. 3200 BC	c. 2800–2000 BC	c. 2750–2000 BC
People start building megaliths in western Europe.	First passage graves are built at Carnac, France.	Newgrange grave is built in Ireland.	Stonehenge is built in England.	Megalithic temples are built in Malta.

Minoans

THE MINOAN civilization was the first major civilization in Europe. It began on the island of Crete and was named after its legendary ruler, King Minos. It was at the height of its power from about 2000 BC.

◄ Legend tells of a monster (half-man, half-bull) that lived in a labyrinth (maze) under the palace of Knossos. It was killed by Theseus, an Athenian prince. Bulls may have been sacred to the Minoans.

THE MINOANS had a rich culture, with a highly organized society and a flourishing economy. Merchants traveled throughout the Mediterranean trading wine, grain, and olive oil from Crete for amber, ivory, and precious metals.

Towns were built around huge palaces. These weren't just royal residences; they also contained workshops, shrines, and storage for goods. By 1450 BC most of the palaces had been destroyed, probably by earthquakes or volcanic eruptions, and Crete was taken over by the Mycenaeans.

▲ Knossos was the largest Minoan palace. Built around a central courtyard used for religious ceremonies, it had 1,300 rooms. The walls of the royal apartments were decorated with frescos. The ruins of Knossos were found by Sir Arthur Evans in 1894.

► Many huge clay jars, used for storing oil, wine, and grain, were discovered at Knossos.

c. 6000 BC	c. 3000–1000 BC	c. 2000 BC	c. 1700 BC	c. 1600 BC	c. 1450 BC
The first farmers settle in Crete.	People on Crete and mainland Greece learn how to make bronze.	The first palaces are built on Crete.	The palaces are destroyed by earthquakes and are later rebuilt.	The Mycenaeans first reach Crete.	A volcanic eruption destroys all the palaces on Crete, Knossos included.

Mycenaeans

FROM ABOUT 1600 BC to 1100 BC the Mycenaeans dominated mainland Greece. They lived in separate, small kingdoms, although they shared the same language and beliefs. They are named after their greatest city, Mycenae.

A gold death mask, once believed to have covered the face of Agamemnon, the legendary king of Mycenae and hero of the Trojan War. Scholars now think the grave it came from dated from 300 years before his time.

THE MYCENAEANS built their great palaces on hilltops surrounded by massive stone walls. This type of fortified city was easier to defend from attack, and was called an *acropolis*, which means "high city" in Greek. The Mycenaeans were farmers and traders. They founded colonies on Rhodes and Cyprus. They also seem to have been brave and successful warriors.

Many pieces of armor and weapons have been found in Mycenaean graves. In 1876, a group of five shaft graves were discovered, containing 16 members of the royal family. Five of them had exquisite gold death masks over their faces, and with them was buried a priceless hoard of golden treasure.

The Trojan War began when Agamemnon led an army to bring back his sister-in-law, Helen, after she had eloped with a Trojan prince, Paris. Legend tells how the Mycenaean soldiers were smuggled into Troy inside a huge wooden horse.

The Lion Gate was the main gateway into Mycenae. The two carved lions may have been symbols of the Mycenaean royal family. The gate was built in about 1250 BC.

c. 1600–1100 BC	c. 1450 BC	c. 1250 BC	c. 1200 BC		c. 1100–800 BC
Mycenaeans dominate mainland Greece.	Mycenaeans become rulers of Crete.	Traditional date of the fall of Troy.	Mycenaean culture begins to decline, possibly due to crop failure and a weak economy. People begin to abandon the great cities.		The Dark Ages in Greece.

Ancient China

THE earliest civilizations in China grew up along the banks of three major rivers – the Chang Jiang, Xi Jiang, and Huang He. Farmers used the water to irrigate their crops, but often suffered bad floods.

FROM ABOUT 2205 BC, China was ruled by a series of dynasties (ruling families). The first for which experts have good evidence is the Shang dynasty, which began in about 1766 BC. The Shang ruled for more than 400 years, until they were conquered by the Zhou.

Zhou rule lasted until 221 BC. During this time many wars were fought between the rival

A terracotta soldier from the enormous underground tomb of Shi Huangdi, who was buried in 210 BC with all that he needed to survive the afterlife. This included a vast army, 10,000 strong, of life-sized clay soldiers.

Early copper "coins" were shaped like tools, and were different in each state. Under Shi Huangdi, all coins were made round with a hole in, so they could be strung together.

kingdoms that made up the Zhou land. But it was also a period of economic growth, with Chinese silk, precious jade, and fine porcelain being traded abroad.

By 221 BC, the kingdoms of China had been at war for more than 250 years. Gradually, the Qin (or Ch'in), a warlike dynasty from the northwest, united the country and established the empire that gives China its name. The first emperor of the united China, Shi Huangdi, reorganized government and standardized money, weights, and measures. A road and canal network was built to link up various parts of

The Great Wall of China (built 214–204 BC) was more than 1,400 miles (2,250 km) long and was wide enough for chariots to pass along. Thousands of peasants worked on the wall. If their work was below standard, they were put to death.

Convicted criminals were used as a workforce

c. 1766–1027 BC
The Shang dynasty rules China.

1027–256 BC
The Zhou dynasty rules China.

c. 551 BC
Birth of the great teacher, Confucius

CONFUCIUS

The philosopher Confucius was born in about 551 BC, at a time when wars were frequent. He dedicated his life to teaching people how to live in peace. His teachings formed the basis of the Chinese civil service up to the beginning of the 20th century.

	Tree	Moon	Bird	Sun	Horse	
About 1500 BC	米	)		○		
Before 213 BC	朮	)		~		
After AD 200	木	月	鳥	日	馬	

The earliest Chinese writing was found on oracle bones (Shang dynasty). Gradually the picture symbols became more abstract in form.

e country, and the Great Wall of China as built across the northern border to ep out the hostile Hsung Nu (the Huns). i Huangdi was a brilliant but ruthless eneral and politician, putting scholars to eath if their ideas did not atch his own. The Qin nasty was overthrown n 206 BC, four years after i Huangdi's death.

Watch towers provided shelter for the army from attackers

Chinese nobles came to watch the construction

Soil was packed down into mud blocks, then lined with cobbles

A pulley on a bamboo scaffold lifted soil from surrounding works

kers carried heavy materials with a balanced yoke

Enlisted soldiers worked as overseers

–221 BC	221 BC	212 BC	210 BC	206 BC
e so-called Warring tes Period, when most China is in a state of l war.	Shi Huangdi unites China and founds the Qin dynasty. He becomes China's first emperor.	The Burning of the Books by Shi Huangdi – his suppression of ideas that did not match his own.	Death of Shi Huangdi.	The Qin dynasty collapses and the Han dynasty rules China until AD 9.

Phoenicians

THE PHOENICIANS were the greatest traders and seafarers of the ancient world. Their cities of Tyre and Sidon became centers of a vast trade network. They also set up colonies around the Mediterranean Sea. One was Carthage, which became a great power and Rome's rival.

◀ By about 1C BC, the Phoenici had developed alphabet of letters. Vowels w later added by Greeks. In time, Greek version was adapted by the Romans writing Latin, and this forms the basis of alphabet we use to write English toc

for export. Goods traded included glassware, timber, cedar oil, and ivory. Bu their most famous export was a purple-red dye made from a kind of shellfish. They were such expert navigators that about 600 BC the Egyptian king Necho hired Phoenician sailors to sail around Africa. The expedition is said to have taken three years.

◀ The Phoenicians were famous for their craft skills. They were particularly skilled in glass-making and glass-blowing. This funeral mask is made from colored glass.

THE PHOENICIANS lived along the eastern coast of the Mediterranean (in what is now part of Syria, Lebanon, and Israel). In large ships made of cedar wood, they ventured as far west as Britain and down the African coast. Potters, ivory carvers, metal workers, and carpenters made goods for everyday use and

◀ Phoenic cargo sh had squa sails and oc A lookout ke watch pirates. On arriv in Carthage, on North African coa merchant ships used port and the navy anoth

c. 1500 BC	c. 1140 BC	c. 1100 BC	c. 1000 BC	c. 814 BC	729 BC	c. 727 BC	332 BC
Phoenician cities flourish under foreign rule.	Phoenicians set up the colony of Utica in North Africa.	Phoenicians independent of foreign rule.	The Phoenician alphabet is well developed.	The city of Carthage is founded in North Africa.	The Assyrian king, Shalmaneser V, invades Phoenicia.	The Greeks adopt the Phoenician alphabet.	Alexander the Great conquers Phoenicia.

Hebrews

THE HEBREWS were the ancestors of the Jews. They lived in the land of Canaan (later called Palestine) and their belief in one God gave rise to the Jewish religion of Judaism. The Hebrews became known as Israelites.

CANAAN was crossed by a number of trade routes. According to the Bible, a shepherd named Abraham led his people to Canaan from southern Mesopotamia. His grandson Jacob had 12 sons, after whom the 12 Hebrew tribes or Israelites were named. The Bible tells how the

▶ The Bible tells how God gave Moses the Ten Commandments (holy laws for a good life) written on slabs of stone.

Hebrews were enslaved in Egypt, but were led to freedom in the 1200s BC by Moses, whose successor Joshua took them back to Canaan.

From about 1029 BC, the Hebrews united to fight their enemies under a strong king, Saul. Saul's successor, David, formed the kingdom of Israel and made Jerusalem his capital. In Jerusalem, King Solomon built the first Temple. After Solomon died, his kingdom split, into Israel and Judah. Both kingdoms fell to invaders from Assyria, Babylonia, and Persia. Many Israelites became slaves or went into exile. In 167 BC, the Jews rebelled and set up an independent kingdom, named Judah, but in 63 BC the Romans conquered Judah, and later drove out most of the Jews.

◀ The Tower of Babel in Babylon, where many Jews were made captive in the 500s BC. The Bible tells how God, angry at this attempt to build a tower to reach heaven, made the workers speak different languages, so the tower was never finished.

c. 1850 BC	c. 1200 BC	c. 1000 BC	c. 1029 BC	c. 982 BC	c. 722 BC	c. 587 BC	c. 538 BC	c. 63 BC
Abraham leads his people from Ur in Mesopotamia to Canaan (Palestine).	Moses leads the Hebrews out of Egypt.	David succeeds Saul as second king of Israel.	Solomon builds the Temple in Jerusalem.	Solomon dies; his kingdom is divided.	The Assyrians conquer Israel.	The Babylonians conquer Judah.	King Cyrus of Persia allows the Jews to return to Jerusalem.	The Romans conquer Judah, which they call Judea.

Ancient America

OVER 3,000 YEARS AGO, two great civilizations grew up in ancient America – the Olmecs in western Mexico and the Chavin along the coast of northern Peru. Their ancestors had come from Asia across the Bering Strait "land bridge" thousands of years before. At first they lived as nomadic hunter-gatherers, but later they settled in farming communities.

The Olmecs made hundreds of sculptures from stone, jade, and clay. These tiny jade and serpentine figures were part of a group found buried at La Venta, Mexico, in 1955.

THE OLMEC CIVILIZATION is thought to have been the first to develop in North America. It started as a small group of villages around the Gulf of Mexico. Gradually these villages merged to form towns, and by 1200 BC the civilization was flourishing. One of the main centers of Olmec culture was the

A Chavin stone vessel carved in the shape of an animal. Chavin craft workers produced large quantities of clay pots and sculptures, which they traded with their neighbors.

This map shows the locations of the Olmec and Chavin civilizations. The Chavin was the most widespread of the early cultures in the Andes mountains. It was followed by the Nazca and the Moche civilizations.

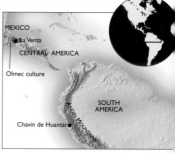

MEXICO
La Venta
CENTRAL AMERICA
Olmec culture
SOUTH AMERICA
ANDES MOUNTAINS
Chavin de Huantar

c. 1200–300 BC	c. 1200–200 BC	c. 1100 BC	c. 1000 BC	c. 850–200 BC	c. 700 BC	c. 400–300 BC
The Olmec civilization flourishes on the coast of Mexico.	The Chavin civilization flourishes on the coast of northern Peru.	The Olmecs build a great ceremonial center at San Lorenzo.	The Olmec city of La Venta becomes a major center for fishing, farming, and trade.	Chavin de Huantar in the Peruvian Andes is at the height of its power.	The Olmecs abandon San Lorenzo.	La Venta is abandoned and destroyed.

y of La Venta on an island off the
exican coast, where the people were
hermen and farmers. The Olmecs built
ge earth pyramids, where religious
remonies were held. Many of their
ulptures and masks depict a half-
man, half-jaguar creature, possibly a
werful god. The system of writing
veloped by the Olmecs influenced
any later cultures, such as the Maya.

▶ The Olmecs built huge stepped pyramids
de of earth. Here they worshiped and
formed religious ceremonies. The pyramid at
Venta was 112 feet (34 m) high. Around it
re several paved areas,
terned to look like
uar masks.

▶ The Olmecs carved
massive stone heads,
some almost 10 feet (3
m) high. These may
have depicted rulers,
gods, or famous
players of a ball-
game, played as part
of religious worship.

The Chavin civilization began in Peru
in about 1200 BC and lasted for about
1,000 years. It is named for the great
religious site of Chavin de Huantar
(c. 850 BC), a huge stone temple
surrounded by a maze of rooms. At the
heart of the temple was a great
statue of the Smiling God, with a
human body and a snarling
face. The Chavin also
worshiped jaguar
spirits, eagles,
and snakes.

Assyrians and Hittites

THE ASSYRIANS and Hittites were two of the most warlike peoples of the ancient world. Their kings led powerful armies, which overran their neighbors. The Assyrians eventually conquered the Hittites and founded an empire that lasted from about 1000 to 612 BC.

THE HITTITES, who are mentioned several times in the Bible, lived in what is now Turkey. By 1500 BC they were a strong power in the Middle East. Their capital was the city of Hattusas, or Bogazkoy, where archeologists have found cuneiform writings. The Hittites were feared for their military skill. They were the first people to use horse-drawn chariots, which carried soldiers at high speed into battle. Hittite armies conquered Babylon, Mesopotamia, and parts of Syria. One of the most famous battles of ancient

▼ The Assyrian army used fearsome assault towers mounted on wheels to break through the city walls of their enemies. The towers' iron-tipped battering rams could be swung to left or right to smash through walls and doors.

◄ Assyrian soldiers used inflated animal skins to help them swim across fast-flowing rivers and mount surprise attacks.

c. 2000–1450 BC	1813–1781 BC	1390 BC	1285 BC	1200 BC	c. 1000–612 BC
The Old Assyrian empire.	Reign of King Shamshi-Adad, a great warrior and empire builder.	Hittite king Suppiluliumas conquers northern Syria and Mitanni.	Battle of Kadesh between Hittites and Egyptians; no clear winner.	Hittite empire collapses under pressure from the Sea Peoples.	New Assyrian empire – a huge empire is conquered.

...mes was fought at Kadesh, ...orth of Palestine, in about ...285 BC between the ...ittites and the Egyptians.

◀ From their fast war chariots, Hittite archers fired arrows and spearmen hurled spears into the enemy ranks.

After about 1190 BC ...ittite power was weakened from ...ttacks by the Sea Peoples – raiders who ...errorized the eastern Mediterranean. In ...17 BC their eastern city of Carchemish was captured by the Assyrian king Sargon II. The Hittites then became part of the new Assyrian empire.

The Assyrians came from what is now Iraq. They were ruled by soldier-kings, who led huge, well-trained, well-equipped armies. The Assyrians were ruthless in using their might against enemy cities. They demanded yearly tribute of goods and crops from conquered peoples; anyone who defied them risked torture, enslavement, or death.

Assyrian kings believed they were chosen by the gods and liked boastful titles, such as "King of the Universe." They built cities and palaces to show off their wealth and power. The earliest Assyrian capital was Ashur, named for their chief god. The last great ruler of Assyria, Ashurbanipal, made Nineveh his capital and collected a huge library there. Soon after his death in 627 BC, the Assyrian empire ended. It had become too large and ungovernable, and fell to the invading Medes and Babylonians.

▶ King Ashurbanipal (668–627 BC) was the last great Assyrian ruler. He was a ruthless military leader, but is also remembered for his splendid palace at Nineveh.

...33–859 BC	745–727 BC	721–705 BC	668–627 BC	612 BC
...eign of King ...shurnasirpal II, ...ho builds a great ...alace at Nimrud.	Reign of King Tiglathpileser III, who conquers Israel.	Reign of King Sargon II, who builds a palace at Khorsabad.	Reign of King Ashurbanipal, who makes Nineveh his capital. He sacks the great cities of Thebes, Babylon, and Susa.	Assyria is invaded and conquered by the Medes and Babylonians.

44

Babylonians

BABYLON, once a small kingdom of Mesopotamia, first grew powerful under the rule of King Hammurabi (c. 1792–1750 BC). He extended the kingdom's frontiers to include Sumer and Akkad, and rebuilt the city of Babylon, making it the capital of the new empire.

King Nebuchadnezzar II ruled c. 605–562 BC) captured Syria and Palestine, and forced many of the people of Jerusalem to live in captivity in Babylon.

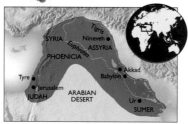

This map shows the extent of the Babylonian empire under Nebuchadnezzar II. His army defeated the Egyptians to take Syria.

Legend says that the Hanging Gardens of Babylon were built for Nebuchadnezzar's Persian wife, Amytis, because she missed the green hills of her homeland. The gardens were one of the Seven Wonders of the ancient world.

HAMMURABI was a just and diplomatic ruler. He is famous for his code of law, th oldest surviving in the world. The laws were recorded on stone pillars for all to see. After his death, Babylon was invade by the Hittites, Kassites, Chaldeans, and Assyrians. The Assyrian king Sennacheri destroyed the city in 689 BC. But Babylor regained its former glory during the 6th century BC under King Nebuchadnezzar II. The king conquered a huge empire and made the city perhaps the grandes in the ancient world.

The awe-inspiring city of Babylon stood on the banks of the river Euphrates (near Baghdad in modern-da Iraq). The capital of the Babylonian empire, it was a major trading center an a flourishing religious complex, especially for the worship of the god Marduk, the city's patron god. In fact,

c. 1894 BC	c. 1792–1750 BC	c. 1595 BC	c. 1595–1155 BC	c. 1126–1105 BC	c. 731–626 BC	c. 626–529 BC
The Amorite people establish the minor kingdom of Babylon in Mesopotamia.	Reign of King Hammurabi. Babylon first rises to power.	Babylon is plundered by the Hittites, then falls to the Kassites.	The Kassites rule Babylon.	Nebuchadnezzar I reigns.	The Assyrians and Chaldeans fight for control of Babylon.	Babylon re-emerges as a major power in the Near East.

BABYLONIAN SCIENCE

The Babylonians were excellent mathematicians and astronomers. They drew the oldest known map of the world, and were the first to use a system of weights (c. 2600 BC). The metal weights were shaped like lions.

☑ The blue-tiled Ishtar Gate was the northern entrance to Babylon. It was named for the goddess of love and war. Bulls and dragons, symbols of the god Marduk, decorated the gate.

the name Babylon means "Gate of the God." Nebuchadnezzar II rebuilt the city in magnificent style. The city walls were enormous, and there were eight massive bronze gates. The grandest, the Ishtar Gate, opened on to the Processional Way, which linked the Great Temple of Marduk inside the walls to an important religious site outside the city. At the New Year's festival, statues of the gods were paraded along this route. Nebuchadnezzar also built a grand palace that became known as "the Marvel of Mankind."

626–605 BC	c. 605–562 BC	c. 597 BC	586 BC	c. 539 BC
King Nabopolassar defeats the Assyrians and rules Babylon. Babylonian army, under Nebuchadnezzar defeats Egypt to win Syria.	Nabopolassar's son Nebuchadnezzar II rules Babylon.	Nebuchadnezzar conquers Judah (southern Palestine) and puts down three rebellions there.	Nebuchadnezzar destroys Jerusalem and exiles its people to Babylon.	Babylon is conquered by the Persians and becomes part of the mighty Persian empire.

Ancient Greece

BY ABOUT 800 BC, Greece saw the rise of a new civilization that transformed the ancient world. Its influence has lasted to the present day. Ancient Greece was divided into small, independent city-states, each with its own government and laws. The two most important were mighty Athens and Sparta.

Pericles was leader of Athens from 443–429 BC. The most famous and popular politician of the "Golden Age," he ordered the rebuilding of Athens after its destruction by the Persians.

MOST CITY-STATES were ruled by a group of wealthy nobles (an oligarchy). Resentment led to revolts, and absolute rulers (tyrants) were appointed to restore law and order. Then, in about 508 BC, a new type of government was introduced in Athens. It was called democracy, meaning "rule by the people," and gave every male free man a say in how the city should be run. Many countries today are democracies, but with votes for all.

The Classical Period (when Greek culture was at its most splendid) lasted from about 500 BC to 336 BC. During that time, Greece was involved in two long-running wars. In 490 BC the Persians invaded. The Greek city-states joined

The Greek army depended on its hoplites, or foot soldiers. Hoplites carried heavy round shields and long spears for stabbing the enemy. The split, skirtlike tunics allowed easy movement.

In battle, Greek hoplites formed a phalanx – a block of soldiers eight or more rows deep.

The phalanx advanced in formation, spearpoints bristling, scattering the enemy foot soldiers

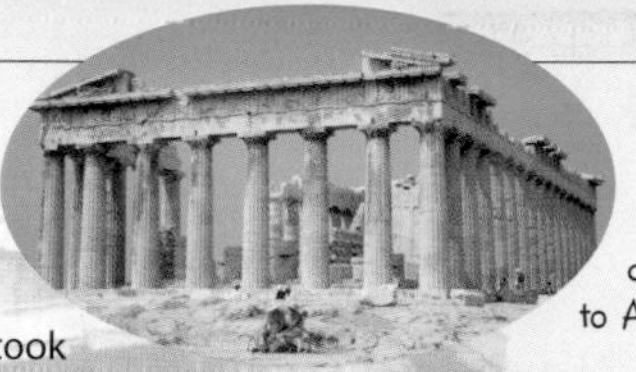

The Parthenon was built on top of the Acropolis (a high hill in Athens) in the 5th century BC. It was dedicated to Athena, goddess of wisdom.

ces and
ntually
eated them in
BC. One of the
st famous battles took
ce at Marathon in 490 BC. A messenger
ned Pheidippides ran the 25 miles
km) back to Athens carrying news of
Greek victory. His run is immortalized
he modern marathon race.

But peace did not last. In 431 BC war
ke out between Athens and Sparta
e Peloponnesian Wars). After laying
ge to Athens, the Spartans starved the
enians into submission. In 404 BC
ens was forced to surrender.

Life in Sparta was very different from life in Athens. Spartan men were trained to be fearless warriors, ready to defend the city-state from invaders and to keep the population under control. Every male Spartan had to train for war. Boys as young as seven were sent away to army camp, where strict discipline and harsh conditions turned them into the toughest fighters in Greece. Girls, too, were encouraged to be fit and strong.

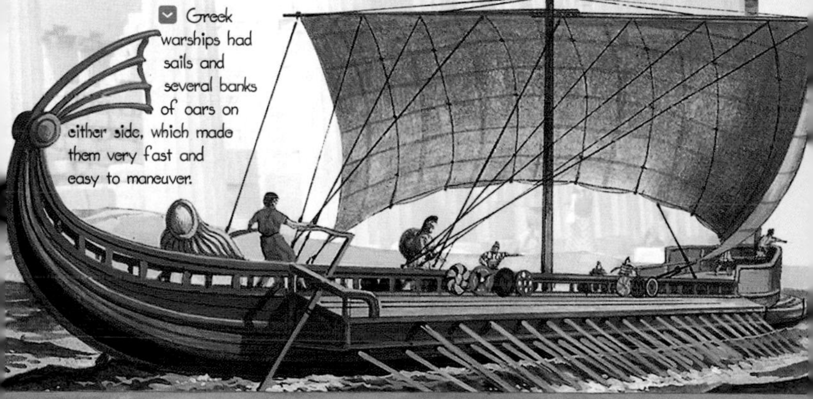

Greek warships had sails and several banks of oars on either side, which made them very fast and easy to maneuver.

o BC
state of
ta is
ded by
Dorians.

c. 800–500 BC
The Archaic Period. Greece revives after a period of decline called the Dark Ages.

776 BC
The first Olympic Games are held at Olympia.

c. 750–550 BC
Many Greek colonies are set up around the Mediterranean.

c. 700 BC
The Greek poet Homer composes the *Iliad* and the *Odyssey*.

c. 508 BC
Democracy is introduced in Athens.

Greek Culture

GREEK CIVILIZATION lasted far longer than the Greek city-states. Greek influence on politics, philosophy, art, architecture, language, and literature had a huge effect on Roman culture and can still be felt today. Many of our ideas about science and art come from ancient Greece.

▶ Greek vases were beautifully decorated with detailed scenes from daily life and stories from mythology. Much of our knowledge about the ancient Greeks comes from vases and vessels.

THE ANCIENT GREEKS were great scholars, thinkers, and teachers. At first they answered questions about life and nature with stories about the gods. Later they started to look for practical and scientific ways of making sense of the world about them. Their scholars were called philosophers, which means "love of knowledge;" they include Socrates, Plato, and Aristotle.

Drama and sport played a very important part in the lives of the ancient Greeks. Greek theater grew from the performance of songs and dances at an annual festival dedicated to Dionysus, the god of wine. These performances were acted out by a group of men called a chorus. At first, plays were performed in a town's market place. Later, open-air theaters were built all over Greece (many can still be seen).

▶ At the Olympic Games, throwing the discus was one of five events in the pentathlon (the others were running, jumping, wrestling, and javelin throwing). The winner of this demanding competition was declared the best all-round athlete at the games. The ancient Olympics ended in AD 395. The modern Olympic Games were begun in 1896.

c. 500–336 BC	490–449 BC	479–431 BC	447–43
The Classical Period. Greek culture reaches its height.	The Persian Wars. The Greeks are victorious.	The Golden Age of Athens, a time of great prosperity and achievement for the city.	The Parthen temple built in Athens

Socrates (c. 469–399), the son of an Athenian sculptor, was one of the most influential of all ancient Greek philosophers. He taught people to think about good and evil. Some people did not approve of his ideas, however, and he was forced to commit suicide.

Sport was important not only as a form of entertainment, but also as a way of keeping men fit and healthy for war. There were many competitions for athletes. The oldest and most famous was the Olympic Games, held every four years at Olympia in honor of the chief god, Zeus. For the five days of the games, a truce was called between the city-

states to allow the athletes safe passage to Olympia. Athletes trained hard for months before the games. Discipline was strict and breaking the rules harshly punished. But for the winners it was worthwhile. Their prize was a simple olive crown cut from a sacred tree, and a hero's welcome, fame, and fortune when they arrived back home.

▶ The Greeks developed two main styles of column for their grand public buildings and temples: Doric (top) and Ionic (center). A third, more elaborate style, called Corinthian (bottom), was introduced in Roman times.

Greek actors were all men. They wore different masks and costumes for characters that were happy, sad, male, female, old, or young. The Greeks were the first to build theaters; the largest could hold an audience of 18,000 people.

Alexander and the Persians

AFTER THE squabbles following the Persian Wars, Macedonia became the dominant force in Greece. Its young king, Alexander, led his armies on an epic march of conquest, crushing the Greeks' traditional enemies, the Persians.

◄ The Persian army's greatest strength lay in its archers and cavalry troops. But it was no match for Alexander's battle tactics.

THE PERSIAN homeland was in what is now Iran. The Persians had come to rule an empire th stretched eastward to India and as far west as Turkey. Great Persian kings, such as Cyrus the Great, commanded huge and efficient armies. Darius I (521–486 B built fine roads for carrying messages quickly across the empire, which he reorganized into provinces called satrapies. From 499 BC, Persia turned against the Greeks, but in 480 BC its invasion fleet was defeated at the battle of Salamis.

Power then swung toward Greece. In 338 BC Macedonia's warrior king Philip I gained control of all the Greek states by victory at Chaeronea. When Philip was murdered in 336 BC, his son Alexander became king, aged 20. It took Alexander just 13 years to conquer the largest empire in the ancient world, spreading Greek (and Persian) culture far and wide

▼ The city of Persepolis, built by Darius I, was the magnificent capital of the Persian kings. The ruins of the city lie near Shiraz in modern-day Iran. When Alexander captured Persepolis in 331 BC, he burned the splendid royal palace to the ground.

In 334 BC Alexander led his army against the Persians. He wanted not only to conquer their lands, but also to replenish his royal treasuries. In 333 BC he defeated the Persian king Darius III at the battle of Issus, and by 331 BC had conquered the whole of Persia and become its king. To strengthen the ties between the two peoples, Alexander included Persians in his government. He also wore Persian clothes and married a Persian princess, Roxane. He went on to invade India, defeating King Porus at the battle of the river Hydaspes. It was to be his final expedition. His exhausted army refused to go on, and Alexander was forced to retreat to Babylon. He died there of a fever in 323 BC, aged 32. After his death, the empire was divided among his leading generals.

Alexander his great war horse, cephalus.

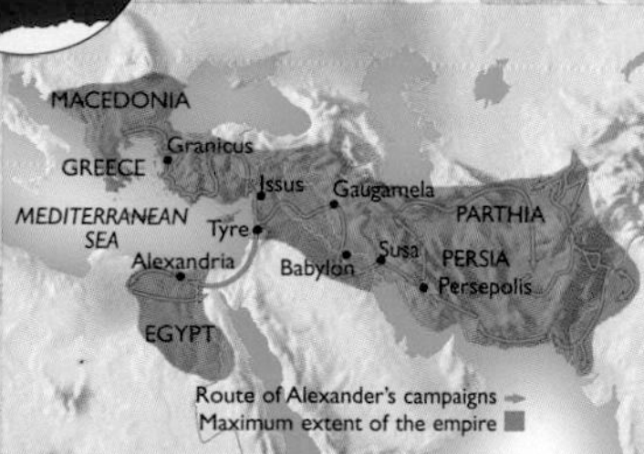

The map shows the extent of Alexander's empire and the routes he took to conquer the east.

MACEDONIA
Granicus
GREECE
Issus
Gaugamela
MEDITERRANEAN SEA
Tyre
PARTHIA
Alexandria
Susa
PERSIA
Babylon
Persepolis
EGYPT

Route of Alexander's campaigns
Maximum extent of the empire ■

BC	331 BC	327 BC	323 BC
ander quers t.	Alexander defeats the Persians at the battle of Gaugamela.	Alexander reaches India. He is forced to turn back in 324 BC.	Alexander dies in Babylon. His generals fight and the empire is divided.

The Celts

CELTIC PEOPLES spread westward across Europe from about 800 BC. They lived in tribal groups, settling in hill-forts and farms. The Celts were unable to unite against a common enemy – the formidable Roman legions.

 Maiden Castle was one of the strongest Age hill-forts in Britain. Approaching invaders could be seen a long way off, and the fort's concentric earthworks made it difficult to cap

THE CELTS were brave and fearless warriors, but they were equally skilled at metal working, making beautifully decorated weapons, jewelry, and drinking cups. They were also gifted storytellers, passing down stories of their gods and history by word of mouth. Roman writers recorded details of Celtic life and culture. They reported

Celtic craftworkers made beautiful metal objects, such as this silver horse harness. Many highly decorated Celtic artifacts have survived.

that the Celts worshiped many differe gods and goddesses, and offered sacrifices in their honor. Religious ritua and ceremonies were performed by priests called druids. In charge of each of the Celtic tribes was a chieftain. On of the most famous was Vercingetorix, a chieftain of the Arveni, a tribe in central Gaul (France). In 52 BC, he led a successful rebellion against the Romans, but was later defeated by Jul Caesar's well-trained army.

Many Celtic tribes built huge hilltop forts surrounded by massive protective earthworks, where they lived safe from attack. Victory in battle was celebrated with feasts that could last for several days, drinking, and the recital of long poems telling of the deeds of Celtic heroes and gods. Their greatest god w Daghdha, the "Good God," who

c. 600–500 BC	c. 400 BC	390 BC	225 BC	58–50 BC	52 BC
Celtic culture develops in Austria and later in France.	The Celts build farms and hill-forts in southern and western Europe.	The Gauls (French Celts) sack the city of Rome.	The Romans defeat the Gauls at the battle of Telamon in Italy.	Julius Caesar conquers all of Gaul (France).	Vercingetorix lead revolt against the Romans in Gaul, is defeated by Caesar.

ntrolled the weather
d the harvest and
ought victory in battle.

Celtic warriors were
med and feared for their
avery in battle. Wars
equently broke out between
al Celtic tribes – a weakness that
lped the Romans to overwhelm
em more easily.

BOUDICCA

The Roman emperor Claudius
invaded Britain in AD 43. Some
Celts fought back fiercely. In AD
60, Boudicca (or Boadicea),
queen of the Iceni, a Celtic tribe
in eastern Britain, led a revolt
against the Romans. The Celts burned
London and killed some 70,000
Romans. But her army was
defeated in AD 61, and
Boudicca killed herself
by drinking poison.

🔺 Safe within
a hill-fort, families lived
with their animals in circular wooden huts. The
huts were thatched and had walls of mud-plastered sticks. A
huge iron cooking-pot hung over the fire in the center.

6₁
udicca is defeated
a revolt she leads
inst the Romans
Britain.

54

The Romans

ACCORDING to legend, the city of Rome was founded in 753 BC by the twin brothers Romulus and Remus. The boys were abandoned by their uncle to die on the banks of the river Tiber in central Italy. But they were rescued by a she-wolf, and later found and raised by a shepherd.

TO REPAY THE SHE-WOLF, Romulus and Remus vowed to build a city in her honor, on the Palatine Hill where she had found them. In a quarrel about the city boundaries, Remus was killed and Romulus became the first king of Rome.

From humble beginnings as a small group of villages, Rome grew to become the capital of the most powerful empire the western world had ever seen.

At first Rome was ruled by kings. The in about 509 BC, King Tarquin the Proud was expelled from Rome, and for the ne 500 years Rome was run as a republic. Power passed to the Senate, a law-making body made up of nobles and headed by two senior officials, called consuls. They were elected each year to manage the affairs of the Senate and th army. By about 50 BC, Rome had conquered most of the lands around th

◀ Octavian, the first emperor of Rome, was known as Augustus, or "revered one." A great politician, he reformed every aspect of government and restored peace and prosperity to Rome.

🔺 This fresco, or wa painting, comes from Pompeii, seaside town in Italy that was destroye in AD 79 by a volcanic eruption. Mar buildings, however, were preserved under th ash and lava that smothered the tow

753 BC	c. 509 BC	264–146 BC	49 BC
The traditional date for the founding of Rome.	The founding of the Roman Republic.	The Punic Wars between Rome and Carthage in North Africa. Carthage is destroyed. Rome controls the Mediterranean.	Julius Caesar seizes power to become dictator of Rome. In 44 BC he is assassinated.

Julius Caesar, a brilliant Roman general, defeated his rivals in Rome to seize power as dictator in 49 BC. He was assassinated on March 15, 44 BC.

Mediterranean. But rivalry between army generals plunged Rome into civil war. In [2]7 BC, Octavian, the adopted son of Julius [C]aesar, became the first Roman emperor, [c]harged with restoring peace. Under the [e]mperors, Rome gained control of much [o]f Europe, North Africa, and the Near East.

HANNIBAL

From 264 to 146 BC, Rome waged a series of wars, called the Punic Wars, against the Phoenician city of Carthage in North Africa, to gain control of the Mediterranean. In 218 BC, the Carthaginian general Hannibal led a surprise attack on the Romans. He marched over the Alps into Italy with 35,000 men and 37 elephants. Carthage was eventually defeated.

A she-wolf [su]ckled Romulus and Remus, [ac]cording to legend, before [the] boys were rescued by a [she]pherd. The legend goes on [to] tell how the twins founded [Ro]me, with Romulus becoming [the] first king. This statue of [the] wolf dates from the [5]th century BC, but the [tw]ins were added much [lat]er in AD 1510.

BC	27 BC	27 BC–AD 14	AD 14–37	AD 37–41	AD 41–54	AD 54–68	AD 64
[Oc]tavian defeats [An]tony and Cleopatra [at] the battle of [Ac]tium, and takes [co]ntrol of Egypt.	End of the Republic, start of the Roman empire.	Octavian takes the title Augustus and rules as the first Roman emperor.	Tiberius rules.	Caligula rules.	Claudius rules.	Nero rules.	Fire devastates Rome.

Roman Society

THE AMAZING expansion and success of the Roman empire was due largely to its army, which was the best trained and best equipped in the world.

Roman coins bore the head of the emperor and were used in trade all over the empire. Peaceful trading was one of the benefits of Roman rule.

THE ROMAN ARMY was originally formed to protect the city of Rome. It was made up largely of volunteer soldiers. General Marius (155–86 BC) reorganized the army into a more disciplined and efficient fighting force. Soldiers were paid wages and joined up for 20 to 25 years.

Ordinary soldiers were grouped into units called legions, each made up of about 5,000 men. The legions, in turn, were made up of smaller units called centuries, of 80 men. These were commanded by soldiers called centurions.

Roman soldiers were well trained and well organized. Wearing heavy armor and plumed bronze or iron helmets, they were capable of marching about 20 miles (30 km) a day carrying weapons, food, and camping kit.

AD 69–79	AD 79–81	C. AD 80	AD 98–117	AD 117–138	AD 166–167	AD 180
Vespasian rules the Roman empire.	Titus is emperor.	In Rome, the Colosseum is completed.	Under Emperor Trajan, the empire reaches its greatest extent.	Hadrian rules.	Plague devastates the empire.	End of the *Pax Roma* (Roman Peace), a ti of stability in the empire.

The Colosseum is one of the most splendid Roman remains in Rome. It was built to stage gladiator fights, a popular form of entertainment. Gladiators were trained slaves or prisoners, who fought each other, or wild animals, to the death. The Colosseum held up to 45,000 spectators.

...e sight of the legions marching into ...ttle behind their silver standards must ...ve been formidable.

Roman society was divided into ...tizens and non-citizens. There were ...ree classes of citizens – *patricians,* the ...chest aristocrats; *equites,* the wealthy ...erchants; and *plebeians,* the ordinary ...tizens. All citizens were allowed to vote ... elections and to serve in the army. ...ey were also allowed to wear togas.

... Emperor Hadrian (ruled AD 117–138) ...ncentrated on strengthening the borders of ... already huge empire. Fortified walls were ...t along vulnerable borders in Germany, ...rica, and Britain. The best preserved is ...adrian's Wall in Britain, built in AD 122 to ... end the empire's northernmost frontier.

Building, mining, and all hard manual labor was done by the vast workforce of slaves. Many slaves were treated cruelly, but some were paid a wage and could eventually buy their freedom.

CHRISTIANITY AND ROME

The Romans worshiped many gods and often adopted new religions from the people they conquered. Jesus Christ was born (probably in 4 BC) in Palestine, then a Roman province. His teachings attracted fervent followers, but upset local Jewish leaders, and he was crucified by the Romans. Christ's followers, among them the apostle Paul, spread the new religion of Christianity throughout the Roman world. Despite persecution, the faith grew and in AD 391 it became the official religion of Rome.

African Cultures

THE first great African civilization, apart from Egypt, grew up in Nubia (now northern Sudan) about 2000 BC. Called the kingdom of Kush, it was conquered by Egypt in 1500 BC. Kush, in turn, defeated Egypt about 728 BC and ruled it for 100 years.

IN THE 3RD century BC, the capital of Kush moved to Meroe, on the river Nile. The city became an important center of iron working. Another early center of iron working developed in what is now northern Nigeria (in West Africa) about 600 BC.

▶ In this wall painting from an ancient Egyptian tomb, Nubians are shown bringing gifts for Egypt's pharaoh. Egyptian expeditions to Nubia brought back gold, cattle, and slaves.

The people of the region were known a the Nok. Their culture flourished until about AD 200. The Nok mined iron and smelted it in clay furnaces. They used th iron to make tools such as hoes and ax used to clear the land for crops. The Nok also made iron

▶ Life in a Nok village centered around farming and iron working. To extract iron from iron ore (a metal-bearing rock), the ore was put into a furnace and heated to a high temperature. Potters used furnaces, too, to fire their terra-cotta heads.

◀ The people of Axum built huge stone obelisks, up to 100 feet (30 m) tall. Carved from single stone slabs, they may have been symbols of power or burial monuments for the royal family.

From 2000 BC	c. 900 BC	c. 600 BC	AD 100s	c. AD 200	AD 320–350	c. AD 350
The kingdom of Kush begins in Nubia.	Kush gains independence from Egypt.	The Nok culture begins in northern Nigeria.	The kingdom of Axum (in what is now Ethiopia) rises to power.	The Nok culture comes to an end, but has a lasting effect on the artistic styles of Africa.	King Ezana rules Axum and converts to Christianity.	Axum overruns the city of Mer and brings the Kushite kingdo to an end.

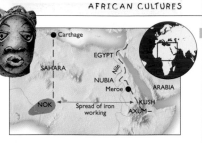

> The map shows the kingdoms of Kush, [A]xum, and Nok. The Nok were named after the village where clay figures, like this head, were found. Nok art influenced later West African cultures.

[arr]owheads, spears, and knives, as well as [sto]ne tools and distinctive clay figures.

The kingdom of Axum rose to power [in] the 2nd century AD. Located in what is [no]w northern Ethiopia, Axum lay on an [im]portant trade route and grew rich [fro]m buying and selling spices, incense, [an]d ivory. Its major trading partners were Arabia, Egypt, and

Persia. In about AD 320 Axum's King Ezana converted to Christianity. In the 6th century AD Axum conquered part of western Arabia. By AD 1000, however, it had collapsed as a new Islamic empire from Arabia expanded its influence.

Map labels: Carthage • ; SAHARA ; EGYPT ; Nile ; NUBIA ; Meroe ● ; ARABIA ; NOK ; Spread of iron working ; KUSH ; AXUM—

[5]00s
[Islam] rules [part] of western [Ara]bia.

c. AD 1000
The kingdom of Axum collapses as Islam expands.

60

Empires of India

IN ABOUT 321 BC, a young prince, Chandragupta Maurya, founded an empire that stretched across northern India from the Hindu Kush in the west to Bengal in the east. This was the first Indian empire.

◀ In early Buddhist art, Buddha was represented by a symbol such as a footprint, a stupa, a wheel, a lotus flower, or a sacred tree.

HINDUISM

The Hindu religion began more than 4,000 years ago as ideas from the Indus Valley civilization mingled with those of invading peoples. Under Emperor Ashoka, Buddhism became the major religion of India. Hinduism enjoyed a revival under the Guptas. Today, more than 75 percent of Indians are Hindu. The main symbol of Hinduism is the word "Om" (shown above).

▶ Exquisite wall paintings cover the Buddhist cave temples at Ajanta in western India. The paintings date from the time of the Gupta empire. Some show scenes from the life of the Buddha.

CHANDRAGUPTA'S grandson, Ashoka, came to the throne in 269 BC. He extended the empire until most of India came under Mauryan rule. In 260 BC Ashoka's army fought a bloody battle against the people of Kalinga in eastern India. Sickened by the bloodshed, Ashoka was filled with remorse. He converted to Buddhism and vowed to follow its teachings of peace and non-violence.

Ashoka traveled far and wide throughout his empire, listening to people's views and complaints and trying to improve their lot. He had edicts carved on pillars for people to see, and sent out special officers to explain his policy of religious tolerance, respect for others, and peace

c. 563 BC	c. 483 BC	c. 321 BC	269–232 BC	260 BC	c. 185 BC	c. AD 320
Birth of the Buddha in Lumbini, Nepal.	Death of the Buddha in Kushinagara, India.	Chandragupta seizes power and founds the Mauryan dynasty.	Reign of Ashoka Maurya, thought by some to be the greatest ruler of ancient India.	Ashoka converts to Buddhism after the battle of Kalinga.	The Shunga dynasty replaces the Mauryans.	The beginning of Gupta power emerge in the Ganges valley

After the collapse of the Mauryan
[em]pire in about 185 BC, India was
[di]vided into small, independent
[ki]ngdoms. In AD 320, Chandra Gupta I,
[rul]er of the kingdom of Magadha in the
[Ga]nges valley, enlarged his kingdom.
[Th]e Gupta empire ruled northern India
[for] the next 200 years. Chandra Gupta's
[so]n, Samudra, extended the empire and
[in]creased its trading links. He was
[su]cceeded by Chandra Gupta II. During
[hi]s reign, India enjoyed a Golden Age.

Under the Guptas, arts and literature
[flo]urished, as did science, medicine, and
[m]ath. Great poets and artists were
[in]vited to the splendid royal court.
[Hi]nduism replaced Buddhism as the
[m]ajor religion of the empire, and many
[ne]w temples and shrines were built.
[Sa]nskrit, the sacred, classical language of
[In]dia, became the language of the court.

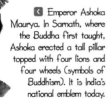

◀ Emperor Ashoka
Maurya. In Sarnath, where
the Buddha first taught,
Ashoka erected a tall pillar
topped with four lions and
four wheels (symbols of
Buddhism). It is India's
national emblem today.

🔺 The gateway
to the great stupa
(Buddhist shrine)
of Sanchi, which
was built during
Ashoka's reign.
The first stupas
contained relics of
the Buddha.
Ashoka had stupas
built throughout
his empire.

BUDDHISM

Buddhism was founded by an Indian prince,
Siddharta Gautama (c. 563–483 BC),
who gave up his comfortable life to seek
enlightenment. He found enlightenment while
sitting and meditating under a Bo tree. He
spent the rest of his life traveling and
teaching. Buddhism teaches that people, like
all living things, are part of an endless
round of birth, change, death, and rebirth.
Buddhism spread from India to other parts
of Asia and beyond.

[A]D 350–550	AD 380–415	C. AD 550
[Th]e Gupta [em]pire brings a [Go]lden Age of [Hi]nduism to [Ind]ia.	The reign of Chandra Gupta II, greatest of the Gupta kings.	Hun invasions weaken Gupta power. The empire splits into smaller kingdoms.

62

The Middle Ages

KINGS AND CONFLICTS
500–1400

THE PERIOD FROM about 500 to 1400 in Europe is known as the Middle Ages, or the medieval period. It began with the fall of the Roman empire and ended with the Renaissance, when a revival of art and learning swept through Europe.

THE MEDIEVAL PERIOD was an age of wars and conquests. Some wars were fought to gain more territory, while others were wars of religion, fought between people of differing faiths in an age when religion dominated most people lives. At this time China's civilization was far in advance of the rest of the world. Africa and America saw the emergence

500s	529	600	c. 610	700	732	751	787	800	802
The Eastern Roman empire is at its height.	The first abbey in Europe is Monte Cassino (Italy).	Teotihuacan civilization in Mexico.	The prophet Muhammad begins preaching in Arabia.	The Mayan civilization is at its height.	The battle of Poitiers checks the Muslim advance into Europe.	The Carolingian dynasty is founded.	The Vikings begin attacks on England.	Charlemagne is crowned Holy Roman Emperor.	Founding of the Khmer empire in Southea Asia.

Byzantium

FOR OVER 500 years the Roman empire brought a unique way of life to a vast area of land. But in 476 the western half of the empire collapsed, overrun by invading German tribes. In the east, Roman rule continued to flourish under what is called the Byzantine empire.

The magnificent church of Hagia Sophia Istanbul was completed in 537. It took only six years to build. The minarets were added later when it became a mosque. It is now a museum.

THE OLD GREEK city-port of Byzantium (modern-day Istanbul in Turkey) was the center of the Byzantine (Eastern Roman) empire. Renamed Constantinople after the first Byzantine emperor, Constantine, it became the seat of the Byzantine emperors and the center of the eastern Christian Church. Within the empire,

Greek and Roman arts and learning were preserved. Byzantine churches, such as Hagia Sophia, were decorated with fine detailed frescos (wall paintings) and mosaics made from hundreds of pieces of glass or stone.

The Byzantine empire reached its peak in the 500s, under the emperor Justinian and his general Belisarius. It included Italy, Greece, Turkey, parts of Spain, North Africa, and Egypt.

Constantine the Great (275-337) was the first Christian emperor of Rome. He moved the empire's capital from Rome to Byzantium and renamed the city Constantinople.

Chariot races mixed thrills with politics. Howling mobs in the Hippodrome cheered for the Blues or the Greens, in support of one or other of the rival political factions.

330	408	445	476	c. 501	527-565	678
Constantinople is founded.	Emperor Theodosius begins building a great wall to protect Constantinople.	Attila the Hun attacks. He is paid to go away.	Fall of the Western Roman empire.	A long series of wars with Persia begins.	Reign of Justinian I.	An Arab siege Constantino is defeated.

ustinian's powerful
vife, Theodora, helped
iim govern. Justinian
ssued a code of laws
n which the legal
ystems of many
uropean countries
vere later based. Constantinople was a
ousy port and meeting place for traders
rom as far away as Spain, China, and
Russia. But invaders from the east –
vars, Slavs, and Bulgars – threatened
his last Roman empire. After Justinian's
leath in 565, Byzantium was weakened
oy many wars and eventually fell to the
urks in 1453.

◀ This map shows the Byzantine (Eastern Roman) empire at its height in the 500s. It extended from the eastern Mediterranean to Spain in the west.

▶ In the 6th century, Byzantine artists in a church in Ravenna, Italy, made this mosaic of the Magi (Wise Men) visiting Jesus.

os	1054	1081	1200	1204	1341–1354	1453
cond Golden Age. e Balkans and ıssia come under zantine influence.	The Christian Church in Constantinople breaks with the Church in Rome.	Alexius I Comnenus seizes power and reforms government.	The Byzantine empire begins to break up under attacks from Turks and Bulgarians.	Constanti-nople is sacked by Crusaders.	Civil war in the Byzantine empire.	Turks capture Constantinople – end of the Byzantine empire.

66

The Franks

THE FRANKS were the strongest of all the western European peoples who struggled for land and power after the end of the Roman empire in 476.

UNDER THEIR first great leader, Clovis, the Franks spread out from their homeland around the river Rhine (in what is now Germany). They fought their neighbors, such as the Visigoths and Burgundians, until by 540 they had conquered most of the old Roman province of Gaul (modern France, which is named after the Franks).

Clovis defeated rival chieftains to bring all the Frankish tribes under his control. His family became known as the Merovingian dynasty, after his grandfather Merovich. Clovis became a Christian and ruled from Paris, governing his lands through Church bishops and nobles. The nobles or lords held estates known as manors, which were plowed and farmed by peasants.

Frankish leaders were always ready to defend their estates and conquer new lands. Their eagerness to ride into battle meant they needed servants for military service. In return, the servants were granted land. This was the beginning of feudalism. Leading families jockeyed for the king's favor. In the 600s two rival clans

◀ This ivory carving shows Gregory the Great, pope from 590 to 604. From the time of Clovis, the Franks were Christian.

▲ Examples of fine metalwork from the Frankish period. These gold and enamel buckles date from the 6th to 7th centuries. They would have been worn by a rich noble.

241	350	428	451	c. 466	486
First mention of Franks, fighting the future Roman emperor Aurelian in Mainz.	Franks are brought under Roman rule.	Salian Franks (living in the Netherlands and lower Rhineland) throw off Roman rule and invade Gaul, led by King Chlodio.	Franks join with Romans to defeat Attila the Hun at the battle of Châlons.	Clovis is born. In 481 he becomes king of the Franks.	Franks defeat the last great Roman army in the West at the battle of Soissons.

◀ The Franks were farmers. They tilled their fields in strips using wheeled plows pulled by oxen. Oxen were slower than horses, but stronger.

▶ A Frankish stone monument, possibly a gravestone. The carving shows a warrior with a long broadsword, a favorite weapon of the Franks.

...ought for power. The Austrasians ousted the Neustrians, and their chief, Pepin of Herstal, founded a new ruling family. Pepin's son, Charles Martel (known as the Hammer), won a historic battle at Poitiers against Muslim invaders in 732. This defeat checked the advance of Islam into central Europe. Martel's son, Pepin the Short, established the new Carolingian dynasty. He was the first Frankish king anointed by the pope, in 754. But the greatest of the Frankish rulers was Pepin's son, Charlemagne.

◣ Tough Frankish warriors rode into battle with shaven heads and topknots, wearing light mail armor. They were formidable cavalry fighters, whose loyalty was rewarded with booty. Frankish armies defeated the Romans, Gauls, and Visigoths who tried to halt their expansion.

496	506	511	540	687	732	751
Clovis defeats the Alemanni near the River Seine.	Franks defeat the Visigoths.	Clovis dies.	Franks control most of Gaul and lands in what is now Germany.	After the battle of Tertry, Pepin of Herstal becomes the most powerful Frankish leader.	Charles Martel defeats a Muslim army at the battle of Poitiers.	Last Merovingian king, Childeric III, is overthrown. Pepin the Short (Charlemagne's father) becomes king.

68

The Rise of Islam

THE NEW FAITH preached by the prophet Muhammad in the 600s changed the course of history. Muhammad's followers spread their religion, Islam, by preaching and conquest. By the 700s, Muslims (followers of Islam) ruled most of the Middle East and North Africa.

The Dome of the Rock in Jerusalem. Muslims believe Muhammad ascended to heaven from the rock to speak with God, before returning to Earth to spread Islam.

BEFORE MUHAMMAD, the Arab peoples were not united in any way. Different groups worshiped different gods. Muhammad was a merchant of Mecca, in Arabia. At the age of about 40 he began to preach of belief in one God, after a dream in which an angel told him he was the prophet of Allah (God). The new religion became Islam, which means "submission to the will of Allah."

Muhammad had to leave Mecca when some townspeople objected to his new teaching. His journey in 622 to Yathrib (now Medina) is commemorated still as the Hegira, which begins the Muslim calendar. In Medina, Muhammad and his followers built the first mosque. His teachings and revelations were written down in the Koran, the holy book of Islam. In 630 Muhammad's followers captured Mecca, and Islam became the new religion of Arabia.

A Muslim star-chart of a constellation. Muslim astronomers studied the stars and preserved many older Greek ideas about the universe.

570	610	622	625	630	632	634	644
Probable birth date of Muhammad.	Muhammad begins preaching in Mecca.	Muhammad's flight to Yathrib (now Medina).	Muhammad's teachings are written down in the Koran.	Muhammad leads an army into Mecca.	Muhammad dies. Abu Bakr becomes the first caliph.	Omar succeeds Abu Bakr.	Othman (head of the Ummayads) succeeds Omar.

SPAIN 711–713
CARTHAGE 687–688
SYRIA 638
ARABIA 632
PERSIA 644
MEDITERRANEAN SEA
Cairo
Medina
Mecca
MAURETANIA 700–705
BARCA 643
EGYPT 639–643
BABYLONIA 637
INDIAN OCEAN

When Muhammad died in 632, his father-in-law, Abu Bakr, was chosen as first caliph (successor). A group called the Shiites thought only the descendants of Muhammad's daughter Fatima could lead Islam. Others, known as Sunnis, thought any Muslim could do so. This split continues today.

THE RISE OF ISLAM

◄ This map shows how rapidly the new religion of Islam spread from Arabia as far west as Spain.

1 2 3 4 5 6 7 8 9 10 0

⌃ Arabic numerals (bottom row) evolved from Hindu numbers (top) through trade with India. They proved easier to use than Roman numerals.

By 644 the Arabs had conquered most of Syria, Palestine, and Persia. After 661, the Ummayad family controlled the growing empire from their capital, Damascus, in Syria. Islam's advance into Europe was halted by the Frankish army of Charles Martel in 732. In 762 the new Abbasid dynasty moved the empire's capital to Baghdad (in what is now Iraq). This city became the center of the Islamic world.

◄ Mecca is the city in Saudi Arabia to which Muslims turn when they pray and to which millions of pilgrims travel. Pilgrims circle the shrine containing the Black Stone, believed by Muslims to have been given to Abraham by the angel Gabriel.

► Harun al-Rashid (766–806) was caliph from 786. The power of the Abbasid dynasty of caliphs peaked during his reign.

656	661	732	750	756
The Shiite leader Ali becomes caliph.	The Islamic capital is moved from Mecca to Damascus.	Abd-al-Rahman, ruler of Spain, invades France. He is defeated by a Frankish army led by Charles Martel.	Abbasid dynasty is founded by Abu al-Abbas.	Last Ummayad ruler flees from Damascus to Cordoba, Spain.

American Civilizations

MANY impressive civilizations flourished in North, Central, and South America. The Native Americans who created these civilizations built cliff-top palaces, huge earth mounds, and pyramid temples. A few fragments of their civilizations' achievements survive today.

The Tlalocan mural, a wall-painting in the Mexican temple-city of Teotihuacan, shows Tlaloc, the god of rain and harvests.

THE ANASAZI people lived in what is now the southwestern USA. They grew corn and built amazing cliff houses called pueblos, in which as many as 5,000 people lived. Their descendants were known as the Pueblo.

Also in the southwest lived the Hohokam people, who dug irrigation canals to water their crops and, like the Anasazi, wove cotton cloth and made decorated clay pottery. Farther east, the Mississippian people built well-planned towns of single-family houses.

About AD 700 the largest city in America was in central Mexico. Teotihuacan was a city of more than

As people moved south across the Americas, rich civilizations developed in areas where the land was best suited for farming and settlement.

ARCTIC HUNTERS
SUB ARCTIC HUNTERS
NORTH AMERICA
HUNTERS AND GATHERERS
Mesa Verde
Serpent Mound
PACIFIC OCEAN
ATLANTIC OCEAN
MEXICO
MAYA CULTURE
Teotihuacan
CENTRAL AMERICA
HUNTERS AND GATHERERS
FARMING PEOPLES
Tiahuanaco
SOUTH AMERICA

Llamas were used by the peoples of the Andes to carry goods. These sure-footed, hardy animals also provided wool and meat.

600	700	750	800	900	968	1000
Teotihuacan (Mexico) is at its most powerful. Tiahuanaco (Bolivia) is at its strongest.	Anasazi culture develops in southwestern USA.	Teotihuacan is destroyed. Tiahuanaco also declines.	Nazcas of Peru lose independence after the Huari move into their lands.	Rise of Toltecs in Mexico.	Toltecs set up their capital at Tula.	Mississippian culture at its height; its main city is Cahokia (in what is now Illinois).

AMERICAN CIVILIZATIONS

71

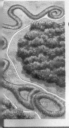

GREAT SERPENT MOUND

This snake-shaped earthwork was made about AD 1000 by Native Americans in what is now Ohio. It is about 1,300 feet (400 m) long. The mound was a sacred burial place. The snake grew bigger as more burials were added. Similar mounds were built by other peoples, including the Hopewell (c. 300 BC to AD 200).

100,000 people, 600 pyramids, and 2,000 apartment blocks. Teotihuacan's time of greatest power was from about AD 350 to 750. From then on it was overshadowed by a new power, the Toltecs, who built their own temple-city at Tula.

In South America, high in the Andes Mountains, was the city of Tiahuanaco, which flourished between 500 and 1000.

Here people used llamas as pack animals and paddled reed boats on Lake Titicaca. Other city-states of the Andes, such as Huari in Peru, were greatly influenced by Tiahuanaco.

The Nazca of Peru marked out giant pictures in the desert with furrows and stones – amazing animal designs that are best seen from the air!

◄ At Mesa Verde in Colorado, the Cliff Palace has more than 200 rooms. The site was abandoned about 1300, possibly due to lack of water.

► A massive stone figure, one of many found at Tiahuanaco in Bolivia. Tiahuanaco was the first planned city in the Andes.

1100	Late 1100s	1200s
Rise of the Chimu kingdom in Peru.	End of the Toltec state; Tula is destroyed.	The Cliff Palace is built at Mesa Verde (in what is now Colorado).

The Maya

THE MAYA lived in Central America. Their civilization lasted more than 700 years. They built huge cities with magnificent stone temples that can still be seen today.

A Mayan calendar. The Mayan number system was based on 20. The farmers' calendar had 18 months of 20 days each.

A jadeite mask made by a Mayan artist. Jadeite is a hard, green gemstone. Much of Mayan art was religious. This mask may have been used by a priest during a ceremony.

grow beans, corn, and squash. They raised turkeys and kept bees, but had no domestic animals other than dogs. The only wheeled vehicles were toy carts.

The largest Mayan city was Tikal, in what is now Guatemala, with a population of 60,000. Crowds filled the large squares around the pyramid-

THE MAYA were at their most powerful from about 200 to 900, although their culture lasted until the Spanish conquest of Central America in the early 1500s. They lived in well-organized city-states, each with its own ruler. The rulers fought wars with neighboring city-states. They also controlled trade in obsidian, cacao, cotton, and other goods such as colorful feathers, used to make headdresses. In the countryside farmers cleared forest and terraced the hillsides to

3372 BC
First date in Mayan calendar.

400 BC
The Maya have built several large pyramid-temples, like those at Tikal in Guatemala.

AD 250
Start of the classic period of Mayan civilization. The Maya borrow some of their ideas from the people of Teotihuacan.

◄ The Maya settled in what is now eastern Mexico. There were some 50 states, each with its own ruler and sacred city, such as Chichén Itzá, Tikal, and Copán.

temples to watch
ceremonies conducted by
sts, who studied the heavens to
dict eclipses of the Moon and Sun.
gion was important to the Maya.
/ made sacrifices to win favors from
many gods. Mostly they sacrificed
nals, but they also threw human

victims into sacred wells. The Maya invented the first writing in America. They wrote codexes (folding books) on pages of tree bark, three of which survive. They also set up tall carved stones to commemorate dates and important events. Many people in Mexico still speak Mayan languages.

▽ A Mayan ruler enters his city. Each city-ruler was a god-king. Everyone worshiped him and offered tribute in the form of goods, food, or work.

c. 900	900	990	c. 1250	1440	1517
each ...st ...ity.	Decline of Mayan civilization. People move to the highlands of Mexico and Guatemala.	Chichén Itzá is the most important Mayan city. It is governed by a council.	Toltec people take over Chichén Itzá.	Mayan culture revives: Mayapán is the chief city.	Rebellion against Mayapán rulers. Maya unity weakened as states fight one another.	Start of Spanish conquest of Maya lands.

Charlemagne

CHARLES I, king of the Franks, was known as Charlemagne (Charles the Great). He founded the Holy Roman empire in Europe and was long regarded by many people as the "ideal ruler."

CHARLEMAGNE was born in 742. His father was King Pepin, son of the famous soldier Charles Martel, and founder of the new Frankish ruling family (later called the Carolingian dynasty, from the Latin name for Charlemagne). In 768 Pepin died, leaving his kingdom to his sons Carloman and Charlemagne. Carloman soon died, and Charlemagne was left in sole control.

A very tall man, convinced of his own destiny, Charlemagne had learned much from his ruthless warrior father. He led his armies out of the Frankish homeland of France into what are now the Netherlands, Germany, and Italy. Wherever he conquered non-Christians, such as the Saxons of Germany or the Avars of Hungary, he forced them to become Christians and to take part i mass baptisms.

There was more to Charlemagne t simply waging wars of conquest. He learned to read Latin and greatly admired scholarship. His capital at

742	768	771	772	774	778
Probable birth date of Charlemagne.	Pepin the Short (Charlemagne's father) dies.	Charlemagne becomes ruler of the Franks.	Charlemagne starts war with Saxons and converts them to Christianity.	Charlemagne makes Lombardy (northern Italy) part of his empire.	Charlemagne fights th Muslims in Spain. His attacked by the Basqu the battle of Roncesva

◀ Charlemagne's empire grew from the lands of Austrasia (France and Germany) he inherited from his father Pepin in 768 and his brother in 771 (in orange on the map). The Frankish empire was at its biggest extent soon after (orange and red).

Charlemagne's position as Europe's strongest leader was recognized in 800 when the pope crowned him Holy Roman emperor. After he died in 814 the Holy Roman empire, weakened by attacks, was soon split between his three grandsons. It survived, however, in one form or another until 1806.

After Charlemagne's death many stories were written about him. A skirmish during his Spanish campaign of 778 became the subject of the medieval epic poem *The Song of Roland*.

Aachen was the glittering center of his empire, with a splendid palace and heated swimming pool. But the emperor himself dressed and lived simply. He had books read aloud to him and invited to his court famous scholars such as Alcuin of York.

◀ The tomb of Charlemagne at the imperial capital, Aachen, dates from 1215. It is decorated with gold and precious stones. Artists working 400 years after Charlemagne's death were able to refer to written descriptions of his appearance, but had no likeness of him to copy.

▶ The iron lance of the Holy Roman emperors was a holy relic as well as a symbol of power. Around the spearpoint is a gold sheath stretched over a nail reputedly from Christ's cross.

800	804	808	814	817
Charlemagne is crowned Emperor of the West by Pope Leo III.	Last of 18 campaigns against the Saxons.	Charlemagne fights the Danes.	Charlemagne dies. His son Louis the Pious succeeds.	The empire is split between Louis's sons.

h ls, s, Avars, and others.

The Khmer Empire

BETWEEN the 9th and the 15th centuries, the Khmer empire of Cambodia dominated Southeast Asia. The Khmers were highly skilled builders and engineers. They constructed cities with massive temple complexes, palaces, lakes, and canals.

At the height of their power the Khmer controlled much of what are now Laos, Thailand, and Vietnam.

BEFORE the Khmer people founded their empire in 802, they set up two smaller states. The first was Funan and the second, dating from 600, was Chenla. The Khmer empire was the creation of a strong king named Jayavarman I, who united people living in what are now parts of Cambodia, Thailand, Laos, and Vietnam. He and his successors we worshiped as gods.

The ancient books of the Khmers have long since been destroyed, so what we kr about them comes mos from Chinese writings (th Chinese bought spices and rhinoceros horn from the Khmers). many stone carvin

Khmer archers rode into battle on great war elephants. Bells and gongs added to the tumult as they attacked. The Khmers held on to their conquests until they were themselves conquered by invaders from Thailand.

802
King Jayavarn founds t Khmer empire.

e ruins of the Khmers' greatest
ings, in the temple of Angkor Wat
n the city of Angkor Thom, also
de a valuable picture of everyday
s well as recording sacred stories
victories in battle.

▶ Traditional houses in
Cambodia are built on stilts
to give them protection
from flooding. Around
Tonle Sap (Great
Lake), the largest
freshwater lake in
Southeast Asia, people
still live by fishing and
trading from boats.

◀ The huge Temple of
Angkor Wat measures
5,100 x 4,500 feet
(1,555 x 1,372 m). Its
tall central towers were
originally gilded. The
temple was first dedicated
to the Hindu god Vishnu. It became
a Buddhist shrine in the 1500s.

e Khmers built
wealth on rice. They
irrigation ditches to water their rice
s and grew three crops a year. Never
g far from water, they built houses
ilts beside rivers and on the shores
e lake named Tonle Sap.

rayavarman II, leader of the Khmers
1113 to about 1150, built Angkor
A successful war leader, he fought

in Thailand and Vietnam. The Khmer
empire reached its height in the reign
of Jayavarman VII (1181–1220). He built
roads, hospitals, and temples. Like all
Khmer kings, he was a Hindu, although
most of the people in the empire were
Buddhist. The Khmers were fierce
warriors, but in the 1400s they were
overrun by the Thais. The great city and
temple at Angkor were abandoned, and
became overgrown by jungle.

ages of	1113–1150	1181	1300s	1431
g the city	Construction	Start of reign	The Khmer empire is	Thai army captures Angkor. End of
kor Thom	of the temple	of King	weakened by extravagant	the Khmer empire. A smaller Khmer
alled	of Angkor Wat.	Jayavarman	building plans, quarrels	kingdom lasts until 1863, when the
arapura).		VII (to 1220).	within the royal family,	French take control of Cambodia
			and wars with the Thais.	and Angkor Wat is rediscovered.

The Vikings

THE VIKINGS were great
explorers. They set sail from
Scandinavia (Norway, Sweden,
and Denmark) looking for new
lands, and reached Greenland,
Britain, and the Mediterranean
and Black seas. Not all came as
raiders; many were peaceful
farmers and traders.

Wooden bucket   **Iron knife**   **Pottery c**
Leather shoe   **Carved stone**   **Antl ska**

⌃ Viking farmers made tools, clothes, fur
and things to sell at market. Wood, ivory, d
antler, leather, clay, bone, and iron were co
materials used.

SCANDINAVIA, the homeland, of the
Vikings, was covered in mountains a
forests, and had little good farmland
Most Vikings lived close to the sea,
tending small fields where they grew
rye, barley, wheat, and oats, and
vegetables such as turnips and carro
They kept cattle and sheep, and caug
fish in the rivers and fjords. Traders
traveled on horseback or by boat to

◩ Many Vikings lived on small farms, often
near to rivers or the sea. They planted cereals
and vegetables, and kept pigs, cows, goats, and
sheep. Women wore linen dresses with wool
tunics on top,
fastened by
brooches.

Late 700s	841	850	c. 860	c. 861	862	874	900s
The trading town of Hedeby in Denmark is founded.	Vikings found Dublin on Ireland's east coast.	Probable date of the Oseberg ship burial in Oslo Fjord, Norway – the richest Viking ship burial found.	Vikings settle around the Baltic. They rule Novgorod in Russia.	Ingolf is the first Viking to reach Iceland.	The Slavs and Finns of north Russia invite the Vikings to rule.	First Viking settlers reach Iceland.	Viking tra visit Constant which the Miklagaa

THE THING

e Viking law court was called
he Thing. Every year local
people came together for
veral days, and any freeman
who had a complaint or an
rgument to settle could raise
e matter. His neighbors would
ten and give a judgement. A
berson refusing to obey the
Thing's verdict became an
butlaw, to be killed on sight.

et towns such as Hedeby in
nark to exchange furs, reindeer
rs, and walrus ivory for weapons,
ls, and pottery.

king families lived in houses made
ood, stone, or turf.
ke from the
ing fire found its
out through a
in the roof.

Around the fire people sat at benches and tables to eat hearty meals, play dice games, and tell stories. The Vikings loved stories, especially those about their heroes and gods. The most important god of Norse (Scandinavian) mythology was Odin, the wise and one-eyed, but the most popular was Thor, the thunder god, whose symbol was a hammer. Physical sports such as wrestling, horse fights, and ice skating were also popular.

Viking farmers often had thralls (slaves) to help with the work, but most men were karls (freemen). A rich jarl, or landowner, was expected to share his wealth with his followers, feasting and entertaining them in his great hall. Powerful jarls became Viking chiefs. As the population increased, farmland became increasingly scarce. From the late 700s, these Viking chiefs and their warriors began to venture from their homelands in search of better farmland and greater riches.

arald ...	982	c. 1000	1000	1030	1100s
oth / nark / es a / an.	Erik the Red reaches Greenland and founds a settlement.	Erik's son Leif Eriksson reaches Vinland (North America).	Jorvik (York), England has a population of 10,000 people.	By King Olaf the Holy's reign, Norway is Christian.	The Swedes are the last Vikings to give up their old religion and convert to Christianity.

THE THING

e Viking law court was called
he Thing. Every year local
people came together for
veral days, and any freeman
who had a complaint or an
rgument to settle could raise
e matter. His neighbors would
ten and give a judgement. A
berson refusing to obey the
Thing's verdict became an
butlaw, to be killed on sight.

et towns such as Hedeby in
nark to exchange furs, reindeer
rs, and walrus ivory for weapons,
ls, and pottery.

king families lived in houses made
ood, stone, or turf.
ke from the
ing fire found its
out through a
in the roof.

Around the fire people sat at benches and tables to eat hearty meals, play dice games, and tell stories. The Vikings loved stories, especially those about their heroes and gods. The most important god of Norse (Scandinavian) mythology was Odin, the wise and one-eyed, but the most popular was Thor, the thunder god, whose symbol was a hammer. Physical sports such as wrestling, horse fights, and ice skating were also popular.

Viking farmers often had thralls (slaves) to help with the work, but most men were karls (freemen). A rich jarl, or landowner, was expected to share his wealth with his followers, feasting and entertaining them in his great hall. Powerful jarls became Viking chiefs. As the population increased, farmland became increasingly scarce. From the late 700s, these Viking chiefs and their warriors began to venture from their homelands in search of better farmland and greater riches.

The Vikings Abroad

WHEN the Vikings sailed overseas in their longships, they were ready to kill and plunder. In slower cargo ships, they went in search of trade and new lands.

VIKING LONGSHIPS were fast and str enough to cross oceans. From the la 700s bands of Vikings set sail from Scandinavia and landed on the coas western Europe. Attacks on England began in 787. Word quickly spread th they were fierce fighters, and the sig of a Viking sail approaching caused panic. Wielding iron swords and axes the Vikings raided monasteries and towns, carrying off slaves and booty.

Viking warriors wore chain-mail tunics or, more commonly, leather jerkins

A Viking sword was heavy and was swung in a wide arc

☑ Raiders rush from longships after rowin up a river. Danish Vikings settled much of eastern England, and even after their defea by King Alfred the Great, the Viking influence on English life remained.

787	795	834	865	866	878	886	911
First reported Viking raids on English coast.	Vikings begin attacks on Ireland.	Vikings raid Dorestad (in what is now the Netherlands).	A great army of Vikings lands in England.	The Vikings capture Jorvik (York), England.	Vikings are defeated by England's King Alfred. England is divided between English and Vikings.	Vikings are paid a huge sum to end their siege of Paris.	Vikin unde Rollo given Norn

◀ From Scandinavian market towns such as Hedeby in Denmark, Viking traders went by sea and overland to Jorvik (York) in England, Dublin in Ireland, and Iceland. They traveled east as far as Kiev in Russia and Constantinople.

The Vikings also came to seize land. y 865 Vikings from Denmark had egun to settle in eastern England, in he Orkney and Shetland islands off the oast of Scotland, in the Isle of Man, and Ireland. They attacked what is now ance, but were bought off with a gift f land (Normandy) in 911. Sailing west to the Atlantic Ocean, Norwegian ikings settled in Iceland (874) and reenland (982), and landed in North merica (c. 1000).

Swedish Vikings traveled east as far as the Black Sea, trading with Greeks and Arabs, who called them the Rus (from which "Russia" comes). Goods from the markets of Baghdad and Constantinople found their way back to Viking settlements in eastern England (the Danelaw).

— **The ax was a fearsome weapon close-to**

WEIGHING COINS

Vikings valued coins by weight. Many traders carried balance scales to check that a customer's money was good and to show another merchant that he wasn't being cheated. Little lead weights such as those below were used to check coins. Small scales for weighing silver have been found at Jorvik and other Viking settlements.

Scales

Silver penny

Lead weights

14
sh victory at
e battle of
ontarf. Viking
minance of
land ends.

1016–1035
Reign of Canute,
Viking king of
England,
Denmark, and
Norway.

1066
Last big Viking attack on
England, by Harold Hardrada
of Norway. His army is defeated
by King Harold at the battle of
Stamford Bridge.

1066
William, Duke of
Normandy, defeats King
Harold at the battle of
Hastings, England.

1072–1091
Norman
armies
conquer
Sicily.

Feudal Europe

IN WESTERN Europe, land was distributed in return for service. This arrangement, known as feudalism, lasted from the 700s to the 1300s.

▶ This 15th-century painting, "March," by the Limburg brothers shows peasants at work on their lord's land around his castle. It comes from a book made for a French nobleman, the Duc du Berry.

IN THE FEUDAL "system," the king was at the top and the poor at the bottom. In the middle were lords, churchmen, merchants, and craftworkers in towns. The king and the noblemen (lords and barons) granted land to people who worked and fought for them (their vassals). In return, the lord protected his vassals against attack.

Vassals had to supply soldiers on a certain number of days, usually 40, each year. They also had to pay taxes in the form of money, farm produce, or goods.

Feudalism developed among the Franks. It was based on the traditional idea that a strong leader should protect

Bishop

Scribe

Lady

Lord

Falconer

Knight

Late 400s	700s	1066	1100
Fall of the Roman empire leads to a breakdown in law and order across western Europe.	Feudal system starts among the Franks, based on arrangements for landholding and defence.	Normans use the feudal system in England to strengthen their grip on the land after the conquest.	It is now usual for a lord's oldest son to inherit his landholding or fief. (The word "feudal" comes from a Latin name for fief.)

A medieval king had enormous power to govern. William the Conqueror kept a fourth of England's land for himself and granted the rest to his followers, in return for military service. Every landholder had to swear allegiance (loyalty) to the king.

and reward followers for their loyalty. Alongside this military arrangement was the manorial farming system. Poor peasant-farmers worked on manors (large areas of land held by a lord). A peasant could own a small plot of land, but also had to work the lord's land.

Feudalism strengthened as kings granted more land to their knights, the

DOMESDAY BOOK

The Domesday (Doomsday) Book was a survey of England made on the orders of William the Conqueror in 1085. Commissioners took details of who owned what land, and how many people lived in each village, collecting figures for 1066 and 1085. Most old English villages and towns are listed.

warriors on whose loyalty and fighting skills they depended. The system began to fall apart in the 1200s, when people began using money more, and preferred to pay rent for land rather than be bound by service. The importance of knights and their castles began to lessen in the 1300s, when new gunpowder changed the nature of warfare. The disaster of the Black Death further weakened the system.

In feudal Europe, the king held most land and power. Next came the lords, bishops, and knights, followed by merchants and town craftworkers. Foot soldiers and peasants were the poorest.

Merchant   Archer   Peasant   Beggar

1200s	1215	1265	1300s
Feudalism becomes more complex, with layers of vassal-lord relationships from the king downward.	King John signs the Magna Carta, limiting the powers of the king of England.	Simon de Montfort, a baron, calls citizens to a meeting with barons and churchmen – the first real Parliament in England. De Montfort's rebellion against King Henry III fails, but royal power in England is never the same again.	Crossbows and cannon render knights less effective. The new technology of war speeds the end of feudalism.

Church and Monastery

IN MEDIEVAL Europe thousands of men and women devoted their lives to the Christian Church, working, praying, and studying in monasteries and nunneries. Monasteries became centers of learning.

An illuminated manuscript page. Some monks made the parchment. Others, called scribes, wrote out the words, decorating them with paint and gold.

MEN AND WOMEN who became monks or nuns obeyed a rule, or way of life, originally set down in the 500s by, amongst others, St Benedict of Nursia. He taught that a monk or nun should be poor, unmarried, and obedient. Monks wore simple robes,

shaved their heads, and lived together in communities known as monasteries. The head of the monastery was the abbot. Some later abbots managed large estate and even commanded knights. The head of a nunnery, a religious house for women, was called an abbess.

Monks and nuns followed a daily program of prayer and worship, attending eight services every day. Monks ate together in the refectory, and worked in the fields or

Dormitory

Cloisters

Infirmary

A monastic community followed a daily routine of work and worship. At its heart was the chapel. There were herb gardens and cloisters (covered walks), an infirmary for the sick, workshops, and farm buildings.

Refectory (dining hall)

Kitchen

Late 400s	c. 480–550	500s	529	597	910	966	1042
Simple monasteries are founded in Ireland, for hermits living in huts.	Life of St Benedict of Nursia. He founds his order of monks in 529.	St Columba founds a monastery on the island of Iona, Scotland.	Abbey at Monte Cassino in Italy is founded. The Benedictine rule is formulated.	St Augustine founds the first English Benedictine monastery at Canterbury.	Cluniac order is founded.	Mont St Michel in France is built by the Benedictines.	Edward the Confessor founds Westminster Abbey, England.

Founded in 909, Cluny Abbey in France is one of many abbeys in Europe built during the Middle Ages. An abbey was a large community of monks or nuns, who lived quietly within its walls.

Monks at prayer

Chapel

Library

Vegetable garden

in workshops. Later, lay brothers (workers who were not monks) did the heaviest work. Monks cared for the sick, gave food and shelter to travelers, and carefully copied books, creating brilliantly colored letters and pictures, called illuminations. These books were kept in monastery libraries, so preserving ancient knowledge.

There were several organizations, or orders, of monks. These included the Benedictines, Carthusians, and Cistercians. In the 1200s new orders of traveling preachers, known as friars, were formed. Friars of the Franciscan order (founded by St Francis of Assisi) did not live behind monastery walls, but wandered the countryside preaching Christianity to the people.

CHRISTIAN PILGRIMS

Pilgrims in the Middle Ages made long journeys to visit holy places or shrines (the bones or tomb of a saint, for example). In England, the most famous shrine was that of St Thomas à Becket at Canterbury.

1084	1098	1100	1119	1181–1226	Late 1100s	1225–1274
Order of Carthusians is founded.	Cistercian order is founded.	Knights of St John (the Hospitallers) found a monastery "hospital" for pilgrims journeying to the Holy Land.	Order of the Knights Templar is founded.	Life of St Francis of Assisi, founder of the Franciscan friars.	University of Paris is founded. Monastery libraries help start Europe's universities.	Life of St Thomas Aquinas, monk and scholar.

Knights and Castles

KNIGHTS were the most heavily armored soldiers of the Middle Ages. Clad in metal, they rode to battle on horseback. Their base was the castle, a strong fortress. There were castles all over Europe, the Middle East, and India, and as far east as Japan. A castle was also home to a lord and his family.

Feasting in the great hall. The lord and lady sit on a raised dais, with other members of the household at lower tables. Servants carry in food, and dogs wait for scraps.

THE EARLIEST medieval castles were earth mounds with wooden stockades on top. Castles like these were built by the Norman invaders of England in 1066, often on the site of earlier Saxon and Roman forts. They were soon enlarged and strengthened, with water-filled ditches or moats, stone walls protected by towers, and a massive central stronghold called a keep. Castles were often built on hilltops, or to guard harbors, rivers, and vital roads.

Medieval castles were private fortresses for the kings or lords who owned them. A castle was also a family home. Early castles were cold and drafty, with no glass in the windows and dry reeds on the stone floor. The lord and his followers feasted in the great hall. Food was brought by servants from the

Jousting was combat on horseback between two knights with blunt-tipped lances. A joust was a social occasion with a large audience. In a tournament, groups of knights fought mock battles, sometimes with fatal results. Safety measures, including blunt swords, were only introduced in the 1300s.

500	800s	950	1000s	1078	1100s	1142	1150–1250
Byzantines build strong stone castles and walled cities.	Arabs build castles in the Middle East and North Africa.	Earliest known French castle built (Doue-la-Fontaine, Anjou).	Normans develop the motte (mound) and bailey (enclosure).	In England, building of the Tower of London begins.	Stone keeps become the main castle stronghold.	Crusaders take over Krak des Chevaliers in Syria.	Thousands of castles are built across what is now Germany.

86

...tchen. At night, everyone slept on the ...oor around the central fire, except the ...rd and his lady, who retired to a private ...oom called the solar. Before about 1300 ...eople rarely took baths, and lavatories ...mptied into the moat. The castle was ...efended by foot soldiers and mounted ...nights. When a castle was attacked, the ...efenders needed enough food and water to withstand a

Knights carried shields to ward off blows and to identify themselves. A shield bore its owner's coat of arms (family badge).

siege lasting weeks or even months. Castle walls had to be thick enough to withstand catapults and battering rams. In due course, cannon and barrels of gunpowder placed in tunnels proved so effective at blasting down walls that castle-building came to an end.

...80s	1200s	1205	1220s	1280s	1320s	1400s
...astles with ...quare-...alled ...owers are ...uilt.	Concentric or ring-wall castle design is used in Europe.	Krak des Chevaliers is rebuilt by the Knights Hospitallers.	Castles with round-walled towers are first built.	Edward I of England orders many castles to be built in England and Wales.	Cannon are first used in Europe.	Castle-building declines in Europe.

The Crusades

88

FOR European Christians, the Crusades were holy wars, with the promise of plunder in the service of the Church. For more than 200 years, Christian and Muslim armies fought for control of the Holy Land, the territory around Jerusalem in the Middle East.

Catapults threw flaming tar and rocks

Round towers gave defenders better angles for arrows

KEY
— First Crusade
— Second Crusade
— Third Crusade

HOLY ROMAN EMPIRE — Ratisbon — Milan — Vienna — Marseilles — Genoa — Belgrade — Adrianople — Lisbon — Rome — Durazzo — Const... — Cadiz — Jebel Tarik (Gibraltar) — Antioc... — Trip... — Acr... — Jerusalem

The journey to the Hol... Land was long. Crusaders endure... sickness, thirst, and attacks as they struggled over rough, often desert, terrain.

MANY CHRISTIAN pilgrims visited Jerusalem, which was a holy city to Jews and Muslims, as well as to Christians. But Jerusalem was held by Muslim Turks, and in 1095 they banned Christian pilgrims from the city. This angered both the western Christian Church, based in Rome, and the eastern Christian Church in Constantinople. From Rome, Pope Urban II called on Christians to free Jerusalem, and so launched the First Crusade, or war of the cross. In 1096 a European force joined with an army from Constantinople. Their leaders were

Both sides built strong castles. To capture a castle, soldiers besieged it, sometimes for months. They battered at the gates and tried to blow up the walls, while being bombarded with missiles from inside.

1096	1099	1147	1187	1189	1191	1202
First Crusade, called by Pope Urban II. Peter the Hermit leads a peasant army across Europe.	Crusaders defeat the Turks and capture Jerusalem.	Second Crusade. German and French armies are beaten.	Saladin captures Jerusalem.	Third Crusade, led by Frederick I Barbarossa of the Holy Roman empire, Philip II of France, and Richard I of England.	Crusaders capture the port of Acre in Palestine.	Fourth Crusade attacks Egypt.

Saladin (1138–1193) was the [gre]atest of the Muslim leaders. [He] took Jerusalem, but in 1192 [made] peace with Richard I, allowing [Chri]stian pilgrims to enter the city.

[ins]pired by religious faith, but also by a [des]ire to increase territory and wealth. In three years they captured Jerusalem and went on to set up Christian kingdoms in Palestine. None of the seven later crusades matched this success.

The Crusades inspired many stories of bravery and honor on both sides. But [the] Crusaders found the weather in the Holy [Land] very hot, and soon learned from Muslim [fight]ers that it was best to wear airy, loose [robe]s over their armor.

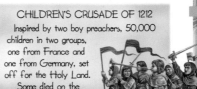

CHILDREN'S CRUSADE OF 1212
Inspired by two boy preachers, 50,000 children in two groups, one from France and one from Germany, set off for the Holy Land. Some died on the journey, and many others were sold as slaves in North Africa.

disasters also happened. Before the First Crusade even set out, a peasant army known as the People's Crusade wandered across Europe and was eventually massacred by the Turks. Then the Fourth Crusade of 1202 turned aside to loot the Christian city of Constantinople.

The Crusaders never did win back the Holy Land. But Europeans learned more about Eastern science, food, and medicine as trade between Europe and Asia grew.

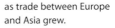

◄ Ships were loaded with soldiers and equipment bound for the Crusades. Groups of knights, including the powerful Knights Templars, protected journeying Christians.

A Medieval Town

IN THE Middle Ages, towns in Europe were noisy and crowded by day, but quiet and dark at night. The silence was broken only by watchmen calling out the hours. Churches, guilds, fairs, and markets all drew people into the towns.

▶ This medieval painting shows French tradesmen at work in their shops. Tailors stitch richly colored cloth and a grocer sets out his goods. Up the street a barber is shaving a customer.

IF YOU WALKED through a medieval town, you took care where you stepped, because people threw out their garbage into the muddy streets. Open drains ran alongside and smelled foul. People either fetched water from the town well or bought it from the water-seller, hoping it was

clean. Pigs and chickens wandered in and out of small yards. Houses were b close together, with the top floors oft jutting out over the streets. Since mos houses were made chiefly of wood, th caught fire easily. At night, the curfew bell warned people to cover or put ou their kitchen fires.

Many houses doubled as workshops and shops. Craftworkers and traders formed groups

◀ Stained-glass windows told stories in pictures. In church, people who could not read looked at the colorful Bible stories to learn more about the Christian faith.

1136	1162	1200s	1209
Fire destroys many old, straw-thatched buildings in London.	Work begins on the cathedral of Notre Dame in Paris, which by 1210 is a city with paved streets, walls, and twenty-four gates.	Many new towns are founded in Europe. City-states develop in Italy and Germany.	A new London Bridge built.

MONEY MAKES MONEY

European merchants usually carried silver coins, but Arabs preferred gold. As international trade increased, Italian merchants set up the first banks, using written bills of exchange to pay for goods instead of heavy bags of coins.

churches, and defensive walls. Large trading cities in Europe, such as Hamburg, Antwerp, and London, grew rich from buying and selling wool and other goods. About 90 cities in northern Europe formed the Hanseatic League to fight pirates, win more trade, and keep out rivals.

d guilds to organize their businesses to set standards of work. Guilds also ed pageants and plays in the streets. e towns were famous for their fairs, h attracted merchants from all over pe, as well as entertainers, fake ors, and pickpockets.

towns, work was to be found ding magnificent cathedrals,

Market day in a medieval town. People brought in farm produce to sell, visited stalls and shops, gossiped, and drank at the ale house. Acrobats, actors, and dancing bears amused the crowds.

| erman towns eck and urg form a association, nown as the atic League. | 1285 English merchants are banned from selling their goods in churchyards. | 1300 The wool trade is at its peak in England. Large churches are built in prosperous wool towns. | 1348–1349 People flee towns during the Black Death in England. | 1377 London by now has at least 50 guilds and a population of more than 35,000. | 1400s Morality plays, in which actors stage tales of good against evil, are performed in churches or in the streets. |

The Mongol Empire

"INHUMAN and beastly, rather monsters than men..." is how the English historian Matthew Paris described the Mongols in the 1200s. Mongol armies sent a shockwave of fear around Asia and Europe, conquering a vast area of land that formed the largest empire in history.

▶ Genghis Khan's empire extended from the river Danube in the west to the Pacific in the east. The capital was Karakorum.

THE MONGOLS lived on the plains of Central Asia, from the Ural mountains to the Gobi Desert. They were nomads, wandering with their herds and living in portable tents (yurts). Their leaders were called khan 1206, Temujin Khan brought all the tr under his rule and was proclaimed Genghis Khan, "lord of all." In a lifetim conquest, he seized an empire that extended from the Pacific Ocean to th river Danube, incorporating t Persian emp

▶ Mongols preferred to fight on horseback. Warriors controlled their horses with their feet, leaving their hands free to shoot bows and hurl lances. Mongol cavalry charges usually overwhelmed the enemy.

1206	1211	1215	1217	1219	1224
Temujin is chosen to be khan of all the Mongols. He takes the name Genghis Khan.	The Mongol army attacks China.	Beijing, capital of China, is taken by the Mongols.	China and Korea are controlled by the Mongols. Their new capital is Karakorum.	The Mongols sweep west to attack the empire of Khwarezm (Persia and Turkey).	Mongol ar invade Ru then Pola and Hung

92

> The Mongols roamed in search of fresh grassland for their sheep, horses, and goats. They carried their felt tents (yurts) with them on ox carts.

Mongols continued their attacks Genghis Khan died. In 1237 a gol army led by Batu Khan, one of ghis's sons, invaded Russia.

Europe, people panicked as word ad of the Mongols' speed and city in battle. Mongol soldiers eled with five horses and were expert with s and lances. In victory, were merciless,

slaughtering the people of a city and carting away treasure. Western Europe was saved only when the Mongols turned homeward on the death of their leader Ogadai Khan in 1241.

> Genghis Khan was ruthless in battle, but kept peace in his empire and ruled fairly, if sternly. Trade flourished during his rule.

MARES' MILK

Horses were vital to the Mongols, who drank fresh mares' milk. They also fermented the milk in skin bags hung from wooden frames to make a strong drink called kumiss. At victory celebrations, kumiss was drunk and fiddles strung with horsehair were played.

Kublai Khan and China

GENGHIS KHAN'S grandson was called Kublai Khan. When he became leader of the Mongols he moved from the windswept steppes of Central Asia to rule the most splendid court in the world, in China. At this time, China was the most sophisticated, technologically advanced country in the world.

Nutmeg **Cinnamon** **Clov**

 Spices for flavoring food and disguisi taste of bad meat were traded from the I Indies and India to China and the West.

KUBLAI KHAN'S armies overthrew th ruling Song dynasty in China. By 127 controlled most of the country. The r emperor moved his capital to Beijing China at this time had the world's big cities, including Kaifeng and Hangzh (each with more than one million pe

Chinese silks, porcelain, and other luxuries astonished travelers from Eu and Africa. They were also amazed by Chinese gunpowder

◀ In China, Kublai Khan (1216–1294) founded the Yuan dynasty, which lasted until 1368. Yuan means "origin of the Universe."

▶ Merchants traveled in caravans (groups of laden camels and horses) for protection against bandits. From China, they followed the Silk Road across mountains and deserts to the markets of the Middle East. The Silk Road provided the only regular contact between Europe and China.

1216	**1260**	**1271**	**1274**	**1276**	**1279**	**1281**
Kublai Khan is born.	Kublai is elected Great Khan of the Mongols.	Marco Polo sets out from Venice, Italy, for China.	Kublai Khan sends an army to invade Japan, but it is driven back by a storm.	The Mongols defeat the Song fleet near Guangzhou.	Kublai Khan rules all China.	A second Mongol a on Japan is foiled b typhoon, which the Japanese call kami the "divine wind."

◄ Writing was a government tool and an art form in China. More than 40,000 characters, originally picture-signs, were written with a fine brush.

MARCO POLO
In 1271 an Italian merchant-explorer named Marco Polo (1256–1323) traveled to China from Venice. He stayed for 24 years, touring China in the service of Kublai Khan. Later he wrote in praise of China's cities, with their baths and restaurants, the fine mail system, and the paper money, as yet unknown in Europe.

...kets. Other inventions included paper ...king, the magnetic compass, and ...ting with movable type.

...ublai Khan was a fair ruler and a ...iant general. He strengthened his ...pire by building long roads to connect ...flung territories. He organized charity ...the sick and food supplies in case of ...ine. He also twice tried to invade ...an, without success. After his ...th in 1294, the mighty Mongol ...pire began to decline and by ...mid 1300s had largely broken ...Then in 1369, Timur "Leng" (the ...e), known as Tamerlane, made ...self ruler of Samarkand in ...tral Asia. He set out to re-create ...Mongol empire, and conquered ...sia, Iraq, Syria, Afghanistan, and ...t of Russia. In 1397 he ...ded India, and died on the ...y to China in 1405.

☑ The Chinese began making paper about 105. In the imperial workshops, paper-makers used hemp or mulberry tree bark for fiber. Pulp was spread on mesh trays to dry into sheets. Early paper was used for wrapping and clothes, not for writing on.

1325	1368	1395	1398	1402	1405
Ibn Battuta begins a 24-year journey from his homeland, Morocco, through Persia, India, and Indonesia, and on to China.	The Mongols are driven from China by Ming forces.	Tamerlane, a descendant of Genghis Khan, invades large parts of southern Russia.	Tamerlane takes Delhi in India.	Tamerlane defeats the Ottoman Turks at Ankyra.	Death of Tamerlane.

THE MIDDLE AGES

The Black Death

THE Black Death was the most horrific natural disaster of the Middle Ages. It was a devastating plague that killed many millions of people in Europe and Asia. One Italian historian wrote: "This is the end of the world."

THE PLAGUE came to Europe from As 1347. Disease ravaged a Mongol arm fighting in the Crimea (southern Russ The desperate Mongols catapulted diseased corpses over the walls of a fortress defended by Italians. When th Italians sailed home to Genoa, they carried the disease with them.

The disease was bubonic plague, passed to humans from infecte rats through flea bi The nam

1344	1347	1348	1349	1350	1353
Bubonic plague breaks out in China and India.	The plague reaches Genoa in Italy and spreads west.	In the summer, the disease hits southern England. In the winter, it reaches London.	The Black Death spreads to Ireland, Wales, and Scotland. Also affected are France, Spain, Germany, and Russia.	The epidemic reaches Scandinavia.	The Black Deatl epidemic eases many as 20 mil people in Europ are dead.

A picture of the time shows a procession penitents whipping themselves in the streets.

...ack Death" came from the black spots ...at appeared on victims, who also ...veloped swellings in their armpits and ...oin, and coughed up blood. Many ...ople died the same day they fell ill. No ...edieval doctor knew why the Black ...ath struck or how to cure it. To many ...hristians it seemed a punishment from God, and some took to the streets, whipping themselves as a penance for the sins of humanity.

◀ Neither town governments nor local doctors could fight the plague. Many people fled, leaving the sick to die. Crosses on doors showed the disease had struck. Carts carried the dead away.

The Black Death raged from China to Scandinavia. As it spread, panic-stricken people fled from the towns. Wherever they went, the plague went with them. So many people died (at least 25 million, or a third of the people in Europe) that villages were left deserted and fields overgrown. The Church lost many priests, the only educated men of the time. Half of England's monks and nuns died, and three archbishops of Canterbury died in one year.

Repeated plague attacks throughout the 14th century left Europe short of people to work and farm the land, and pushed up wages. Unrest over wages and taxes led to an uprising in France in 1358 and to the Peasants' Revolt in England, led by Wat Tyler, in 1381.

BLACK DEATH

The black rat carried the fleas that transmitted the disease. The rats traveled on ships from port to port, and as they moved the Black Death spread at terrifying speed. There were rats and fleas in every medieval town and in most houses. Garbage in the streets and poor sanitation made towns an ideal breeding ground for disease. Many towns lost half their populations to the plague, and some villages were abandoned.

| ...asants' ...sing in ...ern France ...vagely ...down. | 1381 The Peasants' Revolt in England, with rioting in the southeast (in Essex and Kent). | 1400 Further outbreaks of the Black Death continue until this date. |

African Kingdoms

IN THIS period, the abundant riches of the mightiest kingdoms in Africa impressed Muslims and Europeans who visited their courts. Much of this wealth came from trade in gold, salt, and slaves.

MANY NORTH AFRICAN kingdoms were Muslim. From there, preachers took Islam to West Africa. In the kingdom of Ghana (modern-day Gambia, Guinea, Mali, and Senegal), Muslim traders marveled at warriors with gold-mounted swords and shields guarding the king in his capital, Koumbi Saleh. Even the guard dogs around the royal pavilion wore gold collars.

◀ Cowrie shells like these were use currency in trade. Goods of equal v were also exchanged, or "barte

Ghana reached the peak of its power in the 10th century, when controlled both the gold and salt tra

In the 1300s, Muslim camel caravans crossed the Sahara Desert to the city o Timbuktu. They carried cloth and luxur items, to be exchanged for slaves, leath goods, and kola nuts (used as a drug). Timbuktu was the capital of Mali, an Islamic kingdom that replaced Ghana as the most powerf empire in West Africa. Mali's most famous ruler, Mansa Musa, ma a pilgrimage to Mecca in 1324, with an entoura of 60,000 followers. His fame spread a far as Europe, where his kingdom was shown on maps as a la of gold.

▶ Many people in Africa were skilled in metalworking. This bronze hand altar shows a Benin king with his wives, servants, and soldiers. The lost-wax process was used to make bronzes of superb quality.

750	770	800	800s	900s	969	1043	1062
Arab armies have overrun most of North Africa. Islam spreads westward.	Soninke people begin to build the kingdom of Ghana, led by King Maghan Sisse.	Ife kingdom in Nigeria becomes prominent.	Arabs and Persians set up trading posts in East Africa.	Ghana controls gold and salt trade and buys cloth from Europe.	The Fatimid dynasty conquers Egypt.	Mandingo empire of Jenne is founded in West Africa.	Muslim Ber (Almoravids build their capital of Marrakech.

◄ The kingdom of Ghana rose to power by the 900s, but was later swallowed up by the Islamic empire of Mali. Other African kingdoms also flourished in West Africa.

prosperity lasted until almost 1500, when the Portuguese took control of trade in the region and the trading cities were destroyed.

arther south were kingdoms just as ndid, such as Ife, Oyo, and Benin, re trade made powerful rulers rich. craftworkers of Benin made cast ze figures, the finest metal ptures in Africa. Benin's r, the oba, lived in a ed city with his 100 or vives. The people of Benin ed with the Portuguese, began sailing along the t African coast in the 1400s.

East Africa, people living in t are now Somalia, Kenya and zania traded in ivory, animal s, and slaves with cities on the st. These were visited by ships n Arabia and India. The East Coast

Mansa Musa on his mage to Mecca at the head large army, with camels, es, and foot soldiers. His spread as far as Europe.

1100	1163	1173	1200s	1250	1307	1440–1480
a is ered ravids.	All Muslim Spain is now part of the Almoravid empire.	Almohads overthrow Almoravids and rule northeast Africa and Spain.	Saladin declares himself sultan of Egypt.	Founding of Benin kingdom under the first oba, Eweka.	Mamelukes rule in Egypt.	Mali empire at its height under Mansa Musa, with its capital at Timbuktu.	Reign of the most famous oba of Benin, Ewuare the Great.

Japan's Warlords

EMPERORS in medieval Japan had little power, relying on warlords, or shoguns, who led armies of warriors and ruled the land.

JAPAN'S EMPERORS were dominated by powerful military families. From these soldier clans came the shoguns, such as the powerful Minamoto Yoritomo (1147–1199). The shoguns drove off attacks from Mongol China with their fiercely loyal samurai warriors. Like a knight in Europe, a samurai held land that was farmed by peasants, while he hunted or trained with sword and bow.

> A Samurai warrior wore a steel horned helmet and fought with bow, sword, and lance. His body armor was made in pieces from leather or lacquered iron strips, and so was fully flexible.

The samurai eventually came to form elite warrior class. They practised Zen Buddhism, a philosophy brought to Japan from China in 582.

From the 1300s, Japan was torn by civil wars between daimyos – lords w built castles to guard their lands. The daimyos led armies of samurai warrio The most powerful daimyo was Hideyoshi Toyotomi (1537–1598 peasant who rose to become samurai warlord. He controlle all Japan from 1585 until his death. One of his lieutenant Ieyasu, became shogun in 1603 and founded the Tokugawa dynasty.

DIVINE WIND

The Japanese believed the gods protected them. In 1274 and 1281 Kublai Khan sent fleets to conquer Japan. The first fled before a storm. The second was sunk by a typhoon (shown here as a god), which the Japanese called kamikaze, or "divine wind."

582	995	1192	1219	1274	1333	1338
Buddhism reaches Japan.	Literary and artistic achievements under Fujiwara Michinaga (to 1028).	Minamoto Yoritomo sets up military government or shogunate.	Hojo clan rules Japan (to 1333).	Mongols try to invade Japan, but are driven back by the "divine wind."	Daigo II overthrows Hojo shoguns and rules to 1336.	Ashikaga family rule as shoguns until 1573

The Hundred Years' War

EDWARD III became king of England in 1327. He believed he also had a claim to the French throne so, in 1337, he declared war on France. War between England and France lasted on and off until 1453.

EDWARD'S FORCES won a sea battle at Sluys and two great land victories at Crécy and Poitiers, but were driven back by the French king, Charles V, and his commander Bertrand du Guesclin. In 1360 Edward gave up his claim to the French throne in return for land.

Years of truce followed until England's king Henry V renewed his claim to the throne in 1414. He led his troops to France where, in 1415, they defeated a much larger French army at Agincourt.

Soldiers fought with (left to right) halberd, longbow, sword, cannon, and crossbow. Only knights wore full armour. If knocked from his horse, a knight was often imprisoned and ransomed.

To make peace Henry married the French king's daughter, but he died in 1422 before his baby son could become king of France. Fighting continued as the French were inspired by a peasant girl named Joan of Arc (1412–1431), who claimed to hear voices from God. She fought until the English burned her as a witch. Under the weak rule of Henry VI, the English lost first Paris, then Rouen, and by 1453 all French lands except Calais.

The death of Joan of Arc. The English hoped this would end French resistance, but the French were inspired to fight on and win back their lands.

1337	1340	1356	1380	1415	1431	1453
Edward III goes to war with France, claiming the throne.	Sea battle of Sluys (off Belgium) won by English.	English victory at Poitiers, led by Edward III's son, the Black Prince.	France's Charles V dies. Charles VI succeeds him.	England's Henry V gains control of France after victory at Agincourt.	Joan of Arc is burned to death.	End of the Hundred Years' War.

Pacific Voyagers

THE FIRST PEOPLE to settle Oceania – Australia, New Zealand, and the Pacific islands – almost certainly came originally from Asia. They made some astonishing voyages, crossing stretches of the world's largest ocean in wooden canoes.

THE FIRST HUMANS to settle in New Guinea and Australia had arrived there by 40,000 years ago. Until about 10,000 years ago, these two landmasses formed one large continent, of which Tasmania (now an island) was also part. So it was

▶ Aboriginal paintings on rocks and tree bark often depicted animals and people. They were painted in pigments made from coloured earth and were drawn to keep ancestor spirits alive.

relatively easy for humans from Asia t migrate there, either overland or by crossing narrow stretches of water.

The first peoples of Australia probal arrived from the islands of Southeast Asia. Although they never made meta tools, they survived in Australia's ofter harsh environments, spearing fish anc using boomerangs to kill animals for food. They became expert at finding seeds, insect grubs, roots, tubers, and fruits to eat. The modern Aboriginal

▼ The Maoris of New Zealand built wooden stockades, called pas. Warri fought from platforms on the walls. To capture an enemy's fort was great triumph. The victors took the food stored inside.

40,000 years ago
People move from Southeast Asia to the islands of Indonesia, New Guinea, and Australia.

c. 25,000 years ago
Aborigines settle in southeast Australia. This part of Australia later becomes the island of Tasmania (when the sea level rises about 12,000 years ago).

c. 4000 BC
People from New Guinea settle in the Solomon Islands (Melanesia).

c. 1000 BC
People from Melanesia sai east to settle on Fiji. Other people from Polynesia also make voyages to colonize Fijian islands.

eoples of Australia preserve some of
ese ancient skills.

Humans settled the islands of the
estern Pacific, known as Melanesia, by
sland-hopping." To reach the more
mote islands of Micronesia (such as
uam, the Marianas, and Nauru) and
olynesia (including Fiji, Tonga, and
amoa) was more difficult. About 4,000
ears ago the intrepid colonists set sail
outrigger canoes, loaded with the
ssentials of life – coconuts, taro, yams,
ananas, breadfruit, pigs, and chickens.
hey relied on skill and luck to land on
ands dotted across the vast Pacific
cean. Canoe voyagers traveled as far
west as Easter Island and, about
2,000 years ago, to the
Hawaiian islands.

▶ One of the 600 mysterious stone
statues scattered around Easter Island.
The tallest figure is 36 feet (11 m)
high. No one knows why the stone
heads were carved and set up.

One of the last places
the voyagers colonized
was New Zealand.
Polynesian
Maoris had
landed in New
Zealand by
about AD 750.

Australia was
isolated, apart from
occasional visits
from Indonesian and
possibly Chinese
traders, until the 1500s.
The great southern
continent and the
Pacific islands remained
unknown to Europeans.

◀ A Maori war canoe sets out on a raid. Like other
Pacific islanders, the Maoris built wooden canoes
for sea travel, often twin-hulled like modern
catamarans. Some settlements were
the result of accidental voyages,
others of planned migrations.

100	c. 400	c. 750	900
ynesian tlers arrive in Hawaiian ands.	The first settlers land on Easter Island. They probably came from Polynesia, though some historians claim that the island was colonized by South Americans.	Maoris start to settle New Zealand. They probably came from eastern Polynesia. They do not use the name Maori until much later.	Earliest recorded rulers of Tonga, an island group in the South Pacific settled earlier by Polynesians, probably from Samoa.

The Age of Discovery

EXPLORERS AND EMPIRES 1400-1700

THE 1400s mark the end of the Middle Ages. In Europe, the new ideas of the Renaissance and Reformation transformed the way people thought about themselves and the world, and the way they lived.

THREE EVENTS are often picked out as marking the end of the medieval period and the start of the modern age. They are the fall of Constantinople in 1453, which ended the last traces of the old Roman empire; the development of printing in the 1450s, which made books cheaper and more widely available; and the first voyage of Christopher Columbus to the Americas in 1492.

1464	1492	1497	1500	1501	1517	1522	1526	1535	1543
Rise of Songhai empire in Africa.	Columbus sails from Spain to America.	Portuguese explorers sail to India.	Renaissance is at its height in Italy.	Start of Safavid dynasty in Persia.	Martin Luther begins the Reformation in Europe.	First round-the-world voyage by Magellan's expedition.	Babur founds the Mughal empire in India.	Spain completes conquest of Aztec and Inca empires.	Copernicus argues that the Sun, not the Earth, is center of the solar system.

The "Age of Discovery" was a time when the peoples of the world came to increasing contact with each other. People in America, Africa, and Asia had greater contact with Europe. Europeans increased their power in the world through trade, through the use of new technology such as cannon and muskets, and through a restless search for new lands and wealth that sent explorers and adventurers across the oceans. By the 1600s, several European countries had established permanent colonies overseas.

This period also saw many new ideas and challenges to old beliefs. Religious quarrels led to bitter wars. There were power struggles between kings and parliaments, as democratic government slowly developed. From the 1500s, there were startling advances in science, with inventions such as the telescope and microscope revealing new wonders, and prompting new questions. Great scientists such as Copernicus, Galileo, and Newton challenged the old ideas, and a new freedom of thought began to shake the foundations of society.

	1588	1590	1616	1609	1618	1620	1642	1643	1665
the battle of epanto, istians defeat slim oman Turks.	Spanish Armada fails to invade England.	Japan is united by Hideyoshi.	First known European landing in Australia.	Galileo uses a telescope to study the stars and planets.	Thirty Years' War begins.	Mayflower pilgrims from England land in America.	English Civil War begins.	Louis XIV becomes king of France.	Isaac Newton reveals the nature of light.

The Renaissance

THE RENAISSANCE was a "rebirth" of interest in the art and learning of ancient Greece and Rome. Many historians say that it marked the end of the Middle Ages and the beginning of our modern world. It began in Italy, and in the 1400s spread throughout Europe, changing the way people thought about the world.

THE RENAISSANCE began among the scholars, artists, and scientists of Italy. They had new ideas, but also turned to the past, rediscovering the learning of ancient Greece and Rome. Many old handwritten books were brought to Italy by scholars fleeing from the city of Constantinople (the ancient capital of the Eastern Roman empire), which was captured by the Ottoman Turks in 1453. With a greater knowledge of ancient science and beliefs, European scholars were inspired to think again about established religious teaching. In literature, great Italian poets such as Petrarch began to explore human emotions. By the early 1500s, three painters of genius – Leonardo da Vinci, Michelangelo, and Raphael – were bringing a new energy and realism to

A print workshop in Denmark, about 1600. The technology of printing with a screw press and metal type spread throughout Europe, and for the first time books became widely available.

1306	1308	1387	1416	1453	1454
Italian artist Giotto di Bondone paints frescos that are more lifelike than earlier medieval paintings.	Dante Alighieri begins writing "The Divine Comedy" in his native Italian, not Latin.	Geoffrey Chaucer begins The Canterbury Tales, written in English.	Italian sculptor Donatello breaks new ground with free-standing figures, including his nude David.	Constantinople is captured by the Turks; many of its scholars flee to Italy.	Johannes Gutenberg perfects printing with movable type. By 1476, William Caxton is printing in London.

▶ The great dome of Florence Cathedral in Italy, designed by Filippo Brunelleschi, the first major architect of the Italian Renaissance. Begun in 1420, it took 14 years to complete.

▶ The new universe, as conceived by Polish astronomer Copernicus in 1543. He put the Sun, not the Earth, at the center of the universe. This challenged the established theory of the 2nd-century Greek astronomer Ptolemy.

...rt. Architects designed new and elegant ...uildings that echoed the classical styles ...f ancient Greece and Rome.

The Renaissance was fueled by new technology. Printing with movable type, developed by Johannes Gutenberg in Germany, made books cheaper and more plentiful, so new ideas could be read by more people. Some new ideas were astounding, such as Copernicus's theory that the Sun was the center of the solar system. The Renaissance changed the Western world forever.

▶ A flying machine drawn by the Italian artist ...onardo da Vinci. As well as being an artistic ...ius, Leonardo was a visionary, devising several ...uristic machines.

▶ Dante Alighieri, whose poem *"The Divine Comedy"* explores love, death, and faith. Dante wrote in his own language, Italian, and not Latin, which was the language of scholars.

466–1536	**1478**	**1508**	**1513**	**1516**	**1543**	**1590**
...fe of ...asmus. He ...blishes ...udies of the ...ld and New ...staments.	Lorenzo de Medici makes Florence a center of art and learning. Sandro Botticelli paints *Primavera*.	Michelangelo paints the ceiling of the Sistine Chapel in the Vatican, Rome.	Italian Niccolo Machiavelli writes *The Prince*, on the theory of government.	Sir Thomas More publishes *Utopia*.	Nicolas Copernicus's theory about the solar system.	William Shakespeare is writing plays in England.

The Aztecs

THE AZTECS were fierce warriors. They conquered an empire that eventually extended right across Mexico, and was at its height in the early 1500s. But in 1521 Aztec rule came to a sudden end. The Aztecs lost their empire to a small band of Spanish treasure-seekers.

🔺 Aztec warrior chiefs wore feather headdresses (feathers and jaguar skins were traded throughout the empire). But most people wore simple clothes woven from plant fibers.

THE AZTECS came to dominate other Native Americans in Central America by fighting constant wars with them. Their capital, Tenochtitlan, was founded in 1325 on an island in the middle of Lake Texcoco (now the site of Mexico City). Tenochtitlan was a walled city of 100,000 people, with stone temples and a network of canals. Causeways linked the main island to the mainland, and smaller islands were specially built as a place to grow vegetables.

▶ Like the Maya, the Aztecs built pyramid-temples. This Mayan pyramid at Uxmal gives an idea of what the Aztec Great Temple at Tenochtitlan may have looked like before it was destroyed.

c. 1200	1325	1440–1469	1500	1502	1519
Aztecs settle in the Valley of Mexico.	Traditional date for the founding of Tenochtitlan.	Reign of Montezuma I. The empire is extended.	The empire is at its height. The Aztecs rule more than 10 million people, most of whom belong to other tribes.	Montezuma II becomes emperor.	Spaniards led by Hernando Cortés march on Tenochtitlan. They are aided by tribes hostile to the Aztecs

The great Calendar Stone shows the face of the Sun-god Tonatiuh. The stone measures feet (3.7 m) across and weighs about 25 ns. It was unearthed in Mexico City in 1790.

The Aztecs were skilled in sculpture, oetry, music, and engineering. They orshiped the Sun as the giver of all life. ach year priests sacrificed thousands of ctims to the Sun-god, cutting out their earts as offerings, in the belief that this ould bring good harvests and rosperity. Other sacrificial victims were rowned or beheaded.

Farmers grew corn, beans, and matoes, and merchants traded hroughout the empire. The ruling class vere warriors. All warriors had to capture at least one enemy for sacrifice, and conquered peoples were forced to pay taxes to the emperor.

In 1519 Spanish treasure-seekers led by Hernando Cortés attacked the Aztecs. Emperor Montezuma II welcomed them, believing Cortés was the god Quetzalcoatl, but he was taken prisoner. Aztec spears and clubs were no match for Spanish guns, and by 1521 the Aztec empire was at an end.

The heart of the Aztec empire was the fertile Valley of Mexico, where the capital, Tenochtitlan, and most of the major cities were located. These thrived as busy market centers. The empire extended east into present-day Guatemala.

GODS AND SACRIFICE

One of the reasons that the Aztecs went to war was to capture prisoners, for sacrifice to the gods. They believed that the hearts and blood of their victims nourished the gods. Priests cut open the bodies using sacrificial knives like the one above. Sacrifices had to be performed on the right day, according to the sacred 260-day calendar.

20	1521
e Aztecs rise up ainst the Spanish vaders. Montezuma wounded and dies.	Cortés and his men attack and capture Tenochtitlan. End of the Aztec empire.

The Incas

FROM the mountains of Peru, the god-emperor of the Incas ruled a highly organized empire. Civil war and Spanish invasion finally caused the empire to fall.

A mosaic mask made from mussel shells. Masks of gods' faces were worn by Inca priests for ceremonies, and were often richly decorated.

THE INCAS took over from the Chimu as rulers of the Andes mountains of South America. Their civilization reached its peak in the 1400s under the ruler Pachacuti, who defeated an invading army from a neighboring state.

Pachacuti reformed the way the kingdom was run. He appointed a central administration to control the building of towns and ensure that farms and workshops were run efficiently. From the capital, Cuzco, he and his successors expanded the Inca empire to include parts of Chile, Bolivia and Ecuador.

The Incas communicated over long distances by sending fast runners with messages in the form of quipus (knotted cords). A message could be sent 120 miles (200 km) in a day along a system of paved roads.

The Incas built stone cities and fine roads, which were used by traders. Goods were bartered – exchanged for goods of equal value (the Incas did not use money). Farmers terraced the mountain slopes to grow corn, cotton, and potatoes. Although they had neither writing nor wheeled vehicles, the Incas' many skills included music, bridge-building, and medicine.

In 1525 the Inca empire was at its greatest extent. But in 1527, after Emperor Huayna Capac died, the empire was split between his two sons and civil war broke out. In the 1530s a Spanish expedition led by Francisco Pizarro arrived, seeking gold. The Europeans were impressed by Cuzco's

1200
Incas begin to conquer neighboring peoples in the Andes region.

1438
Inca empire starts, under Pachacuti, the 9th Inca (king). He fights off an invasion from a neighboring state, the Chanca, and rebuilds Cuzco as the capita

aces, temples, and
ter supply, and
the fortress of
csahuaman,
ich was built from
ge stones that fitted
gether perfectly without mortar.

Though few in number, the Spaniards
d horses and guns, which were both
w to the Incas. In 1532, Pizarro

The Spanish were fewer in number than
Incas. But they had horses, armor, and
s. Many Incas fought
vely, but with their
murdered, they
e quickly
eated.

A gold raft depicting
El Dorado, a legendary ruler
whose body was said to be
dusted with gold every year.
Such tales made European
invaders greedy for gold.

captured the Inca ruler
Atahualpa and demanded for a ransom a
room full of gold and two rooms full of
silver. The ransom was paid, but Atahualpa
was killed anyway. The leaderless Inca
armies were swiftly defeated, although
resistance to Spanish rule continued from
scattered mountain forts, such as Machu
Picchu, until 1572.

–1500	1525	1527	1532
er Topa Inca and his son, yna Capac, the empire is nded from Peru into ern-day Bolivia, Chile, ador, and Colombia.	About this time, the first potatoes are taken to Europe from South America.	Death of the emperor Huayna Capac; civil war starts between his sons Atahualpa and Huascar.	Atahualpa defeats Huascar, who is imprisoned and later killed. Francisco Pizarro, with 167 soldiers, attacks Atahualpa's forces and captures Cuzco.

112

Voyages of Discovery

IN THE late 1400s, Europeans began to explore the oceans. In stronger ships capable of longer voyages, they went in search of trade, treasure, and new lands. Their voyages took them west to the Americas and east to Asia.

AFTER THE Byzantine empire fell to the Ottoman Turks in 1453, the old land trade routes between Europe and Asia were cut off. Europeans anxious to get spices – essential for flavoring and preserving their food – had to find a new way to reach India and the islands of Indonesia. This need, coupled with a growing curiosity and a spirit of adventure, sent Europeans to sea.

▶ European explorers sailed in ships called carracks with three masts and square sails. Columbus's ship "Santa Maria" probably looked like this.

First to go exploring were the Portuguese. Their prince, Henry the Navigator, took a keen interest in shipbuilding and navigation. He directe his sailors west into the Atlantic and south to explore the west coast of Afri There they set up forts and traded for gold and ivory. Spanish, French, Dutch, and English sailors followed. Some explorers, like Christopher Columbus, headed farther west, and ended up in the Americas – much to their surprise.

Portugal and Spain began to settle and plunder the America dividing it between them by treaty. By 1517 the Portugues

◀ Seafarers used simple naviga instruments such as the astrol (top) and cross-staff to their ships' positions by and stars. The magn compass showed North, was not always relia

---

1419	1431	1488	1492	1494	1497	1500
Portuguese sail to the Madeira Islands.	Portuguese reach the Azores.	Bartolomeu Dias of Portugal explores the west coast of Africa as far south as the Cape of Good Hope.	Christopher Columbus, an Italian, leads a Spanish expedition to America.	Spain and Portugal divide the Americas between them by the Treaty of Tordesillas.	John Cabot, an Italian in the service of England, sails to Canada. The Portuguese explorer Vasco Da Gama sails around Africa to India.	Pedro Alva Cabral fro Portugal s to Brazil, South America.

d landed in China (by sailing east
ound Africa to India and onward).
arly 30 years later they reached Japan.

The ships used by the explorers were
all, but more seaworthy than the
msy vessels of the Middle Ages. They
ed a mixture of square and lateen
angular) sails for easier steering and
eater maneuverability. Sailors had only
ude maps and simple instruments to
ide them on voyages that lasted many
onths. In 1519 a Portuguese captain,
rdinand Magellan, set out from Spain
th five ships. The ships sailed around
uth America, across the Pacific Ocean
the Philippines (where Magellan was

NEW WORLD FOODS

As well as gold and silver, European
explorers brought back new foods from the
Americas. Potatoes, tomatoes, and peppers,
plants native to America, were all
unknown in Europe before 1500.
Potatoes were at first a luxury,
served only to the rich at banquets. Chocolate,
from the cacao tree, was first brought to
Spain from Mexico in 1520. Also
from the New World came
tobacco, turkeys, and maize.

killed) and across the
Indian Ocean to Africa. Only one ship,
commanded by Sebastian Del Cano,
found its way home to Spain, becoming
the first ship to sail around the world.

The
ages of
overy
ealed to
opeans that
world was
er than
ent
graphers
believed.
ors crossed
ans and met
les unknown
earlier
opeans.

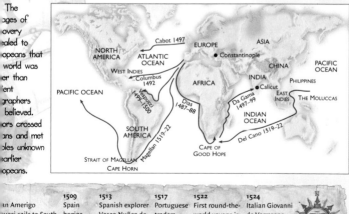

an Amerigo
ucci sails to South
rica. A map
ished in 1507
es the continent
erica" after him.

1509	1513	1517	1522	1524
Spain begins settlement of the Americas.	Spanish explorer Vasco Nuñez de Balboa is the first European to see the Pacific.	Portuguese traders reach China.	First round-the-world voyage is completed by Ferdinand Magellan's Spanish crew.	Italian Giovanni da Verrazano searches for a northwest passage from Europe to Asia.

Spain and Portugal

MEDIEVAL Spain was divided between Christian and Muslim kingdoms. After wars, two Christian monarchs ended Muslim rule in Spain: they were Ferdinand of Aragon and Isabella of Castile.

◄ In the early 1400s, Spain was not yet on kingdom. Aragon and Castile were the strongest Christian kingdoms, while Granada was ruled by Muslim emirs.

IN 1469 Ferdinand and Isabella were married, uniting Spain's two strongest Christian kingdoms. By 1492 their forces had captured Granada, the last Muslim outpost in Spain. The new rulers were intolerant of other religions and set up the Spanish Inquisition to seek out heretics – both Christians who held different beliefs from the Roman Catholic Church and peop of other faiths, such as Jews.

In the 16th century, Spain became Europe's strongest nation. Its army fought wars in Europe (against the Dutch, for example) and its navy controlled the profitable trade in gold and silver from Spain's new empire in the Americas.

◄ Catherine of Aragon (1485–1536) was the daughter of King Ferdinand and Queen Isabella of Spain. In 1509 she became the first of the six wives of King Henry VIII of England.

► Columbus leaves the court of Spain, having won the support of King Ferdinand and Queen Isabella for his westward voyage. He set sail in 1492, convinced that the Atlantic was a narrow ocean.

711	Early 1000s	1143	Late 1200s	1479	1492	1512
Muslims invade southern Spain (which includes what later becomes Portugal).	Muslim central rule of Spain collapses in civil war.	Portugal gains independence from Castile.	Granada is the only Moorish kingdom in Spain.	Aragon and Castile become one kingdom.	Moors are forced out of Granada. Jews are expelled from Spain. Columbus sails to America.	Ferdinand seizes Nav to comple unification of Spain.

Spanish power reached its peak during the reign of Charles I (1516–1556). He became Holy Roman Emperor in 1519, which gave him control of lands in Germany, Austria, and the Netherlands, as well as parts of France and Italy. On his death, his lands were divided between his son Philip II (who ruled Spain, the Netherlands, and Spanish colonies in the Americas) and his brother Ferdinand (who became Holy Roman emperor).

By 1580, the Spanish empire included Portugal. Portugal had led the

◀ Arabic script on Spanish stonework. The Muslims left a rich legacy of architecture in cities such as Granada and Cordoba in southern Spain.

way in European exploration of the oceans. Its sailors had opened up new trade routes to Asia. The Portuguese already controlled an overseas empire that included large stretches of coastline in East and West Africa, Brazil, and India, as well as trading posts such as Goa in India, Macao in China, and many islands in Southeast Asia.

▶ Philip II ruled Spain from 1556 to 1598. A devout Catholic, he dreamed of a Spanish-led Catholic empire embracing Europe and America.

HENRY THE NAVIGATOR

Prince Henry of Portugal (1394–1460) had a passion for exploration. He brought together seamen, shipbuilders, and mapmakers to plan voyages in carracks and caravels (right).

African Empires

AFRICA was a continent of many kingdoms and empires. The richest African rulers commanded trade in gold, ivory, and slaves – goods that by 1500 were attracting European traders.

KANEM
BORNU
Timbuktu • Gao • Ngazergama
SONGHAI
Axum •
ETHIOPIA

KONGO

GREAT
ZIMBABWE

▶ African kingdoms, c. 1400–1600. Because transportation across much of Africa was so difficult, Africans often had more contact with Europeans and Asians (who traded with them by sea) than with other African states.

☑ Timbuktu, on the southern edge of the Sahara Desert, was the center of the gold and salt trade, and merchants came from as far as Morocco to sell cloth and horses there. Muslim scholars from the city advised the ruler of the Songhai empire, Askia Muhammad I.

PORTUGUESE traders sailing the coast of West Africa heard tales of wondrous kingdoms in the heart of the continent. The strongest was Songhai, a Muslim kingdom that controlled trade across the Sahara Desert. In 1464 King Sonni Ali freed Songhai from control by the Mali empire, and expanded its borders. A new Songhai dynasty was founded in 1493 by Askia Muhammad I, who gained great wealth from the trading cities of Jenne and Timbuktu. Songhai rule lasted until 1591, when the army was defeated by a Moroccan force, which was better-armed with guns.

1300s	1335	1341	1430s	1460s	1464	1468	From 1480s
European rulers try to contact the legendary Prester John. Great Zimbabwe is the heart of a powerful Bantu kingdom.	The Songhai ruling dynasty is founded.	Suleiman is king of Mali to 1360.	Portuguese begin exploring the west coast of Africa.	Portuguese explorers buy ivory, pepper, palm oil, and slaves from the kingdom of Benin.	Songhai breaks away from Mali's control.	Sonni Ali captures Timbuktu.	Portuguese traders set up forts as bases to trade with African rulers

Great Zimbabwe as it looks today, with parts of its massive defensive walls still standing. In the 1400s the walled citadel was surrounded by village houses and grazing cattle.

Another Muslim empire, Kanem-Bornu, extended through parts of present-day Chad, Cameroon, Nigeria, Niger, and Libya. Kanem-Bornu thrived on trade between northern and southern Africa. It reached its peak about 1570, under Idris Alawma.

In northeast Africa was the Christian empire of Ethiopia. Europeans heard tales of its legendary ruler, Prester John. Here, people lived by farming and cattle herding.

By 1450 a settlement at Great Zimbabwe in southern Africa was at its greatest extent. Built over about 400 years, Great Zimbabwe was probably a royal stronghold. It was surrounded by massive walls and a high tower. The people of this prosperous kingdom used copper and iron, and traded in gold with Sofala on the east coast (present-day Mozambique). By 1500, however, the civilization that built it was in decline.

Ethiopian Christians cut down into solid rock to build their cross-shaped churches, which were hollowed out inside. Fifteen rock churches survive at Lalibela (then named Roha), capital of the Ethiopian empire in the 1200s.

PRESTER JOHN

Travelers told tales of Prester ("priest") John, the fabulously rich Christian king of Ethiopia. One story claimed he had a magic mirror in which he could see everything that went on in his empire. Another story tells of giant ants that dug up gold for his treasury.

1488	1493	1506	1511	1520	c. 1530	1591
Portuguese explorer Bartolomeu Dias rounds the Cape of Good Hope.	Songhai is at its peak. Askia Muhammad I takes over the Mandingo empire.	The kingdom of Kongo has its first Christian king, Afonso I.	A Portuguese explorer reaches Great Zimbabwe, now in decline.	Portuguese mission to Ethiopia (lasts until 1526).	The slave trade from Africa to the Americas begins.	Songhai is defeated by Moroccans, aided by Spanish and Portuguese soldiers.

The Reformation

THE REFORMATION was a protest movement to reform the Catholic Church. It came about at a time when there was a new interest in humanism – the belief that humans are in control of their own destinies. Aware of the growing discontent with the way the Western Christian Church was run, reformers suggested new forms of worship, to create a new relationship between the people, Church, and God.

◀ Martin Luther believed that people were saved by faith alone, that the Bible was central to that faith, and that church services should be in everyday languages, not in Latin.

IN 1517 Martin Luther, a German monk, protested publicly at what he saw as the Church's corruption and called for reform. His campaign led to a religious movement known as the Reformation. His ideas were taken up and spread by other reformers, such as Ulrich Zwingli in Switzerland and John Calvin in France. This led to the formation of Protestant ("protesting") Churches

The technology of printing spread these ideas. The Bible, which previously had been available only in Latin (the language of scholars) was translated into local languages for all to read. Some rulers used discontent

▶ King Henry VIII made himself head of the Church in England. He always considered himself a Catholic, despite his quarrel with the Pope in Rome over his divorce from Catherine of Aragon.

1498
Savonarola, an Italian friar who preached Church reform, is burned at the stake in Florence.

1517
Martin Luther pins 95 written arguments critical of the Catholic Church on a church door in Wittenberg, Germany. This sets off the Reformation.

1519
Ulrich Zwingli starts the Reformation in Switzerland.

1521
Luther is expelled from the Church.

1532
John Calvin starts the Protestant movement in France.

1534
Ignatius Loyola founds the Jesuits. Henry VIII becomes head of the Church of England.

1536
Dissolution of the monasteries in England

th the Church for their own ends.
nry VIII of England, for example,
nted to divorce Catherine of Aragon.
en the Pope refused to grant the
orce, Henry broke with the Church in
me to get his own way.

From 1545 the Catholic Church fought
ck with a movement known as the
unter Reformation. It sent out Jesuit
ests to campaign against the spread
Protestantism and convert the
oples of the Spanish empire. The split
tween Christians in Western Europe
d to wars as countries struggled with
w religious alliances. Catholics and
otestants persecuted one another,
en in the cruelest ways.

◄ John Calvin, religious reformer, was born in France. He believed that only people chosen by God would be saved from damnation. His reforms became known as "Calvinism."

■ The Spanish sent the Armada against England in 1588 to restore Catholic rule. An English fireship attack off Calais helped fight off the planned invasion. The great Spanish fleet was eventually wrecked by storms around the coasts of northern Britain.

Ottomans and Safavids

THE Ottoman capture of Constantinople in 1453 marked the beginning of a Turkish golden age. The Ottoman Turks controlled the eastern Mediterranean and the Near East, and their armies moved west to threaten Europe. They also fought many wars against the Safavids, their Muslim rivals in Persia.

The battle of Lepanto in 1571 was fought between a large Turkish fleet and a smaller European fleet. The Turks were defeated, losi at least 20,000 men. The Europeans lost about 8,000.

The Ottoman sultan Suleiman I made the Ottoman empire a power to be respected and feared. Europeans called him Suleiman the Magnificent.

AFTER taking Constantinople, the Ottoman Turks renamed the city Istanb It became the center of a Muslim empi that, at its peak, encircled the eastern Mediterranean. Most of the Ottoman conquests were made during the rule of Suleiman I (1520–1566). The Turks invaded Persia (modern-day Iran), captured Baghdad, took control of the island of Rhodes, and crossed the river Danube into Hungary, where they won the battle of Mohacs in 1526.

By 1529 the Turkish army was outside the city walls of Vienna and looked likely to invade

1288	1402	1453	1501	1516	1520	1526	1529
Osman becomes ruler of the Ottoman Turks.	Tamerlane rules most of the Ottoman empire until his death in 1405.	Constantinople is captured by the Ottomans. They rename it Istanbul.	Safavid dynasty in Persia is founded by Shah Ismail I.	Ottoman Turks conquer Egypt, defeating Mamelukes.	Suleiman I becomes sultan of the Ottoman empire.	Battle of Mohacs in Hungary is won by the Turks.	At the sie of Vienna the Turks to capture the city.

estern Europe. The siege of Vienna was
fted, however, and Europe relaxed. But
ttoman warships continued to control
e Mediterranean. Turkish pirates, such
s the ferocious Barbarossa (Khayr ad-
in Pasha), raided ports, captured
nerchant ships, and carried off Christians
o be slaves. Ottoman sea power was
hecked in 1571, when a European fleet
efeated the Turks at the battle of
epanto in the Gulf of Corinth, Greece.

Suleiman tried three times to conquer
ersia, which from 1501 was under the
rule of the Safavid dynasty,
founded by Shah
Ismail I.

A map showing the
Ottoman empire (in red)
and the Safavid empire (in pink).
Poets, architects, and scholars from all over the
Islamic world visited their rulers' royal courts.

Here the people were Shiites, not Sunni
Muslims as in the Ottoman empire.
Safavid rivalry with the Ottomans
continued under Shah Abbas I (1557–
1628). From his capital of Isfahan, Shah
Abbas I ruled not only Persia but also
most of Mesopotamia (modern-day
Iraq). Wars between the two empires
continued throughout the 16th century
and helped to keep the Ottoman Turks
from advancing into Europe.

Istanbul's Blue Mosque was built on the
orders of Sultan Ahmet I (reigned 1609–1616).
After capturing the city in 1453, the Muslim
Ottomans took over Christian churches and
built new mosques, like this magnificent example.

A Persian carpet
of the 1500s.
Designs traditionally
included flowers and
geometric shapes.

34	1565	1571	1590	c. 1600
rks capture nis, aghdad, and esopotamia.	Turks attack Malta, but are fought off by the Knights of St John.	Battle of Lepanto. Don John of Austria destroys the Ottoman fleet, led by Ali Pasha.	Turks and Persians make peace.	The Ottoman empire declines. It eventually ends in 1918.

The Mughal Empire

THE Mughal dynasty ruled a mighty empire in India for nearly 300 years. The dynasty was founded by Babur. Under his grandson Akbar, India saw a rich flowering of Mughal art and learning.

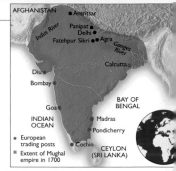

A map of the Mughal empire at its peak. Akbar ruled from Agra and Fatehpur Sikri.

BABUR was a Muslim chieftain from Afghanistan. After capturing Samarkand, he moved into northern India with an army skilled at using cannon. In 1526 his army defeated the sultan of Delhi's army at the battle of Panipat. This was the start of the Mughal dynasty. But the shrewd and able ruler Babur died just four years after his triumph. His son Humayun succeeded him. Faced with rebellions, in 1540 he was driven out of India.

Babur (1483–1530) was a descendant of Tamerlane and Genghis Khan. He was a writer as well as a warrior.

The golden age of Mughal India began in 1556 under the rule of Babur's grandson Akbar (then aged only 13). Akbar defeated several Hindu kingdoms and widened the empire farther by war and skillful diplomacy. His conquests included the capture of Bengal, with its riches of rice and silk. To govern his vast empire, Akbar organized an efficient land tax system. Famed as a wise and just ruler, he tolerated all religions, even permitting Hindus and

1526	1530	1540	1556	1565	1567
Mughal dynasty founded by Babur. His victory at Panipat against the sultan of Delhi, Ibrahim Lodi, gives him control of northern India.	Humayun becomes emperor.	Humayun is defeated by Sher Shah, a ruler of eastern India, and exiled to Persia.	Start of Akbar's reign; he wins a second battle of Panipat against the Hindus.	Akbar extends his rule to southern India.	Akbar subdues the Rajput princes, storming the fortre of Chitor with min and artillery.

122

tuguese Christians to discuss their
hs at his court at Fatehpur Sikri. Akbar
ed until his death in 1605.

Akbar was succeeded by his son
angir, who preferred the company of
nters and poets to ruling a large
pire. Jahangir was succeeded in 1627
hls son Shah Jahan, who enlarged the
pire. Shah Jahan was a great patron of
arts and paid for many splendid
ldings, including the Taj Mahal in
ra. In 1657 he fell ill, and an argument

◀ This 1568 painting shows Mughal soldiers, equipped with firearms, storming an enemy fortress. During Akbar's brilliant wars of conquest, war elephants were used like tanks by Akbar's armies in India.

broke out between his sons over who
should rule. His third son Aurangzeb
killed his brothers, locked up Shah Jahan,
and seized the throne.

Aurangzeb, the last great
Mughal ruler, expanded the
empire to its greatest extent.
A strict Muslim, he over
taxed his non-Muslim
subjects and destroyed
many Hindu shrines. After
his death in 1707 the Mughal
empire began to break up.

◀ The Taj Mahal was built between
1631 and 1648 as a tomb for the favorite
wife of Mughal emperor Shah Jahan. 20,000
workers and artists helped create this
beautiful white marble building.

▶ A Sikh today. The Sikh
religion was founded in the
early 1500s. The Sikhs
fought for freedom from
Mughal rule.

	1627–1657	1658–1707	1664	1720s
ers d.	Rule of Shah Jahan.	Rule of Aurangzeb.	Hindu Marathas overrun western India.	Mughal empire breaks up.

Ming China

IN THE 1300s the Mongol grip on China weakened. A revolt drove out the last Yuan (Mongol) emperor, and in 1368 a Buddhist monk calling himself Ming Hong Wu became China's new ruler. The Ming dynasty ruled China for almost 300 years.

The Forbidden City in Beijing. The third Ming emperor Yung Lo made Beijing his capit in 1421. The emperor lived there secluded fro both foreigners and his own people.

UNDER MING HONG WU, the first Ming emperor, Chinese self-confidence and national pride returned. An able and efficient ruler, though despotic later on, Hong Wu established peace and prosperity. He reformed Chinese society by abolishing slavery, confiscating large estates and redistributing them among the poor, and demanding higher taxes from the rich. China began to reassert its

power over its neighbors, and its stror army was able to fight off foreign atta

At sea, Chinese ships (then the large in the world) made a series of voyages during the early 1400s as far as Africa and Arabia. The fleets were commanded by Admiral Zheng He.

Chinese soldiers defended their empire against foreigners such as Japanese warlords (samurai), who tried to invade Korea in the 1590s, but later withdrew.

This is a "Ming vase." The Ming period was one of elegant artistry, especially in porcelain.

1368	1398	1405–1433	1421	1449
Foundation of the Ming dynasty in China.	Death of the first Ming emperor, Hong Wu.	Zheng He leads seven voyages to India and East Africa. He may have reached Australia.	Beijing is made the capital.	The Ming empe is captured by Mongols. He resumes the throne in 1457

The Ming period was one of great ~ativity. Ming emperors supported the ~s, and built many fine palaces. From ~21 they lived within the Forbidden ~y in Beijing, a huge complex of ~laces, temples, and parks. Foreigners ~d most Chinese were not allowed ~ide the city. Only the emperor's family ~d the officials and servants of the royal ~usehold were permitted.

China's first contacts with European ~ders began in the 1500s, when ~rtuguese ships arrived. By 1557 the ~rtuguese had set up a trading ~tlement in Macao. Western traders were eager to buy porcelain, silk, and tea. Tea

CROSSBOW

An arrow fired from a powerful Chinese artillery crossbow could travel over 650 feet (200 m) and pierce a wooden shield. The Chinese developed a number of other ingenious weapons, including gunpowder rockets and bombs, which they first used about AD 1000.

was a new drink for Europeans. It first reached Europe in 1610.

The Chinese had seldom looked far beyond their borders and after the mid-1500s the government banned voyages overseas. Ming rulers regarded China as the center of the world. Ming rule weakened in the early 1600s and ended in 1644.

> Christian missionary Matteo Ricci, an Italian, went to China in 1583 and spent 30 years there. In 1601 he visited the emperor in Beijing, giving two clocks as gifts.

Oceania Explored

ALTHOUGH European sailors crossed the Pacific Ocean in the 1500s, Australia and New Zealand remained "undiscovered" by Europeans until the 1600s.

The first Europ[ean] visitors to New Zeal[and] were respectful of [the] warlike Maori, whose weapons included club[s] spears, and long staves.

IT SEEMS CERTAIN that Chinese and Indonesian sailors knew about the northern coastline of Australia long before European ships arrived. Asian fishermen and seafarers traded with the Aborigines, handing over iron knives, for example. Rumors of an unknown "Southern Land" reached Europe in the 1500s, for a vague landmass begins to be shown on maps made after 1540.

The first European to see Australia a[nd] return was Dutch explorer Willem Jans[z] He sailed into the northern Gulf of Carpentaria in 1606, where he saw "wil[d] black men." The first known landing w[as] in 1616. A Dutchman named Dirk Hartog, skipper of a ship bound from t[he] Cape of Good Hope to Java to pick up [a] cargo of spices, was blown off course. H[e] sailed too far east, and landed on the

To mark his landing in Australia in 1616, Dirk Hartog put up a metal plate on the shor[e] of what is now Dirk Hartog Island. The plate was later returned to the Netherlands, and ca[n] be seen in an Amsterdam museum. The Dutch never attempted to settle in Australia.

The Aborigines of Australia had a way of life perfectly in tune with their environment. Before the 1700s, their only contacts with the outside world were occasional trade exchanges with Asian fishermen and merchants.

1500s	1519–1521	1526	1567	1577–1580	1606	1615
Portuguese navigators begin to explore the Pacific.	Ferdinand Magellan's ships cross the Pacific Ocean during the first-ever circumnavigation of the globe.	Portuguese land on Papua New Guinea.	Spanish explorer Mendana de Neyra visits the Solomon Islands.	English explorer Sir Francis Drake explores the Pacific during his round-the-world voyage.	Dutch sailor Willem Jansz sights the north coast of Australia.	Luis Vaez de Torres of Spa[in] explores coas[t] of New Guine[a] and northern[n] Australia.

Dirk Hartog's route to the spice islands in 1616 should have taken him north of Australia (dotted line) to the Dutch East Indies (Indonesia). But driven off course by winds known as the Roaring Forties, he and his crew reached the west coast of Australia.

round-the-world voyage of 1577–80. Much later, in the 1680s, the English pirate William Dampier explored the coasts of Australia and New Zealand. There seemed little trade or treasure to be gained, so until the 1700s Europeans largely ignored the new southern lands.

est coast of Australia. Other Dutch ships took the same wrong route and w this vast new land. They explored its estern and southern coasts, but did ot attempt to settle.

In 1642 Abel Tasman, another Dutch aptain, sighted the island of Tasmania, which he named Van Diemen's Land. iling on eastward, his ship came in ght of a bigger island. He had scovered New Zealand's South Island. s first contact with the Maori people ho lived there ended violently, with ur of the Europeans killed. Tasman ported that the new land was best left one. And so it was, until the arrival of mes Cook in 1769.

Crossing the vast Pacific Ocean was a sky adventure. The English sailor ancis Drake managed it during his

Francis Drake sailed around the world in the "Golden Hind." He was the second explorer to make the voyage.

The Thirty Years' War

THE RELIGIOUS conflicts in Europe that started after the Reformation continued into the 1600s. The Thirty Years' War began in 1618 as a protest by the Protestant noblemen of Bohemia (now part of the Czech Republic) against their Catholic rulers, the Holy Roman emperors.

BOHEMIA'S noblemen chose Protestant Frederick of Bohemia to become their king. Then, in 1619, Ferdinand II, a member of the powerful Habsburg royal family, became the new Holy Roman emperor. Determined to turn the empire back to Catholicism, Ferdinand sent his army to attack Bohemia.

By 1620 Ferdinand's army had forced Frederick and his family to flee to the Netherlands. Catholicism was now the only form of Christianity allowed in Bohemia. A year later Spain, also ruled by the Habsburgs, joined the war on the side of the Holy Roman empire and sent an army to fight the Protestant Dutch. In 1625 the Dutch asked Denmark and England for help. Many English soldiers died not by fighting, but from plague, and by 1629 Habsburg armies had also defeated the Danes.

The Protestant Swedish king Gustavus II Adolphus led his army to war against

In 1618, a group of Bohemian nobles threw two Catholic governors out of a window in Prague Castle. This act, known now as the Defenestration of Prague, sparked off the Thirty Years' War.

King Gustavus II Adolphus of Sweden leading his troops into battle, as was his custom. He went to war against the Habsburgs to defend Protestant beliefs, and also to protect Swedish trade in the Baltic, which was being threatened by Spain.

1618	1619	1620	1625–1629	1630	1631
War starts with the Defenestration of Prague.	Ferdinand II is crowned Holy Roman emperor.	Ferdinand's army enters Bohemia and defeats Protestant King Frederick.	Denmark and England join the war in support of the Dutch.	King Gustavus II Adolphus of Sweden joins the war on the side of the Protestants.	Swedish victory at the battle of Breitenfeld.

◄ Europe after the war ended in 1648. Many small German states were devastated, while France emerged as Europe's strongest nation.

► The French statesman Richelieu (1585–1642) ruthlessly suppressed Protestantism in France, but to defeat Spain supported the Protestant states in the Thirty Years' War.

Finally France entered the war to weaken Habsburg power. At first Spain was victorious, but from 1637 the French and their Protestant allies were able to defeat them. The Treaty of Westphalia ended a war that, together with disease, had halved the populations of many German states.

...pain and the Holy Roman empire in ...630. He won in Saxony at Breitenfeld in ...631 and again at Lutzen in 1632. But ...ustavus was killed just after the battle of Lutzen. Two years later Sweden withdrew from the war.

...32	1634	1635	1637	1643	1648	1659
...ustavus is ...lled after ...e battle ...Lutzen.	Sweden withdraws following defeat at Nordlingen.	Richelieu takes France into the war against the Habsburgs.	The French and their allies start to defeat Spain.	French victory at Rocroi over Spain.	The Treaty of Westphalia ends the Thirty Years' War.	Spain and France cease fighting. France becomes the most powerful country in Europe.

130

Tokugawa Japan

THE Tokugawa, or Edo, period in Japan marked the end of a series of civil wars and introduced a long period of stability and unity. It began in 1603, when Tokugawa Ieyasu became the first of the Tokugawa shoguns – the powerful military leaders and effective rulers of Japan.

◀ Tokugawa Ieyasu (1543–1616) as shogun encouraged agriculture and Confucianism in Japan. He firmly controlled the nobles and their families.

IN 1543, when Tokugawa Ieyasu was born, Japanese warlords were fighting for control of the country. As a boy, Ieyasu learned the skills of fighting from a rival family that he was sent to as a hostage. When he finally returned

1543	1550	1560	1582	1584	1600	1603	1605
Birth of Tokugawa Ieyasu.	Ieyasu is sent as a hostage to the Imagawa family.	Ieyasu returns to his own lands and allies himself with the warlord Nobunaga.	Nobunaga commits suicide. He is succeeded by Hideyoshi.	After several small battles Ieyasu allies himself with Hideyoshi.	Ieyasu defeats rival warlords at the battle of Sekigahara.	Ieyasu becomes shogun. The Tokugawa period begins.	Ieyasu abdicates, but retains great power.

ne, he began a long and well-planned
ggle for power. By 1598 Ieyasu had
biggest army in Japan and the most
ductive estates, centered on the
ing village of Edo. In 1603, the
peror appointed him to the position
hogun, giving him power to run the
ntry on the emperor's behalf.

Ieyasu turned Edo into a
fortified town (later
known as Tokyo). He
reorganized the

ORNAMENTAL WOMEN
Under the Tokugawas, wealthy
women were regarded as
ornaments. They wore high
platform shoes and complicated
ornamental hairstyles that greatly
restricted movement. The rules of
society were rigid, too. People were
expected to commit suicide if they
were disgraced in any way.

country into regions, each led by a
daimyo, who controlled the local
warriors (samurai).

Ieyasu abdicated in 1605, but he
continued to hold real power and, in
1612, fearful that Christianity might
undermine his rule, he discouraged visits
by foreign missionaries. He died in 1616,
but this policy was continued and in
1637 missionaries were banned
altogether. All Japanese Christians had
to give up their religion or be put to
death. The shogun next banned all
foreign traders, apart from the Dutch
who were allowed to send one trading
ship a year to the port of Nagasaki.
Japan flourished, despite its isolation
from the rest of the world.
The Tokugawa dynasty
ruled until 1867.

◄ Himeji castle was
the stronghold of the
warlord Hideyoshi,
who ruled Japan from
1582 to 1598. Under the
Tokugawas, the power of the
warlords was greatly reduced.

◄ Samurai warriors
fought on foot or on
horseback. They
wore armor
and masks to
make them
look more
frightening,
as well
as for
protection.

▶ Kabuki drama,
with its elaborate
costumes, developed
as a popular art
form in the 1600s.

	1616	1637	1830s	1867
has about	Death	All foreigners	Peasants	The last
000	of	apart from	and samurai	Tokugawa
le. 80,000	Ieyasu.	the Dutch are	rebel	shogun is
em are		forced to	against the	overthrown.
urai.		leave Japan.	Tokugawas.	

The Dutch Empire

UNTIL 1581 the countries we know as Luxembourg, Belgium, and the Netherlands (Holland) were part of the Low Countries, a group of 17 provinces. The Dutch people of the Netherlands won their independence from Spanish rule in 1581. They sent ships west and east to trade, and by the 1600s a Dutch empire had come into being.

◀ William of Or (1533–1584) led Dutch in several revolts against Sp rule. He was elec the first ruler of Republic of the Ur Netherlands, but wa killed by a Spanish a

FROM 1516 the Dutch were ruled by Spain as part of the Holy Roman empire. This came about because the Holy Roman Emperor Charles V was also king of Spain. Charles's son Philip II was an ardent Catholic, whereas most of the people in the northern Low Countries were Protestant. The Spanish tried to crush the Protestants, but the Dutch, led by William of Orange, rose in revolt. Seven northern provinces broke fror Spain, declaring themselves the Repub of the United Netherlands in 1581.

▶ After the Netherlands gained independence from Spain, there was a flowering in Dutch art. This painting of a woman writing a letter is by the Dutch artist Jan Vermeer (1635–1675).

1568	1576	1577	1579	1581
William of Orange led a Dutch revolt against Spanish rule.	Spanish troops destroy Antwerp. Many inhabitants move to Amsterdam.	The Netherlands makes a pact with England to fight against the Spanish.	Seven northern provinces of the Netherlands form the Union of Utrecht.	The Republic of the United Netherlands declares independen William of Orange i elected ruler.

While still at war with Spain, the Dutch [be]gan to build a trading empire overseas, [in t]he Caribbean and Asia. In 1599 they [beg]an to wrest control of the Moluccas, or [Spic]e Islands, from Portugal. In 1602 the [Dut]ch East India Company was set up to [enc]ourage trade with the East Indies [(Ind]onesia). Its headquarters, founded in [161]9, were at Batavia [(now] Jakarta) on the

island of Java. It later took control of Ceylon (Sri Lanka) and several ports in India.

▶ Coffee, tea, cinnamon, and cloves were among the valuable goods traded by the Dutch East India Company.

Coffee

Tea

Cinnamon

Cloves

Other Dutch merchants headed west, and in 1621 set up the Dutch West India Company. This controlled islands in the Caribbean, and Dutch Guiana in South America. It traded in slaves, sugar, and tobacco. Their jealously guarded trading empire increased Dutch wealth, but led to rivalry and wars with England in the late 1600s.

▼ This map shows the Dutch trading empire. Goods traded included spices, sugar, rice, and slaves. The chief Dutch city, Amsterdam, was home to merchants and bankers.

[...] Dutch East India Company traders sailing [fro]m the Netherlands to the East Indies would [brea]k their journey at the southern tip of [Afr]ica (the Cape of Good Hope) to buy [supp]lies for their onward journey. The Dutch [set] up a colony there in 1652.

	1602	1621	1648	1651–1674	1689
[...]Dutch [...]control of [...]Moluccas [...]gal.	The Dutch East India Company is founded.	The Dutch West India Company is founded.	Spain recognizes Dutch independence at the end of the Thirty Years' War.	Three Anglo-Dutch wars between the Netherlands and England are fought over trade.	William III of Orange and his wife Mary (daughter of James II of England) are offered the English throne.

Colonizing North America

THE Spanish and French were the first Europeans to explore North America. French traders and missionaries explored the north, which they named Canada. To the south, the Spanish founded what is now New Mexico, and explored California and Texas.

A replica of the *Mayflower*, the ship that [brought] the Pilgrims to America in 1620. They planne[d to] land in Virginia, but were blown north near to [the] Cape Cod. It was mid winter, and only 54 o[f the] 102 passengers survived until spring.

Sir Walter Raleigh (1552–1618) was a favorite of Queen Elizabeth I, England's "Virgin Queen." He named Virginia in her honor. In 1615 he led an expedition to South America in search of gold, but failed. On his return he was imprisoned by King James I, and later executed.

THE FIRST serious attempts at Europea[n] colonization were made in the 1580s [by] English explorer Sir Walter Raleigh, in [an] area he named Virginia. These early colonies failed, but in 1607 Raleigh se[t] up a more successful colony named Jamestown. The colonists struggled against hunger, disease, and battles w[ith] the Native Americans, whose land the[y] were occupying, but they survived.

In 1620, a group of religious dissenters, the Pilgrims, left Plymouth[,] England and sailed to North America seeking a place where they could practice their religion in peace. They landed near Cape Cod in Massachuset[ts] and founded a small settlement – the Plymouth Plantation. Only with help from the Native Americans were they

ole to survive. In 1624, the
Dutch West India Company
founded the colony of New
Netherlands on the Hudson
River, and in 1625 the Dutch
built a trading post on
Manhattan Island, naming it
New Amsterdam.

French colonization
started in Canada. Samuel de
Champlain founded Quebec in 1608, and
from there explored beyond the St
Lawrence River as far as Lake Huron,
claiming all the land for
France. Later, other French
explorers traveled along
the Mississippi River
and claimed the
whole river valley for
France, naming it
Louisiana, after King
Louis XIV of France.

◀ Native
Americans taught
the settlers how to
grow their new crops.
They exchanged
animal furs for guns
and alcohol.

EUROPEANS FIGHT FOR NORTH AMERICA

The English, French and Spanish
claimed large areas of North
America for themselves, even though
many Native Americans lived there.
Some tried to convert the Native
Americans to Christianity. The
colonists fought battles with Native
Americans and with rival colonists
over land ownership.

☑ European settlers cut down trees to build
simple log cabins to live in and barns for their
animals. The cleared land was fenced in and
used for growing crops such as corn and
squash. Turkeys were kept for food, and
tobacco, indigo, and rice were grown
for export to Europe.

30 v this date ere are about ,000 English ttlers in assachusetts.	1636 Harvard College is founded in Cambridge, Massachusetts.	1664 The English capture New Amsterdam from the Dutch and rename it New York.	1670 The Hudson Bay Company is set up to encourage trade, especially in furs, between Canada and England.	1679 Fur traders from France are the first Europeans to see Niagara Falls.	1682 The explorer La Salle claims the whole Mississippi river valley for France.	1683 The first German settlers arrive in Pennsylvania.

The English Civil War

THE ENGLISH Civil War broke out during the reign of Charles I, who became king in 1625. The royal army fought the army of Parliament. Charles lost and was executed. For a time England became a republic under Oliver Cromwell.

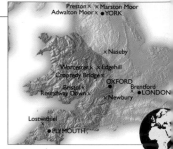

This map shows the main battles of the war. The pink area is land held by Charles I after 1644, when he lost control of the north. Parliament controlled the rest of the country.

◄ The king's soldiers were called Royalists, or Cavaliers. Some wore their hair long and dressed flamboyantly in wide-brimmed hats and shirts of fine linen. Armor was little protection against bullets. Most soldiers on both sides wore leather jerkins and iron breastplates to protect their chests.

▶ Parliament's soldiers were known to their enemies as Roundheads, because of their short haircuts. Cavalrymen wore long boots with spurs. Iron helmets with neck and face-guards protected them from sword blows.

THERE WERE religious, economic, and political reasons for the war. Puritans (extreme Protestants) thought Charles favored Catholics – he had a French Catholic wife, Queen Henrietta. Charles believed that only God gave him the right to rule and to choose his advisers. He came into conflict with Parliament over raising taxes, and from 1629 tried to rule without Parliament.

In 1640, Charles had to recall Parliament, to raise money through taxes to fight rebelling Scottish Protestants. He tried to arrest his five leading opponents in the House of Commons, but they escaped. London mobs rioted in their

1625	1629	1637	1639	1640	1642	1645
Charles I becomes king. He marries Henrietta Maria of France.	Parliament tries to curb Charles's power and is dismissed.	Charles forces the English Prayer Book on Scotland.	Rebellion breaks out in Scotland.	Charles calls, dismisses, then recalls Parliament.	Charles tries to arrest five Parliamentarians. Civil war begins.	New Model Army defeats Royalists at Naseby.

PURITANS

Puritans were Protestants who wanted to "purify" the Church of England of its bishops and ritual. They dressed in simple clothes. The Pilgrims were Puritans.

Oliver Cromwell (1599–1658). He helped recruit, train, and command the New Model Army, his "Ironsides." As Lord Protector he tried to impose parliamentary rule in Scotland and Ireland by force.

...pport and Charles
...t London. Both sides then raised
...mies of volunteers.

...Neither side won the first major battle,
...ught in August 1642 at Edgehill.
...anks largely to Cromwell's New Model
...my, Parliament beat the Royalists at
...arston Moor (1644) and, decisively, at
...aseby (1645). Charles fled to the Scots,
...ho handed him over to Parliament. He
...caped and plotted with
...e Scots to fight again
...648), but his forces
...ere soon crushed.
...e was tried for
...eason, found
...uilty, and

The execution
...King Charles I
...ok place in
...hitehall on
...nuary 31, 1649.

executed in January 1649. In 1651 his son Charles, invading with Scots help, was beaten at Worcester. This battle ended the Civil War. England was governed as a Commonwealth (republic) by Parliament, until its members quarreled. From 1653, Oliver Cromwell ruled as Lord Protector, backed by his army. When he died in 1658, his son Richard was soon removed from office. In 1660 a new Parliament invited Charles II back from exile.

...6	1647	1648	1649	1651	1653–1658	1660
...arles ...renders to ...Scots.	Charles is handed over to parliament. He escapes to the Isle of Wight.	Charles, aided by Scots, starts second civil war, but is defeated.	Charles goes on trial for treason. He is executed on January 31.	Charles's son goes into exile in France.	Cromwell rules as Lord Protector.	Restoration of the monarchy; Charles II comes to the throne.

The Slave Trade

AFRICA had a long history of slavery. Until the early 1500s most slaves were prisoners of war. Some were sold to Arab traders. Then Europeans visited the coasts of Africa and a new slave trade began, to the New World.

> Slave ships carried more than 400 people, packed in as tightly as possible, on the two-month voyage from West Africa to the Americas.

conditions and European diseases killed many native people, so the colonists started to look elsewhere for workers to replace them. Some convicts were brought from Europe, but they soon fell ill and died. The colonists then looked to Africa for slaves.

EUROPEAN explorers to the New World set up colonies on mainland America and the islands of the Caribbean. They grew crops such as sugar cane on large plantations, and in many places enslaved the native population to do the work for them. But terrible

< Slaves were often brutally ill-treated. Some were made to wear heavy iron collars so they could not lie down and rest. Many were worked to death.

> On a sugar plantation, slaves worked in the fields and processing factories. The work was heavy, conditions were bad, and hours were long. Some plantation owners even beat and starved the slaves who worked in their grand houses.

1441	1448	1493	1502	1570s
The Portuguese bring gold and slaves to Europe from West Africa for the first time.	The Portuguese set up the first trading post in Africa.	Christopher Columbus introduces sugar cane from Europe to the Caribbean.	The Spanish take the first slaves from Africa to America to work on plantations.	The Portuguese take slaves from Africa to Brazil to work on sugar plantations.

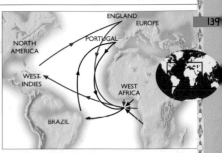

> From Europe, slave ships sailed to Africa with guns and cloth to buy slaves. The slaves were carried to the Americas, where they were sold. On the return journey to Europe the ships carried sugar, rum, and cotton.

Soon huge numbers of people were being captured in central Africa. Chained together, they were forced to march to the coast, where they were sold to European slave traders. Then, still chained, they were crammed into ships and taken across the Atlantic. Conditions on board ship were terrible, with not enough light, air, food, or water. As many as a third of the slaves died on each eight-week journey to America.

Slaves faced a hard life on the plantations. They were often badly fed and whipped for the smallest mistake. Many died soon after arriving at the plantations. The strongest rarely survived for more than ten years, and few ever saw Africa again.

The slave trade reached its peak in the 18th century, when between six and seven million people were shipped from Africa to America. The impact on some traditional African societies was devastating. From the 1780s, European reformers at last began to realize how cruel slavery was and started to campaign against it.

A SLAVE AUCTION

When African slaves arrived in the Caribbean, South America, or the colonies of North America, they were sold at auction to the highest bidder. Africans from different cultures and with different languages were grouped together to work.

1619	1681	1683	1700s	1730	1780s
African slaves arrive in Virginia to work on tobacco plantations.	By now there are about 2,000 slaves in Virginia.	By now, almost all the native peoples of the Caribbean have been wiped out.	The slave trade is at its peak. Cities such as Bristol, Liverpool, and Nantes grow rich on the profits.	About 90 percent of Jamaica's population are of African origin.	People start to campaign against slavery.

140

Louis XIV

LOUIS XIV of France was the most powerful of all European monarchs in the 17th century. An absolute ruler, he governed alone. This brought him into conflict with both the nobility and the ordinary people.

In 1661 Louis dismissed the council of nobles and took into his own hands the government of France, by then the most powerful country in Europe. His chief adviser, Jean Colbert, reorganized taxes and reformed the legal system. He set up new industries and a network of roads and canals, and increased the size of the merchant fleet to encourage trade. Louis spent much of France's wealth on building a magnificent

LOUIS XIV came to the throne in 1643, when he was just five years old. His mother ruled on his behalf until 1651. The council of nobles argued with her constantly, because they wanted a share of the power. There was also a rebellion by the people in 1648, over the heavy taxes they had to pay. When the nobles revolted, too, Louis fled from Paris and did not return until 1653. He was determined such a rebellion would never happen again.

◄ The Hall of Mirrors the most magnificent room at Versailles. Everything in the palace reflected the king's magnificence, and its style was copied throughout Europe

▶ The palace of Versailles (built 1662–1710). The nobility were encouraged to live here, under King Louis XIV's watchful eye.

1638	1643	1648	1653	1660	1661
Birth of Louis, son of Louis XIII of France and Anne of Austria.	Louis succeeds to the throne as Louis XIV.	At the end of the Thirty Years' War, France is the most powerful nation in Europe.	Cardinal Jules Mazarin finally puts down the five-year uprising known as the Fronde and Louis returns to Paris.	Louis marries Marie-Thérèse of Austria, daughter of the king of Spain.	Mazarin dies and Louis takes control of France.

Louis XIV (1638–1715) was glorified by artists and writers as the Sun King. He ruled France for 72 years.

new palace at Versailles near Paris, and on wars. He wanted to expand French territory to reach the Alps, the Pyrenees, and the Rhine river. Between 1667 and 1697 he fought three major wars.

The peasants were heavily taxed to pay for the king's extravagance, while the

MOLIERE

Louis XIV was a great patron of the arts and literature. One of his favorite dramatists was Jean Baptiste Poquelin, known as Molière (1622–1673), the father of modern French comedy. From 1659 to 1673 Molière wrote and directed many plays at Versailles. He also acted in his plays.

nobles and clergy paid nothing. Two bad harvests left thousands starving, but protests were quickly crushed. When Louis died in 1715, his five-year-old great-grandson succeeded him, inheriting a country left financially weak after years of warfare.

1667 Start of war with Spain over the Netherlands. Louis gains control of Flanders, but has to retreat in 1668.

1672 Start of six-year Dutch war, which ends in victory for France.

1678 Louis moves his court to Versailles.

1685 Persecution of the Huguenots (French Protestants) forces many of them to leave France.

1689–1697 War of the Grand Alliance, led by Britain against France, ends in French defeat.

1701–1713 War of the Spanish Succession, in which Louis fights for control of the Spanish empire.

1715 Death of Louis XIV at the age of 77.

Revolution and Industry

THE WORLD IN TURMOIL
1700–1900

THE TWO centuries between 1700 and 1900 were a time of conflict, revolution, and change in many parts of the world. Empires were won and lost, kings and governments toppled, and agriculture, industry, and transportation developed rapidly.

THE COUNTRIES of northwest Europe grew more powerful, while Spain and Portugal declined. The 13 American colonies declared their independence from Britain in 1776 to become the United States of America. They were helped by the French, who in 1789 had their own revolution. The French overthrew their king and became first a republic and then an empire. By 1793 this action had led to wars between France and Austria, Britain, the Netherlands, Portugal, Prussia, Russia, and Spain. The wars lasted until 1815 when the French emperor Napoleon was finally defeated.

1644 Manchus overthrow the Ming dynasty of China.	**1682–1725** Peter the Great rules Russia.	**1740** Frederick the Great becomes king of Prussia, which dominates Europe.	**1756–1763** Seven Years' War: France, Austria, and Russia clash with Britain and Prussia.	**1768** James Cook's first of three voyages to the Pacific.	**1769** James Watt builds the first efficient steam engine.	**1776, July 4** The Continental Congress in America adopts the Declaration of Independence.	**1789, July 14** A mob seizes the Bastille in Paris. Start of the French Revolution.

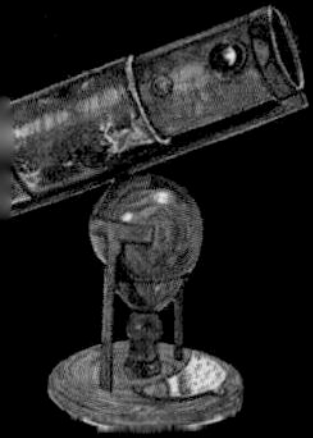

The Spanish and Portuguese colonies South America took advantage of the ırs in Europe to gain their ləpendence, and by 1830 were all free foreign rule. Later conflicts in Europe ited the separate states of Germany d of Italy into two countries. In the ıited States of America, conflict over very led to a four-year civil war.

Revolutions in agriculture, industry, d transportation affected the lives of en more people, especially in Europe d America. Canals and railways made vel overland easier, while steam-wered ships were faster than sailing ps had been. New methods of ming made it possible to feed more ople, and large numbers left the countryside to make a living in the rapidly expanding towns. Factories in towns used machines to produce vast quantities of goods once made by hand.

To provide raw materials and a ready market for these factory goods, many European countries built up empires overseas. Britain tightened its control on India and laid claim to Australia and New Zealand. In the Scramble for Africa (1880 to 1900), European powers divided most of Africa between them. China, Japan, and Russia stayed largely isolated from the rest of the world. The rising power was the United States, where millions of Europeans settled, their westward movement forcing Native Americans from their ancient homelands.

	1804	1808	1830	1837–1901	1848	1857	1861–1865	1869
nas e's *The* *s of* is shed.	Napoleon declares himself emperor of France.	Independence struggles begin in South America.	First all-steam railway, in England.	Queen Victoria's reign; the British empire includes a fourth of the world's people.	Year of Revolutions affects most of Europe.	Indian Mutiny.	The Civil War.	Union Pacific Railroad links east and west coasts of America.

The Russian Empire

PETER THE GREAT changed Russia from an isolated, backward nation into a major European power. Nearly 40 years after his death, another great ruler, Catherine the Great, carried on his ambition.

🔺 The Summer Palace and St Petersburg's other grand buildings and palaces were built b European architects for Peter the Great. Th city was built on many islands, linked by bridge

IN 1682, aged just 10, Peter the Great (Peter I) became czar of Russia. At first he ruled with his half-brother Ivan V. When Ivan died in 1696, Peter ruled on his own until 1725. Russia had been expanding rapidly since

1639, but it was still backward compare with the rest of Europe. Peter was determined to change this. For 18 months he toured Europe, meeting kin scientists, and people in industry, farm and ship-building. In the Netherlands h even worked in a shipyard for a while. When he returned to Russia, Peter put knowledge he had gained to use. He b

🔻 Throughout the long Russian winters, carriages used runners instead of wheels, so could glide through snow like a sleigh.

🔺 Peter the Great ruled Russia from 1682 to 1725. He was an immensely tall, strong, energetic man. But he could also be brutal – he imprisoned and tortured his own son, for example.

1638	1696	1700–1721	1703	1712	1722–1723	1725	1729
Peter the Great is born.	Peter becomes sole ruler of Russia.	Great Northern War against Sweden.	St Petersburg is founded. Peter calls it his "window on Europe."	St Petersburg becomes Russia's capital and main port.	War with Persia gives Russia access to the Caspian Sea.	Peter the Great dies.	The future Catherine the Great is b in Prussia

p the navy and encouraged industries nd farming. He improved and xpanded the army and built new ads and canals to help trade.

Peter also gained a Baltic oastline for Russia through ar with Sweden. This gave ussia a seaport that was not ice-ound in winter. He moved Russia's apital from Moscow to St Petersburg on he Baltic. Under Peter, the serfs peasants) were made to pay more tax, nd were worse off. But in 1725, when eter died, Russia as a whole was more ecure and advanced than it had been hen he came to power.

In 1762, another powerful uler came to the throne. atherine II (the Great) was ussian by birth, but narried the heir to the ussian throne in 1745. e was murdered six nonths after he

Catherine the Great was ruthless and ambitious. She was interested in new ideas, but her plans to improve Russia's education system and reform the law came to nothing.

became czar, and Catherine declared herself empress. Like Peter, she encouraged western ideas and gained territory for Russia, fighting the Ottoman empire in 1774 and 1792, and Sweden in 1790. She also claimed much of Poland. Conditions did not improve for the serfs, however, and a revolt in 1773 was harshly put down.

Life was a constant ruggle for Russia's serfs. hey paid heavy taxes and, the harvest was bad, ften went hungry.

45	1762	1773	1787	1796
atherine marries r cousin, Peter , heir to the ussian throne.	Catherine becomes empress of Russia after her husband's death.	A revolt by the serfs is brutally crushed.	On a tour of Russia, Catherine meets healthy, well-fed, well-dressed actors while the real serfs are hidden from sight.	Catherine dies and is succeeded by her son.

Manchu China

IN THE early 1600s in China, rebellions broke out against the Ming emperor's unpopular government and its high taxes. At the same time, tribes in Manchuria (the region to the northeast of China) were uniting.

◄ Beautifully shaped vas made from fine porcelain ar decorated with patterns of flowers and animals were expor to the West during the Qing dyn

BY 1618 THE MANCHU were strong enough to take control of and hold on to the Ming province of Liaotung. Then, in 1644, a rebellion in China led to the capture of Beijing, the capital. Ming officials asked the Manchus to help them

defeat the rebels. Instead, the Manchus seized power and set up a new dynasty the Qing, which ruled China for more than 250 years.

The Manchus considered themselve superior to the Chinese and lived apart from them. They forbade marriages between Chinese and Manchus, and made Chinese men wear their hair in pigtails. But as soon as they had seized power they adopted the Chinese way government, and employed former Mir officials. Gradually they also adopted th Chinese way of life, which made their r more acceptable to the Chinese people

◄ Beijing expanded greatly under the M who built many new palaces temples, and a new wall and m around the city. The Q left the inner c unaltered, but b new pala and temp outside city w

1618	1630s	1644	1661	1692	1704
United Manchu tribes take control of the Chinese province of Liaotung.	The Chinese start to rebel against the high taxes imposed by the Ming dynasty.	The Manchus take control of Beijing and overthrow the Ming dynasty.	Kangxi becomes the second Qing emperor. He conquers Taiwan, Outer Mongolia, parts of Siberia, and Tibet.	Kangxi gives Jesuit missionaries permission to spread Christianity to the Chinese.	All missionari except the Jesu are expelled fo not tolerating Chinese traditions.

The Qing empire (in red) was larger than China today (boundary shown in blue).

Under the Qing dynasty, China flourished once more. Its empire grew to three times the size it had been under the Ming, and the population trebled from 150 million to 450 million people. Production of silk, porcelain, lacquerware, and cotton expanded, and trade, especially with Europe, increased. The Chinese considered their products to be better than anything else in the world, and accepted only gold and silver in exchange for them. Tea was grown for export, and China also produced almost all the food its people needed.

The Manchu emperors, resplendent in silk robes, were immensely powerful. Under their rule China prospered in the 1600s and 1700s.

A British tall ship lies at anchor in Guanzhou (Canton), the only port in China open to Europeans and Americans.

In 1792 Britain sent its first ambassador to China with a request for greater trade rights. The emperor refused, wanting China to stay isolated. This meant China was slow to take up new technology, and by the 1840s the weakened empire was unable to resist Western pressure.

The Enlightenment

THE ENLIGHTENMENT was the name given to a time of new ideas, beginning in the 1600s and lasting until the end of the 1700s. It was also called the Age of Reason, because people began to look for reasons why things happened as they did. Modern science grew out of this questioning. New ideas about government and how people should live were also central to the Enlightenment.

> The *Encyclopédie*, compiled by the French writer and critic Denis Diderot, was written by experts in many subjects and aime cover all branches of knowledge. First publish between 1751 and 1772, the work comprised volumes of text and 11 volumes of pictures.

SOME EUROPEAN RULERS took up Enlightenment ideas with enthusiasm did ordinary people who were no long willing to be told what to do, and wan a say in government. Others feared tha the new thinking would overturn the world for ever. The French philosopher René Descartes (1596–1650) argued that only an idea that could be

> The telescope opened new worlds of discovery. Improved telescopes made by Newton in 1668 and Cassegrain in 1672 used mirrors to reflect light, and gave astronomers clearer images of the Universe.

> A botanical drawing of sunflowers from *Philosophia Botanica* by Carl von Linné (Linnaeus), published in 1751. Linnaeus was the first person to classify the plant and animal kingdoms, defining and grouping living things into species.

1632–1704
Life of English philosopher John Locke. He believed that all men were equal and free and that the authority of government comes only from the consent of the governed.

1687
Sir Isaac Newton sets out his theories about light and the visible spectrum, the three laws of motion, and the existence of gravity.

1743
Benjamin Franklin sets up the American Philosophical Society in Philadelphia. Its members are interested in science as well as philosophy.

1743–1794
Life of French chemist Antoine Lavoisier, who was first to establish t combustion (burning) form of chemical actic

INFLUENTIAL WOMEN

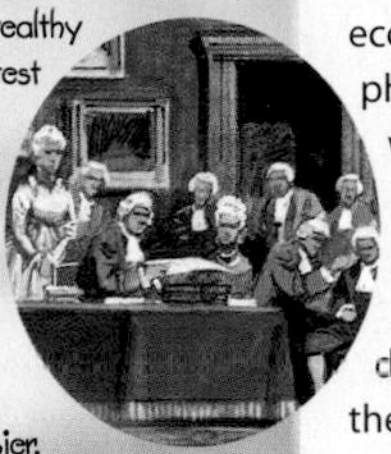

New ideas were exchanged at meetings of rtistic and educated people. They gathered, often in the homes of wealthy omen, to discuss the latest scientific discoveries, plays, books and issues of the day. Two such women were Madame Geoffrin, seen here in 1725, and Marie-Anne Lavoisier, wife of the chemist Antoine Lavoisier.

inventor, and statesman, Adam Smith the economist, David Hume the historian, the philosopher Immanuel Kant, and the writer Mary Wollstonecraft. The belief that every person had the right to knowledge, freedom, and happiness inspired a new revolutionary and democratic fervor, which was to shape the world of the 19th century.

own to be true, by evidence or by soning, was true. Such arguments ubled the Christian Church, and also gs and queens who believed they d a "divine" (God-given) right to e. Another French thinker, taire (1694–1778), criticized th the Church and government his day. So did Jean-Jacques usseau (1712–1778), whose as helped shape the events ding to the American and nch revolutions. Other leading nts of the Enlightenment were njamin Franklin, scientist,

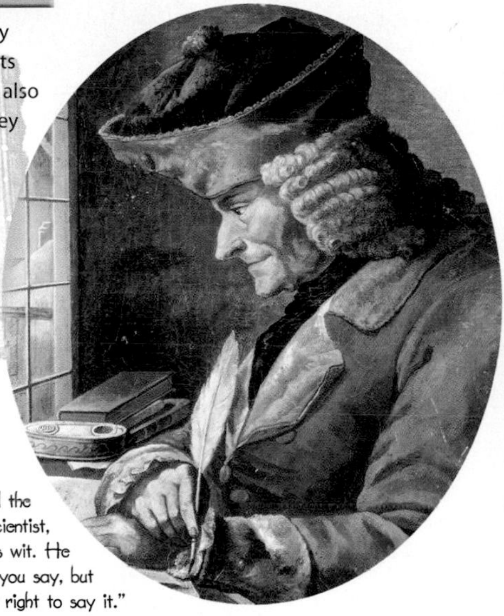

François Marie Arouet used the pen-name Voltaire. He was a scientist, thinker, and writer, noted for his wit. He declared: "I may disagree with what you say, but I will defend to the death your right to say it."

	1751	1755	1768	1788	1791	1792
first me e clopédie ıblished.	Linnaeus publishes his *Philosophia Botanica.*	Samuel Johnson's *Complete Dictionary of the English Language* is published. It contains over 43,000 words.	The *Encyclopaedia Britannica* is first published.	*The Times* newspaper is first published in London.	Thomas Paine's *The Rights of Man* influences Americans in their fight for independence from Britain.	Mary Wollstonecraft's *A Vindication of the Rights of Women* argues for equal opportunities in education.

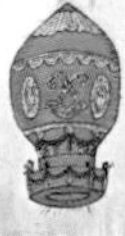

The Agricultural Revolution

UNTIL the end of the 17th century, farming methods in Europe remained unchanged from the Middle Ages. Most people still lived in the country and were able to grow just enough food to feed themselves, with a little spare to sell at the local market.

New, larger breeds of farm animals were bred during the 18th century. Artists often painted portraits of prized animals with their owners, as in this picture, "Mr Healey's Sheep".

PEOPLE FARMED small strips of land, scattered over three or four large, open fields that surrounded their village. To keep the land fertile, each year one field was left unplanted, or fallow, and so produced nothing. This system worked well while the population was small. But in time the population increased, and more people moved to the newly expanding towns, where there was no land on which to grow crops. If everyone was to be fed, better ways of growing crops had to be found.

Some of the earliest experiments in agriculture were carried out in the Netherlands, where more land was needed that was suitable for farming.

The Dutch drained lakes and reclaimed land from the sea, using pumps powered by windmills to keep the water out. Dutch farmers could not afford to leave any fields unplanted. Instead, they experimented with crop rotation, in which four different crops were planted in the same field over a four-year period. This idea was copied

The fantail windmill was invented in 1745. The fantail moved the main sails when the wind shifted. Before this, a windmill's main sails needed moving whenever the wind changed, so that they faced into the wind.

ritain. The plow was improved and the
orse-drawn seed drill and hoe were
vented. These allowed several rows of
eeds to be sown at the same time, and
ter weeded.

In many places, the land was
organized. Large, open fields were
ivided into smaller ones, separated by
edges or walls. Laws were passed in
ritain giving landowners the right to
nclose common land, which everyone
ad previously used for grazing. Whole
illages were even demolished to make
ay for bigger fields.

CROP ROTATION

Crop rotation increased the fertility of the
soil. A farmer planted wheat in the first field,
turnips in the second, barley in the third, and
clover in the fourth.
Each year the crops
were rotated, so in the
second year wheat was
grown in the second
field, and so on.

As more people moved to the new
industrial towns, fewer farmers had to
provide more food. Agricultural changes
between 1700 and 1850 helped farmers
to feed the growing population.

A seed
rill made a
eries of
ven holes
to which
eeds fell. A
orker then
ked over the
les. Before
is, seeds were
cattered on the
round by hand.
hey fell
nevenly and
ften failed to
erminate, or were
aten by birds.

701
ritish
ventor
thro Tull
vents the
ed drill.

1715
The Dutch
have reclaimed
large areas of
land from
the sea.

1730
Four-crop
rotation is
introduced
in England.

1759–1801
In Britain the
Enclosure Acts
enclose huge
areas of
common land.

1796
A school for
farmers is
set up in
Hungary.

1800
In Britain, careful breeding
has more than doubled the
weight of the average cow
from 100 years earlier.

1840
Publication of
the first book
on using
chemicals in
farming.

Austria and Prussia

EUROPE in the 18th century was dominated by absolute monarchs. Rulers of all they surveyed, they built magnificent palaces and attracted artists, musicians, and intellectuals to their "enlightened" courts. Two of the richest and most powerful states were Austria and Prussia.

⬆ The Schonbrunn Palace in Vienna (built 1696–1711) was the Habsburgs' summer palace. Planned to rival Versailles, it had 1,440 rooms.

AUSTRIA was ruled by the Habsburgs, a family that had dominated Europe since the 13th century. In the early 1500s Charles V, then Holy Roman Emperor, divided his huge realm. One half was ruled from Spain, the other from Vienna in Austria. In 1700 the Spanish Habsburgs died out, but the Austrian

◀ Maria Theresa (1717–1780) inherited the throne of Austria in 1740. War broke out among her rivals, but her position was secured in 1748.

▶ Wolfgang Amadeus Mozart (1756–1791) playing at the court of Maria Theresa. Mozart first played at court when he was only six years old.

1700	1711	1713	1740	1756–1763
Austria has taken Hungary from the Ottomans. The last Spanish Habsburg monarch dies and Spain is ruled by the Bourbons of France.	Charles VI, Archduke of Austria, becomes Holy Roman emperor.	Frederick William succeeds as king of Prussia.	Maria Theresa succeeds Charles VI. Rivals challenge her right to rule. Frederick II (the Great) becomes king of Prussia.	Seven Years' War. France, Austria, and Russia clash with Britain and Prussia.

In the Seven Years' War (1756–1763), France, Austria, and Russia opposed Prussia and Britain. At the end of the war Prussia gained Silesia, seized from Austria. Britain took control of France's colonies in India and America.

...absburgs were still powerful. From ...740 a woman, Maria Theresa, ruled ...ustria (which included Hungary, ...captured from the Turks). She restored ... power and made Vienna the artistic ...nter of Europe. Artists from all over ...rope came to work on its grand building projects. Maria Theresa was succeeded in 1780 by her son Joseph II, a follower of the Enlightenment, though no democrat, who freed the serfs and abolished privileges enjoyed by nobles.

Frederick II (the Great) became king of Prussia in 1740. An outstanding general, he inherited a well-organized state with a powerful army, which he used to make Prussia a major power.

Frederick the Great (1712–1786) of Prussia was a cultured man, but also a stern administrator. He encouraged the study of science and agriculture, and improved education.

...5	1772	1780	1781	1786	1795
...ria Theresa rules ... Holy Roman ...pire with her ... Joseph.	First partition of Poland by Austria, Prussia, and Russia.	Maria Theresa is succeeded by Joseph II.	Joseph II introduces major reforms and frees the serfs.	Frederick the Great dies.	Partition of Poland between Austria, Prussia, and Russia. Poland ceases to exist until 1919.

Birth of the United States

B Y THE MID 1700s there were 13 British colonies in North America. Britain had also won control of Canada, by defeating France in the Seven Years' War (1756–1763). Britain had no thought of changing the way it governed its American colonies, but the colonists, denied a say in governing themselves, rebelled. The American Revolution led to the colonies' independence as the United States.

The Declaration of Independence was signed on July 4, 1776, by delegates from the 13 colonies. It separated them from Great Britain and created the United States.

BRITAIN taxed its American citizens to help pay for the defense of North America. There were about two million British-Americans. They produced most of their own food and other goods, but were unhappy at having to pay taxes on imported tea and legal documents. The Americans had no representatives in the British Parliament, and declared that "taxation without representation is

British troops, trained for fighting in European wars, found fighting in America very different. Standing in close-packed ranks, firing volleys of shot, they presented good targets for the American sharpshooters. British infantrymen (left) wore red long-tailed coats, and so were known as "redcoats."

On Christmas night, 1776, George Washington led his troops across the icy Delaware River and went on to defeat the British at the battle of Trenton. This was one of the first major American victories in the War of Independence.

1765	1770	1773	1775	1776	1777
Protests start against British taxes in the American colonies.	At the Boston Massacre, British troops fire on a crowd of colonists and kill five of them.	The Boston Tea Party; in Boston harbor, colonists throw ships' cargoes overboard as a protest against the tax on tea.	The American War of Independence starts.	On July 4, the Continental Congress adopts the Declaration of Independence.	The British are defeated at Saratoga, New York. France sides with America. The British capture Philadelphia, Pennsylvania.

"tyranny." Britain reacted by sending soldiers. In April 1775, an armed confrontation between colonists and British troops took place at Lexington in Massachusetts. The colonists formed an army of their own, commanded by George Washington, and on June 17 the two armies clashed at Bunker Hill, near Boston. The British were successful, but the War of Independence, or American Revolution, had begun.

While fighting continued, colonial leaders signed the Declaration of Independence on July 4, 1776. The British government refused to accept it. Under Washington's command, the colonists' army began to defeat the British. France, Spain, and the Netherlands all joined the colonists' side. The six-year war ended in 1781, when the British surrendered at Yorktown. Two years later, Britain recognized the independent United States of America.

PAUL REVERE

Paul Revere is one of the heroes of the War of Independence. He rode from Boston to Lexington to warn of the approach of British soldiers. Although he was captured, his mission was successful. Revere was immortalized in a famous poem by Longfellow.

1778	1779	1780	1781
The British capture Savannah, Georgia.	Spain joins the war on America's side.	The Dutch join the war on America's side. British victory at Charleston, South Carolina.	After a siege at Yorktown, Virginia, the British surrender.

The French Revolution

THE FRENCH Revolution of 1789 shook all of Europe. It began as a protest for fairness, food, and democracy. The French people, most of whom were denied a say in government, rose up against the "old order." The years of bloodshed led to the emergence of a dictator, who made himself emperor – Napoleon Bonaparte.

◀ In 1793, Maximilien Robespierre (1758–1794) started the Reign of Terror. Over the next nine months thousands of opponents of the Revolution were put to death, until he himself was denounced and guillotined.

IN THE 18TH CENTURY, society in France was divided into three classes, or estates. The first estate was the nobility, the second was the clergy, and the third was everyone else. Only people in the third estate paid taxes. Educated people, by now familiar with the ideas of the Enlightenment, knew how unfair the system was. Their discontent increased in 1788, when a bad harvest pushed up prices, leaving many people facing starvation. After years of extravagant kings and costly wars, the government had little money to deal with the crisis. When, in 1789, King Louis XVI called a meeting of the Estates General (the nearest France had to a parliament) to raise more money, the third estate said that if they had to pay taxes, they should have a say in how the country was run. Louis XVI refused this request.

The rebels, calling themselves the National Assembly, refused to leave Versailles until the king listened to their demands.

▶ During the Reign of Terror about 500,000 people were arrested and 17,000 of them put to death by public execution on the guillotine. Many of the first victims were aristocrats, condemned as "enemies of the people."

1789, May 15	1789, July 14	1789, August 26	1789, October 5	1791
The Estates General meets for the first time since 1614. The third estate breaks away and forms the National Assembly.	The French Revolution starts when a mob seizes the Bastille.	The Declaration of the Rights of Man is made.	The king and his family are seized by a mob and taken to Paris as prisoners.	The royal family try to escape but are returned to Paris.

MARIE ANTOINETTE

Marie Antoinette (1755–1793), daughter of Maria Theresa of Austria, was married to King Louis XVI of France. At first she was popular, but her extravagance soon turned people against her. On hearing that Parisians were rioting over bread shortages, she is reputed to have said: "Let them eat cake!"

to resist oppression. Louis XVI and his family were arrested and held until 1793. Finally, the king was put on trial and executed. This was the start of the Reign of Terror, led by Maximilien Robespierre, in which thousands of people were put to death. Austria, Britain, the Netherlands, Prussia, and Spain all went to war with France. Alarmed by this turn of events, Robespierre's colleagues ordered his execution. The threat of civil war in 1795 led to the rise of an ambitious French soldier, Napoleon Bonaparte.

n Paris a mob attacked the Bastille, a royal prison, and riots broke out all over France. The National Assembly made a Declaration of the Rights of Man. These included liberty, equality, and the right

792
rance is eclared a epublic.

1793
Louis XVI is executed in January, Marie Antoinette in October. The Reign of Terror starts. The Netherlands, Austria, Britain, Prussia, and Spain are at war with France.

1794
Robespierre's execution ends the Reign of Terror. France is governed by the Directoire, a committee of five.

1795
Napoleon Bonaparte's rise to power starts when he defends Paris against rebels.

Australia and New Zealand

IN THE late 1700s, Europeans rediscovered Australia and New Zealand and the peoples living there, the Aboriginals and Maoris. Settlement of Australia by Britain began in 1788, and in 1840 New Zealand became a British colony. Emigrants from Europe settled in both countries.

A reconstruction of "Endeavour," the ship in which James Cook set out to explore the South Pacific in 1768. Scientists and artists on board recorded the plants, animals and people they saw or met on the voyage.

BRITISH NAVIGATOR James Cook made three voyages to the Pacific during the 1700s. His first expedition left in 1768. Cook sailed around New Zealand, then to the eastern and northern coasts of Australia. He landed at Botany Bay on the southeast coast and claimed the territory for Britain. On his second journey he explored many of the Pacific islands. The third voyage, in 1776, took him back to New Zealand. He then explored the Pacific coast of South America, before sailing to Hawaii.

In 1788 the First Fleet sailed from Britain, transporting convicts to the penal colony of Port Jackson in Australia. Some prisoners stayed on as free men

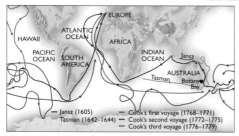

This map shows the voyages to Australia and New Zealand of the 17th-century Dutch explorers Willem Jansz and Abel Tasman, and the three epic explorations (1768–1779) of England's James Cook.

EUROPE
ATLANTIC OCEAN
HAWAII
AFRICA
PACIFIC OCEAN
SOUTH AMERICA
INDIAN OCEAN
Jansz
AUSTRALIA
Tasman
Botany Bay

— Jansz (1605)
— Tasman (1642–1644)
— Cook's first voyage (1768–1771)
— Cook's second voyage (1772–1775)
— Cook's third voyage (1776–1779)

1768–1771	1772–1775	1776	1788	1793	1803	1813
Captain James Cook's first voyage to the South Pacific.	Captain Cook's second voyage to the South Pacific.	Captain Cook's third and last voyage to the South Pacific. In 1779 he is killed in a quarrel with Hawaiians.	Convicts are transported from Britain to Australia.	The first free settlers from Britain arrive in Australia. They settle in Botany Bay.	Settlers from Britain start going to Tasmania for the first time.	By this date merino sheep (from Spain) have been introduced into Australia. Settlers have spread north and west, beyond the Blue Mountains.

ABORIGINALS AND MAORIS

Many Aboriginal Australians were ill-treated by Europeans. Some were shot, others died from European diseases. Many simply lost the will to live. The Maori of New Zealand numbered about 100,000 when James Cook arrived. After the Treaty of Waitangi, Maori rights were not protected, war broke out, and in 1848 the Maori were defeated.

...nd from 1793 were joined by settlers, ...ho made their homes around Botany ...ay. Towns were built and explorers crossed the continent. The settlers showed little respect for the Aboriginal

Australians whose lands they were taking. Transportation of convicts to Australia ended in 1850.

In New Zealand, the French arrived after Cook, but found the Maoris hostile. Contacts resumed with visits by whalers, seal-hunters, and Christian missionaries in the early 1800s. In 1840, by the Treaty of Waitangi, Maori leaders gave up their lands and New Zealand became a British colony.

Captain James Cook and his men meet Maoris for the first time, while charting the coast of New Zealand (1769-1770). Cook was killed by islanders in Hawaii in 1779.

...o	1851
...aori leaders sign the ...eaty of Waitangi. It offers ...nd rights and full British ...izenship. The treaty is ...t honored and war ...eaks out (1843–1848).	Discovery of gold in Victoria results in the Gold Rush.

160

Napoleon's Wars

NAPOLEON Bonaparte (1769–1821) rose from the rank of artillery officer to become emperor of France. Determined to unify Europe under his rule, his wars of conquest dominated the start of the 19th century.

◀ In land battles, Napoleon was a master at using artillery (wheeled guns). At sea, he tried to starve Brita into making peace by cutting its trade links, bu he was unable to defeat the British navy.

headed for Egypt, hoping to disrupt the British trade route to India. He defeated the Egyptians in 1798 at the battle of th Pyramids, but was then stranded when the British navy destroyed the French

NAPOLEON was born on the island of Corsica. He joined the French army in 1785. He supported the French Revolution and in 1793 defeated anti-revolutionary forces at Toulon. In 1795 he was called to Paris to defend the city against rebels, and in 1796 was appointed to command the French army in Italy. He won control of Italy from Austrian forces, and then

▶ At the battle of Austerlitz in December 1805, a French army of 73,000, under the command of Napoleon and his generals Soult and Bernadotte, defeated an army of 87,000 Austrians and Russians.

1785	1795	1797	1798	1799	1804	1805
Napoleon becomes an officer in the French army.	Napoleon defends Paris against rebels and prevents civil war breaking out.	A French army led by Napoleon drives Austrians from much of northern Italy.	The French fleet is defeated by Nelson at the battle of the Nile in Egypt.	Napoleon returns to France and seizes power.	Napoleon declares himself emperor of France.	The French fleet is defeated by Nelson at the battle of Trafalgar. Napoleon's army defeats the Austrians and Russia at the battle of Austerlitz

eet at Aboukir Bay. Napoleon returned
 France and set about making himself
le leader in place of the committee,
e Directoire, that ruled the country. It
ll in 1799. Most people welcomed a
rong ruler, and in 1802 Napoleon was
ade First Consul. He brought in a new
de of laws, the Code Napoleon,
mbodying some of the principles of the
ench Revolution. In 1804 he had
mself crowned emperor.

Napoleon enjoyed a string of
uccesses on the battlefield against
France's enemies: Prussia, Austria, and
Russia. He could not subdue
Britain, however, and naval
defeat by the British
admiral Horatio Nelson
at the battle of
Trafalgar in 1805
ended his hopes of
invasion. In 1807 he
led his army through
Spain to invade
Portugal, and made his
brother king of Spain.
Britain responded by
sending troops, beginning
the long Peninsular War.

This map shows the French empire under
Napoleon I and the main battles of the
Napoleonic Wars.

In 1812 Napoleon led his Grand Army
into Russia, but was driven back by the
bitter Russian winter. By 1813 the French
empire was collapsing. Napoleon
abdicated as emperor in 1814. Escaping
from exile on Elba, he raised a new
army and made a final effort to
win a victory and secure a
peace. Defeat at Waterloo in
1815 ended his hopes, and he
was exiled to Saint Helena,
where he died in 1821.

A caricature of the Duke of
Wellington (who had a boot named after
him). He led the British army in Spain
and Portugal, and defeated Napoleon at
Waterloo, in what is now Belgium.

...6	1807	1808	1809	1812	1814	1815
poleon's	Napoleon's	The Peninsular	Napoleon	Napoleon's army	Napoleon is	Napoleon
ny	army defeats	War starts when	marries the	invades Russia, but is	forced to	escapes from
eats the	the Russians at	Napoleon puts	Austrian	defeated by the winter	abdicate and	Elba. He is
ussians	Friedland.	his brother	emperor's	weather. In Spain the	is exiled to the	defeated finally
ena.	France controls	Joseph on the	daughter,	French army is defeated	island of Elba,	at the battle of
	Portugal.	throne of Spain.	Marie Louise.	at Salamanca.	off Italy.	Waterloo.

Canada

IN 1759 the British captured Quebec from the French, and by 1763 New France (French Canada) had become British Canada. The Canadian people developed a unique culture of French, British, and Native American traditions.

The Royal Canadian Mounted Police or "Mounties" were founded in 1875, with 300 riders to patrol the wilderness.

CANADA was a vast land with few people. During the American Revolution (1775–1783) thousands of United Empire Loyalists moved from America to Canada. Canadians later resisted American attempts to invade them during the War of 1812. Britain split Canada into two: Lower Canada (mostly French-speaking) and Upper Canada.

At first, only the eastern part of the country was settled by Europeans. The west and Arctic north were left to Native Americans and Inuit peoples. But soon fur traders and explorers pushed west, followed by farmers and railroad-builders. Britain reunited Upper and Lower Canada in 1841, and in 1867 Canada became a self-governing dominion.

The Red River Rebellion of 1869 failed to break up Canada, and by the 1890s the country extended from the Atlantic Ocean to the Pacific Ocean and included the Yukon territory.

The building of the first railway across Canada, the Canadian Pacific Railway, in the 1880s united the eastern and western halves of the huge country.

1759	1774	1775	1791	1821	1841	1867	1886
General James Wolfe captures Quebec for Britain.	The Quebec Act recognizes the rights of French Canadians in British-ruled Canada.	Americans try to invade Canada.	Britain creates Upper and Lower Canada.	Hudson's Bay Company takes control of territory west of the Great Lakes.	Upper and Lower Canada reunited.	Canada becomes a Dominion of the British empire.	Canadian Pacific Railway spans Canada.

South American Independence

BY 1800 Spain and Portugal still ruled vast areas in North and South America. Most local people hated being colonists, paying taxes to distant governments. After the Napoleonic Wars in Europe brought chaos to Spain and Portugal, the colonies decided to try and win their independence.

THE MAIN FIGHT against Spanish rule was led by Simón Bolívar from Venezuela and José de San Martin from Argentina. San Martin gained freedom for his country in 1816, but Simón Bolívar's fight was longer and more difficult. He had joined a rebel army that captured Caracas, capital of Venezuela, in 1810, but it was then defeated by the Spanish. Bolívar became the army's leader in 1811

▶ José de San Martin freed Argentina from Spanish rule, then led his army over the Andes mountains to help the people of Chile gain their independence.

and spent three years fighting the Spanish. When he was defeated a second time, he went into exile in Jamaica. In 1819, he led an army over the Andes from Venezuela to Colombia, where he defeated the Spanish in a surprise attack at the battle of Boyoca. In 1821 he freed Venezuela, and in 1822 he freed Ecuador and Panama too. He made them all part of a new state, called the Republic of Gran Colombia, with himself as president. Finally Peru was liberated and part of it was renamed Bolivia after Bolívar.

▶ At the battle of Ayachucho in 1824, Simón Bolívar's army defeated the Spanish to win independence for Peru.

18[1]5	1818	1819	1821	1822	1824	1825	1828
José de San Martin leads Argentina to independence from Spain.	Chile becomes independent from Spain.	Colombia wins independence from Spain.	Simón Bolívar wins independence for Venezuela.	Brazil wins independence from Portugal.	Bolívar wins independence for Peru.	New republic of Bolivia is named after Bolívar.	Uruguay wins independence from Spain.

The Industrial Revolution

THE INDUSTRIAL Revolution began in Britain in the mid-18th century. Society was transformed as people moved from the countryside to the towns to work in factories.

The Rocket, designed and built in England, was the first intercity steam locomotive (1830).

of an improved steam engine, used for pumping water out of coal mines. It was now possible to produce more coal and better quality iron for industry.

TWO EVENTS in the early 18th century helped make the Industrial Revolution possible. The first was Abraham Darby's discovery that coke was a better fuel than charcoal for smelting iron. The second was Thomas Newcomen's invention

Until the 1760s most goods were hand-made by people working at home or in small workshops. Metalworkers made nails, pins, and knives, and spinners and weavers produced woolle

The first public railroad, from Stockton to Darlington in England, opened in 1825. From 1830, steam locomotives were used to draw covered passenger carriages.

1698	1709	1712	1733	1742	1764	1769
Thomas Savery develops a steam engine to pump water out of mines.	Abraham Darby discovers smelting iron with coke.	Thomas Newcomen improves the steam engine.	John Kay invents the flying shuttle, speeding up weaving.	First cotton factories in England.	James Hargreaves invents the spinning jenny.	James Watt designs a more efficient steam engine. Richard Arkwright invents a spinning frame powered by water. Josiah Wedgwood makes pottery.

SPINNING JENNY

James Hargreaves, inventor of the spinning jenny, was a poor spinner. He named his new machine after his daughter Jenny. Other hand-spinners feared his machines would put them out of work, and destroyed them.

...nd linen cloth. But the 1700s saw a ...sing demand for cotton cloth, which at ...rst was imported from India. Then raw ...otton was imported, for ...anufacture into ...oth in Britain.

In 1733 the ...vention of a ...ying shuttle ...eeded up the ...eaving process so ...uch that spinning wheels ...ould not produce enough yarn to keep ...e weavers supplied. Then, in 1764, ...ames Hargreaves invented the spinning ...nny, which allowed one person to spin ...ght threads at once. This was followed ...ve years later by Richard Arkwright's ...eavy spinning frame, which was ...owered by water. Factories were built ...ear fast-flowing streams to house these ...ew machines, and the cotton industry ...oomed. By 1790, James Watt's ...nprovements to the steam engine

meant that steam power could be used to drive machinery. This also increased the demand for coal to heat the water to make steam, and for iron to make the engines and other machinery. Canals (and later railroads) were built to bring raw materials to the factories and take finished goods away. Towns grew rapidly, but housing and working conditions were often very poor and many people suffered from hunger, disease, or accidents at work.

Pit machinery at an English coal mine in 1792. In the centre is a steam pump used to drain water from the mine. Steam engines were used to power machinery in factories too.

Children from the age of five up worked in coal mines. Some pulled heavy loads; others sat all day in darkness, opening and closing doors to let the air circulate.

Europe in Turmoil

IN 1815, at the end of the Napoleonic Wars, Europe was in disorder. Old governments, with old ideas, were restored, but a new age of industrialism and democracy was dawning. At first people's demands for change were either ignored or crushed. Revolution seemed the only weapon to people all across Europe who still had no say in how they were governed.

These were the main centers of unrest in 1848, "the Year of Revolutions." By the end of 1849 all the revolts had been quashed.

REVOLT broke out in France in 1830, when Louis-Philippe was chosen as a "citizen-king" to replace the unpopular Charles X. Newspapers helped to spread reports of the uprising, sparking off protests in other countries. Within two years, Greece declared its independence

from Turkish rule, and Belgium from the Netherlands.

In 1848 so many revolutions and protests broke out again throughout Europe that it was known as the "Year of Revolutions." In Britain the Chartists demonstrated for political reforms and votes for all men. In France a group of rioters in Paris, who were demanding votes for all men and a new republic, were shot by soldiers. In Belgium, Denmark, and the Netherlands reforms were made peacefully.

In Germany, many people wanted all the German states to be united into one country, and Italians wanted a united Italy. In contrast, in the vast Austrian empire the many groups of people who had their own languages wanted the empire to be divided into separate states to reflect this.

◀ The revolutions of 1848 started with a small revolt in Sicily (Jan 20). This inspired a revolt in France on February 24. Soon the spirit of protest had spread across Europe.

◀ Riots broke out in Berlin in 1848. Men, women, and children were attacked by Prussian soldiers as demands for reform and a united Germany were crushed.

The revolutions in 1848 were crushed by the end of 1849. The ideas that drove them did not go away, however. Many governments realized that they would have to make some reforms. Reformers looked for new ways of governing and distributing wealth more fairly. The German socialists Karl Marx and Friedrich Engels published their ideas in *The Communist Manifesto* in 1848. This was to have a huge impact on future events.

▶ Irishman Feargus O'Connor (1794–1855) was elected to the British parliament in 1832. He agitated for votes for all men, and led the Chartists from 1841 until 1848.

1831	1832	1838	1844	1848	1852
Belgium declares independence from the Netherlands.	Greece becomes independent from the Ottoman empire.	In Britain, the People's Charter is published to demand political reforms. Its supporters become known as Chartists.	Friedrich Engels makes a study of the lives of workers in Manchester, England.	The Year of Revolutions affects most of Europe.	In France, the Second Republic is replaced by the Second Empire.

168

Exploring Africa

ALTHOUGH Europeans had been trading with Africa since the 16th century, they knew very little about the interior of the continent. They hardly ever ventured beyond the trading posts on the coast.

The route of the Boers' Great Trek is shown in blue. They went in search of new lands north of the Vaal river (Transvaal). Some tried to settle the Zulu lands of Natal, but were defeated. Later, the British took over Natal.

IN BRITAIN, curiosity about the interior of Africa grew, and in 1788 an association was formed to encourage exploration and trade there. At the same time, many Europeans started to campaign against slavery. The British slave trade was abolished in 1807, with slavery finally ending throughout the British Empire in 1833. In 1822 Liberia was founded in West Africa as a home for freed American slaves.

Christian missionaries traveled to Africa to set up churches and schools. Settlers also went there, most making for Cape Colony (South Africa), which the British took from the Dutch in 1806. This was the largest European settlement in Africa. Most of the colonists were Dutch farmers, known as Boers. By 1835 many of them were unhappy living under British rule, and they set off on the Great Trek into the interior. After much hardship they formed two new republics, the

The Victoria Falls, or Mosi-oa-tunya (the "Smoke that Thunders"), on the Zambezi river. The first European to see the falls was David Livingstone in 1855.

1795	1805	1806	1807	1822	1828	1830	1835
The African Association sends Mungo Park to explore the Niger river.	Mungo Park drowns while leading an expedition along the Niger.	Britain takes control of Cape Colony from the Dutch.	The British slave trade is abolished.	Liberia in West Africa is founded as a country for freed slaves.	Frenchman Rene August Caillie is the first European to visit Timbuktu, Mali, and return alive.	The French invade Algeria.	Start of the Great Trek; the Boers leave Cape Colony and head north.

▶ Journalist and explorer Henry Stanley found David Livingstone encamped at Ujiji on the shores of Lake Tanganyika in 1871.

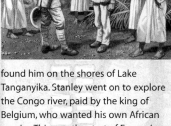

...ansvaal and the Orange Free State. But ...hen they reached the Zulu lands they ...me into conflict with the Zulus. The ...ulus attacked the Boers and the Boers ...taliated. Eventually the Zulus were ...efeated by the British in 1879.

Many British expeditions explored ...rica's interior along its great rivers. ...om 1768 to 1773, James Bruce ...xplored Ethiopia, and in two ...xpeditions from 1795 to 1806 Mungo ...ark explored the Niger river. From 1852 ... 1856 David Livingstone crossed ...e continent following the ...ambezi river. In 1866 he set ...ut to look for the source of ...e Nile, but lost contact ...ith Britain for almost ...ree years. An expedition ...d by Henry Stanley

found him on the shores of Lake Tanganyika. Stanley went on to explore the Congo river, paid by the king of Belgium, who wanted his own African empire. This was the start of Europe's scramble to control the entire continent.

▶ The Zulus were the most ...rmidable soldiers in southern ...rica. They fought the ...ers and the British, but ...re finally defeated by the ...itish in 1879.

Europeans in Asia

BY THE 17th century, European trade with Asia was so important that the British, Dutch, and French set up East India Companies to control and protect their interests. These companies laid the foundations for colonies.

THE DUTCH concentrated on the islands of Indonesia. The British and French fought over India until 1763, when the British East India Company took control of much of India.

In the 1830s, the Dutch decided they wanted to control more than just trade with Indonesia, and so they started to oversee agriculture on the islands.

They set up plantations to grow crops including coffee and indigo (a plant from which a blue dye is made). Enormous profits were made by Indonesian princes and Dutch colonists, at the expense of the ordinary people, who no longer had the time or the land to grow the crops they needed for themselves.

Britain invaded Burma not only to protect India, but also to gain access to Burma's valuable natural resources of teak, oil, and rubies. In spite of having a larger and better-equipped army, the British had to fight three wars before they finally took control.

In India, many Europeans wanted to live in surroundings that reminded them of home. This painting shows Lady Impey, wife of a British judge in Bengal, looking at clothes made by Indian tailors. Her room is furnished in European style in an Indian setting.

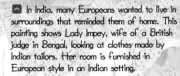

1786	1819	1824	1841
The British take control of Penang in Malaysia.	Foundation of the British colony of Singapore.	Start of the Anglo-Burmese wars.	The Sult Brunei g Sarawak James B

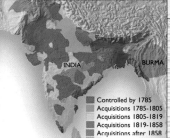

Controlled by 1785
Acquisitions 1785-1805
Acquisitions 1805-1819
Acquisitions 1819-1858
Acquisitions after 1858
Dependent states

and tin mines. From 1824 Britain also tried to take control of Burma (now Myanmar). The Burmese resisted, but were finally defeated in 1885.

France, meanwhile, began to take control of Indochina (now Cambodia and Vietnam), and later added Laos.

Areas of India under British control from 1785 to 1858, when India became part of the British empire. Dependent states were ruled by Indian princes, under British "protection."

As well as controlling India, Britain also began to build up colonies in Southeast Asia. One of the earliest, in 1819, was Singapore on the tip of the Malay peninsula. By 1867 Malacca and Penang had also become British colonies, and in 1896 the remaining Malay states formed a federation under British advisors. Ruling through the local sultans, the British controlled Malaya, setting up rubber plantations

HONG KONG
To force the Chinese to open their ports, Britain went to war against China from 1839 to 1842. Five ports were opened. Hong Kong Island became a British colony, and remained British until 1997.

Officials of the East India Company had many servants and were often carried around in enclosed litters, called palanquins.

1842 China cedes Hong Kong to Britain at the end of the First Opium War.

1857 Indian Mutiny leads to British government taking control of India from the East India Company.

1884 French victory at the battle of Bac-Ninh in Indochina.

1885 Burma becomes part of India at the end of the third Anglo-Burmese War.

1887 French form Indochina, from Cambodia and Cochinchina, Tonkin and Annam (Vietnam).

1893 Laos is added to French Indochina.

172

The British Empire

QUEEN VICTORIA came to the British throne in 1837 and reigned until her death in 1901. During her long reign, Britain became the world's most powerful nation, ruling a huge empire. The British Empire later evolved into the modern Commonwealth of independent nations.

Queen Victoria (1819–1901) was on 18 when she becam queen. She took a keen interest in Britain's empire, and was delighted to become Empress of India in 1876.

MUCH OF BRITAIN'S WEALTH came from her colonies. Colonies and trading posts had been established in the 17th and 18th centuries in places as far apart as Canada, India, Australia, and the Caribbean.

More were added by the Treaty of Vienn at the end of the Napoleonic Wars. Durir Victoria's reign, still more colonies were added, including New Zealand, many islands in the Pacific and Atlantic oceans parts of the Far East, and large areas of Africa. At its greatest extent, in the late 19th century, the empire contained a fourth of the world's land and a fourth of its people.

The British Empire often featured in advertisements. This poster (for a warm drink) played on patriotic feeling during the Boer Wars (1899–1902).

THE CRIMEAN WAR

During the Crimean War (1853–1856), Turkey, France, and Britain fought against Russia. Thousands of British soldiers died from neglect and disease. Florence Nightingale and her team of nurses cleaned up the military hospitals and set up Britain's first training school for nurses.

1763	1788	1808	1815	1829	1830	1839–1842	1840
Britain takes control of Canada.	First British settlement in Australia.	Sierra Leone becomes a British colony.	Treaty of Vienna gives Cape Colony (now South Africa), Ceylon (now Sri Lanka), Mauritius, Malta, and French islands in the Caribbean to Britain.	Britain claims the whole of Australia.	Britain starts to control the Gold Coast (Ghana).	Britain fights Opium Wars to open China to trade.	By the Trea of Waitang Britain gai New Zeala

▶ The British Empire grew throughout the 19th century. The largest empire the world had ever seen was called "the empire on which the sun never sets."

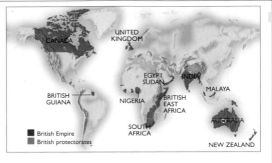

The colonies provided raw materials for British factories and a market for their goods. Some were at first run by trading companies, such as the East India Company in India. But gradually they all came under direct rule from Britain. In many colonies plantations were set up to produce tea, sugar, coffee, spices, rubber, and cotton.

- British Empire
- British protectorates

☑ Indian ports such as Madras and Calcutta became important centers of imperial trade.

The empire affected the lives of millions of people. British laws, technology, and culture were taken all over the world. The British navy defended the empire. By 1900, however, Britain was no longer supreme as an industrial power, and the empire began to break up as countries fought independence.

1843	1853–1856	1857–1858	1860	1867	1875	1876	1882	1901
In West Africa, the Gambia becomes a British colony.	The Crimean War.	The Indian Mutiny leads to India being ruled directly from Britain.	Lagos (Nigeria) is added to the empire.	Canada becomes a British dominion.	Britain buys shares in the Suez Canal Company to control the trade route to India.	Victoria is crowned Empress of India.	Britain controls Egypt.	Death of Queen Victoria.

The American West

AFTER THE United States declared independence from Britain in 1776, many settlers arrived from Europe. Most of the first settlers made their homes in the eastern states, but a few traveled farther west toward what are now Ohio, Michigan, Indiana, and Illinois.

Railroads opened up the West by making rapid settlement possible. The Union Pacific Railroad, opened in 1869, linked the East and West coasts.

MANY MORE people moved into the area around the Great Lakes after 1825, when the opening of the Erie Canal made the transportation of people, farm products, and manufactured goods much easier. To the west of the Mississippi river, in Louisiana, explorers

1803	1821	1825	1835	1836	1842	1845	1846–48
The Louisiana Purchase. The US buys the vast area west of the Mississippi from France.	Opening of the Santa Fe Trail from Missouri to New Mexico.	Opening of the Erie Canal.	Texas claims independence from Mexico.	Mexicans defeat the Texans at the Alamo, then are defeated themselves at San Jacinto.	Border dispute between Canada and the US is settled.	Texas becomes the 28th state of the US.	War between the US and Mexico. US gains California, Nevada, Utah, and Arizona, plus parts of New Mexico and Texas.

d traders set up routes, or trails, to be
llowed by settlers. In 1848, at the end
the Mexican-American War, people
arted traveling to the newly acquired
nd in the West. Known as pioneers, they
ade the journey in long trains of
vered wagons, taking with them food,
othing, tools, and furniture.

On reaching their destinations,
milies chose places to settle. They
opped down trees to build homes,
eared and plowed the land, and sowed
eds. If crops failed, families went
ungry or gathered food from the wild.

GOLD RUSH

The discovery of gold in California in
1848, and in Nevada and Colorado in
1859, attracted thousands of prospectors.
They washed river gravel in large
pans, hoping to find gold, but few
made their fortunes.

In spite of the hardships, the number
of people heading west increased. Then,
in 1862, the US government passed the
Homestead Act, which offered – for a
small fee – 160 acres of land to each
family who would settle and farm for at
least five years. Thousands took up the
offer, and towns sprang up all over the
Great Plains and the West. The land the
government was selling so cheaply was
taken from the Native Americans, who
were forced onto reservations.

▶ White hunters
shot thousands of
buffalo to feed
railroad workers.
With no buffalo
left, the Plains
Indians starved.

◀ Wagon trains took pioneers westward. The wagons were
pulled by teams of oxen or mules. Water was carried in
barrels slung on the side. The pioneers were in constant danger
of attack by Native Americans, whose land they were taking.

49	1858	1859	1862	1867	1869	1882	1893
ight the ld sh.	John Butterfield opens a stage coach route to the West.	Gold mines open up in Nevada and Colorado.	The Homestead Act encourages farmers to move to the Great Plains.	US buys Alaska from Russia.	The Union Pacific Railroad is completed.	Huge copper deposits are discovered at Butte, Montana.	The Great Northern Railroad reaches Seattle.

The Civil War

CIVIL WAR between the Northern and Southern states split the United States of America and left a legacy of bitterness. The war was fought to end slavery, and to prevent the South breaking away from the Union.

Through his determination win, Ulysses S Grant (1822– 1885) led the Union armies victory. He was President of the United States from 1869 to 187.

THE NORTHERN states had the biggest cities and the most factories. Slavery there was banned by 1820, but in the Southern states, which had little industry, plantations relied on large numbers of slave-workers. Here slave-owning was accepted. In 1861 Abraham Lincoln was elected President. He pledged to end slavery in the United States. Many Southerners saw this as a threat to their way of life and in 1861

eleven Southern states announced that they were breaking away from the Unic to form their own Confederacy. When the government told them they had no right to do this, civil war broke out.

The 23 Union (Northern) states had more soldiers and more money than th Confederacy, as well as the industry to provide weapons and supplies for war. With control of the navy, they were able to blockade Southern ports, cutting off supplies to the South from abroad, and preventing the export of cotton – a major source of wealth to the South.

The early battles were won by the South, but in July 1863 Union troops

A NEW KIND OF WARFARE
The American Civil War was fought with new weapons, such as quick-loading rifles, ironclad (armored) ships, submarines, and even balloons (for observing enemy movements). Railroads and telegraphs speeded up communications. Faced with deadly gunfire, soldiers were killed in large numbers as they tried to attack across open ground.

At the battle of Bull Run, Virginia, 1861, Confederate forces (right) led by Generals "Stonewall" Jackson and Beauregard defeated the Union army (left). It was the first major battle of the Civil War.

1861
Civil War starts when Confederate troops attack the Union garrison at Fort Sumter, South Carolina.

GENERAL ROBERT E LEE

Before the war, Robert E Lee (1807–1870) was offered the command of the Union army by Lincoln, but turned it down when Virginia (his home state) withdrew from the Union. He became commander in chief of the Confederate army.

▶ In 1863 Abraham Lincoln (1809–1865) gave his famous Gettysburg Address and announced the abolition of slavery throughout the United States. This was approved by Congress in 1865.

efeated Confederate forces at the attle of Gettysburg, Pennsylvania. nother Union army captured icksburg, Mississippi. In April 1865 the onfederate general Robert E Lee urrendered at Appomattox, Virginia. By

this time, much of the South was in ruins. Over 600,000 soldiers died, more than half from disease. Five days after the surrender, Lincoln was assassinated. Though the war was over and slaves were set free, conditions for them hardly improved.

862	1863	1864	1865
onfederate General Lee revents Union army aking Richmond, irginia, and defeats nother Union army at edericksburg, Virginia.	Emancipation Proclamation is signed. Lee is defeated at Gettysburg, Pennsylvania.	Grant's Union forces besiege Lee's forces at Petersburg, Virginia. Union General Sherman captures Atlanta and Savannah, Georgia.	Grant's forces capture Richmond, Virginia. On April 9, Lee surrenders to Grant at Appomattox, Virginia, bringing the war to an end. On April 15, Lincoln is shot in a theater by actor and Confederate sympathizer John Wilkes Booth.

Native Americans

WHEN Europeans first reached North America in the 16th century, they found many different Native American peoples living there. Each "nation," or group, had its own language and way of life.

◀ The rituals, customs, and languages of the Native Americans are proudly kept alive today.

BEFORE the arrival of Europeans, Native Americans did not have horses or wheeled vehicles, and although they had some knowledge of using metal, most of their tools and weapons were made from wood or stone. West coast Native Americans built wooden canoes for fishing. On the east coast they grew corn in small plots around their villages and trapped animals in the woods. On the Great Plains they hunted buffalo, and in the deserts of the

▶ The Sioux were the largest nation of the Great Plains. They lived in tepees – tents made from wooden poles covered in buffalo hide. Easy to transport, tepees were ideal homes for the hunters as they followed the buffalo herds across the plains.

1830
The Indian Removal Act forces all Native Americans to move to reservations.

1838
Cherokees march west on the "Trail of Tears." Thousands die on the way and soon afterward.

1862
The Homestead Act allows settlers to buy land on the Great Plains very cheaply.

1864
The Navajos are forced to go on "The Long Walk" to Bosque Redondo. Many Cheyennes are massacred at Sand Creek, Colorado.

1865
After the Civil War, many more settlers head west.

The Plains Indians became expert at shooting from horseback, after the Spanish introduced guns and horses in the 17th century.

southwest they built small dams to irrigate the land for growing crops such as corn, beans, and squash.

The arrival of Europeans soon had a disastrous effect on the Native Americans, who had no resistance to diseases such as measles and smallpox. They died, too, in disputes over land, as more and more Europeans moved West looking for places to settle. Then, in 1830, the government passed the Indian Removal Act. This forced all Native Americans in the eastern states to live on reservations. Their lands were taken over by European settlers. One of

the first nations to suffer was the Cherokees, many of whom died on what became known as the Trail of Tears.

Native Americans came under more pressure in the 1860s, when the railroads spread westward. The buffalo, on which many Plains peoples depended, were hunted almost to extinction, partly to feed the construction gangs. In 1876 the Sioux and their allies defeated the US cavalry at the Little Bighorn river. But a final massacre of over 200 Sioux men, women, and children at Wounded Knee Creek in 1890 brought to an end the tragic story of the "Indian wars."

GERONIMO

Geronimo (1829–1909) was a leader of the Apaches. When Mexican troops killed his family, he became a guerilla fighter, feared by both Mexican and American soldiers. He eventually surrendered and in 1905 took part in President Roosevelt's election victory parade.

1876
The US government forces the Chiricahua Apaches to move from their homelands to a reservation in eastern Arizona. In June General Custer's cavalry force is trapped and killed by Sioux and Cheyenne warriors at the battle of Little Bighorn.

1885
By this date only about 2,000 buffalo are left (down from 15 million in 1860).

1890
The US cavalry massacres over 200 Sioux at Wounded Knee Creek, South Dakota.

Unification of Italy

IN THE EARLY 1800s, Italy was united under the control of Napoleon. After Napoleon's defeat in 1815, Italy's states were handed back to their former rulers. Only Piedmont–Sardinia stayed independent.

OF THE ITALIAN states' foreign rulers, Austria was the most powerful. During the 1820s, opposition to foreign rule grew. The "Risorgimento" movement encouraged people to campaign for an independent, united Italy. Revolutions broke out in many states in 1848, but were crushed. In 1858, Piedmont–Sardinia allied itself with France and defeated Austria. This was followed in

◪ The unification of Italy took ten years. The last region to join was that of the Papal States, which surrounds Rome. Rome became the national capital in 1871.

▶ Giuseppe Garibaldi (1807–1882), leader of the "Redshirts," agreeing to hand over the Kingdom of the Two Sicilies to Victor Emmanuel in 1860.

1860 by a successful revolt led by Giuseppe Garibaldi and his army of "Redshirts." Garibaldi conquered Sicily, then Naples. Meanwhile, the northern states had joined up with Piedmont–Sardinia and accepted Victor Emmanuel II as their king. Garibaldi handed Naples and Sicily to him in November 1860 and in 1861 Italy was declared a kingdom.

LOMBARDY
PIEDMONT VENETIA
PARMA Venice
MODENA
LUCCA ROMAGNA
TUSCANY

Piedmont–Sardinia
Area added 1860
Area added 1866
Area added 1870

PAPAL STATES
Rome ★

ADRIATIC SEA

SARDINIA

Naples ●

KINGDOM OF THE
TWO SICILIES

SICILY MEDITERRANEAN
SEA

1815	From 1820s	1848	1849	1852	1860	1861	1866	1871
The Italian states are given back to their former rulers.	The Risorgimento – secret societies are formed to oppose foreign rule.	Unsuccessful revolutions in many states try to bring about unification.	Victor Emmanuel II becomes king of Piedmont–Sardinia.	Count Camillo Cavour unifies northern Italy.	Garibaldi and his Redshirts set out to conquer the Kingdom of the Two Sicilies.	Victor Emmanuel II becomes king of a unified Italy.	Venice becomes part of Italy.	Rome become part of Italy.

Unification of Germany

GERMANY, like Italy, was made up of separate states in the early 1800s. In 1815, after Napoleon's defeat, 38 states joined together as the German Confederation. Austria and Prussia were the two most powerful states to join.

Otto von Bismarck (1815–1898) went to war with Austria and France so that he could unite the northern German states and make Prussia the ruler of a united Germany.

FROM THE START, Austria and Prussia competed against each other for leadership of the Confederation, and in 1866 Prussia declared war on Austria. After Prussia won a battle at Sadowa on the Elbe river, Otto von Bismarck, the chief Prussian minister, set up a separate North German Confederation dominated by Prussia.

In 1851 Napoleon III (1808–1873) declared himself emperor of France. He transformed Paris and encouraged industry. After the Franco-Prussian War his empire collapsed and he went into exile.

The French, threatened by the growing power of Prussia, declared war in 1870. Napoleon III's army of 100,000 men was heavily defeated at the battle of Sedan, however, and Napoleon III was taken prisoner. The people of Paris rose up against him and the French Second Empire was overthrown. The Prussian army then besieged Paris.

When the Franco-Prussian War ended on May 10, 1871, Germany had taken control of Alsace and Lorraine from the French. The German Second Empire was declared, with William II, king of Prussia, as emperor and Otto von Bismarck as chancellor.

This map shows the extent of the German Confederation in 1815. It included much of the old Holy Roman Empire (in red).

PRUSSIA

GERMAN CONFEDERATION

FRANCE

AUSTRIA

The Holy Roman empire
Extent of the German Confederation

1815	1862	1864	1866	1870–1871	1871
38 German states form the German Confederation.	Bismarck becomes Prussia's foreign minister. He determines to make Prussia the most powerful state in the German Confederation.	Austria and Prussia declare war on Denmark and seize Schleswig-Holstein.	Prussia defeats Austria in the Seven Weeks' War. Venice is taken from Austria and given to Italy.	The Franco-Prussian War is won by Prussia.	Creation of the German Second Empire, ruled by William II, the former king of Prussia.

Scramble for Africa

IN 1880, less than five percent of Africa was ruled by European powers. Most European nations had been content with trading colonies around the coast. Only the British and the Boers in South Africa had moved inland and set up new settlements. But within 20 years the situation changed completely, in what is known as the Scramble for Africa.

MOROCCO
ALGERIA LIBYA EGYPT
RIO DE ORO
SAHARA
FRENCH WEST AFRICA
ANGLO EGYPTIAN SUDAN
ITALIAN SOMALIL
GAMBIA
IVORY COAST NIGERIA
SIERRA LEONE
ETHIOPIA
LIBERIA
GOLD COAST
BELGIAN CONGO
BRITISH EAST AFRICA
TOGOLAND
CAMEROUNS
GERMAN EAST AFRICA
ANGOLA
UNION OF SOUTH AFRICA
MADAGASCA
GERMAN SOUTH WEST AFRICA
PORTUGUES EAST AFRICA

- British
- French
- German
- Italian
- Portuguese
- Belgian
- Spanish

In 1914, European powers had control of most of Africa. Only two countries were independent: Ethiopia and Liberia.

SEVEN EUROPEAN nations took control of the whole of Africa, apart from Liberia and Ethiopia. By 1884 Belgium, Britain, France, Portugal, and Spain had started to claim new colonies in Africa or expand their old ones. The newly unified countries of Germany and Italy also wanted shares of the continent. To prevent serious conflict, the European

At Isandhlwana in southern Africa, the Zulus fought the British, killing 1,700 British soldiers at the start of the Zulu War in 1879. Later the Zulus were themselves defeated.

1880	1882	1884	1889	1890	1891	1893
Leopold II, king of Belgium, claims the Congo as his own personal territory.	Britain takes control of Egypt to secure access to the Suez Canal.	Conference of Berlin divides Africa among seven European countries.	The British conquer the Matabele and take their land, calling it Rhodesia.	The Italians take Eritrea and try, but fail, to conquer Abyssinia (now Ethiopia).	Tanganyika (now Tanzania) becomes a German protectorate. The French make northern Algeria part of France.	The French take control of Mali.

powers met at an international conference on Africa held in Berlin. The conference allowed the Europeans to divide Africa, with little regard for the African peoples, their cultures, or their natural boundaries. Resistance by black Africans, or indeed by white Boers in southern Africa, was crushed by well-equipped European armies. Thousands of Africans died in the fighting, and others suffered hardship and hunger as their traditional ways of life were destroyed. Some were forced to work as cheap labor in mines and on plantations, growing cotton, tea, coffee, and cocoa for export to Europe. Europeans started farms in suitable areas, and built roads and railroads.

In the better-run European colonies, schools and medical centers were set up for local people. In the worst-run colonies, African people were treated little better than slaves. Under European rule, Africans gained access to new ideas, but had no say in how their lives were run.

CECIL RHODES
British-born Cecil Rhodes (1853–1902) went to Natal in southern Africa when he was 17 years old. He became a member of the Cape Colony parliament in 1881 and prime minister in 1890. Rhodes helped to bring more territory under British control, but failed in his ambition to give Britain an empire in Africa that extended from the Cape to Egypt.

▶ On the Great Trek during the 1830s, many Boers left Cape Colony and headed north to escape British rule.

1894	1895	1899	1910	1911	1912
Uganda becomes a British protectorate.	Kenya comes under British control and is known as the East African Protectorate.	Start of the Boer Wars between Britain and the Boer people for control of southern Africa.	The Union of South Africa is formed.	The British colony of Rhodesia is divided into Northern Rhodesia (now Zambia) and Southern Rhodesia (now Zimbabwe).	Morocco is divided into Spanish and French protectorates.

The Modern World

INTO A NEW MILLENNIUM
1900–2000s

WHEN the 20th century began, large areas of the world were controlled by European powers, including Britain, France, and Germany. China and Russia lagged behind in industrial might. The new power in Asia was Japan, while the United States was fast becoming the world's industrial giant. During the 1900s, the tide of power ebbed and flowed, but overall the 20th century was dominated by the wealth and culture of the United States.

IT WAS A CENTURY of rapid change in society, in science and technology, and in everyday life. It was the age of aircraft, television, space rockets, computers, and genetic engineering. The world's population increased dramatically to over six billion people. Many of these people were poor and hungry, while others living in rich countries enjoyed comforts and entertainments unimaginable in earlier times.

Everywhere people demanded equal rights. There were revolutions in many countries. The revolution in Russia in 1917 made some people believe that Communism was the new

1914–1918
World War I sees more than 8.5 million soldiers killed.

1917
The Russian Revolution starts when the Bolsheviks, led by Lenin, seize power. They gain control of all of Russia by 1921.

1929
The Wall Street Crash sparks the Great Depression.

1933
Nazis, led by Adolf Hitler, come to power in Germany.

1936–1939
Spanish Civil War.

1939–1945
World War II. The USA enters the war in 1941. In 1945 Germany and Japan surrender.

1947
Pakistan and India gain independence from Britain.

1948
Israel is founded. First Arab-Israeli war.

...orld order. Anti-Communist revolutions ...eastern Europe in the 1980s and 1990s ...owed this was not so. There were two ...orld wars (1914–1918 and 1939–1945), ...d many smaller wars. World War I ...ded in defeat for Germany and its ...ies, but the peace that followed was an ...easy one and did not last long. World ...ar II was the most costly war of all time, ...d the most horrific.

...By 1950, the United States was the ...rongest power, for a while challenged ...the Communist Soviet Union in what ...came known as the Cold War. Europe, ...dly damaged by war, reshaped itself as ...e European Union. Japan modernized ...d became an industrial powerhouse.

Old empires ended, and new alliances were made. New independent nations, including India and the new nations of Africa, joined the United Nations. China emerged from years of isolation.

New communications such as the Internet, satellite TV, and world tourism made the world seem smaller. Problems in one country often affected others. Global concerns, such as the threat to the tropical rainforests or fast-dwindling oil supplies, could not be contained within national borders. Terrorism became a new threat to peace. So fast was the pace of change that it is hard to predict what the world will be like when the 21st century draws to a close.

	1960s	1965–1975	1969	1990	1991	1994	2001
...mmunists ...by Mao ...ong gain ...trol of ...na.	Most countries in Africa gain independence from colonial rule.	The Vietnam War.	US astronaut Neil Armstrong is first to walk on the Moon.	East and West Germany are reunited.	The Soviet Union collapses and the Cold War ends.	Free elections in South Africa.	Terrorists crash airliners into the World Trade Center in New York City and the Pentagon in Washington DC. US-led forces invade Afghanistan to remove Taliban government.

Votes for Women

WOMEN'S right to vote, suggested by British author Mary Wollstonecraft in her book *A Vindication of the Rights of Women* (1792), was a long time coming. Groups campaigning for political reform in the 1830s were only concerned with obtaining the vote for all men. Women were not included.

▶ Women's rights campaigners, or suffragettes, argued their case at elections. This woman is speaking during the run-up to the British general election of 1910.

IN THE MID-1800s, however, a movement was started in the USA that aimed to win voting rights for women across the world. It held its first meeting in Seneca Falls, New York, in 1848. Many other public meetings followed, often fiercely opposed by those who did not want women to have the right to vote. Speakers included Sojourner Truth and Harriet Tubman, both of whom had been born slaves.

1848	1890	1893	1897	1902	1903	1905
First women's rights convention held in Seneca Falls, New York, USA.	Wyoming allows women to vote in local elections.	New Zealand gives women the vote in national elections.	The National Union of Women's Suffrage Societies is formed in Britain.	Australia gives women the right to vote.	In England, Emmeline Pankhurst forms the Women's Social and Political Union.	The first two suffragettes are sent to prison in Britain.

The movement grew, and 1890 Wyoming became he first US state to allow women to vote in local ections. Three years later ew Zealand became the first ountry to allow women to ote in national elections. In ritain, this triumph ncouraged various women's uffrage (right to vote) ocieties to unite in 1897. At first their ampaigns were peaceful, but in 1903 mmeline Pankhurst set up a new ociety, the Women's Social and Political nion (WSPU), which advocated action ther than words.

◀ Women's rights campaigner Emmeline Pankhurst was arrested several times for destroying property. Protesters refused to pay taxes and disrupted political meetings.

The WSPU held demonstrations and attacked property in protest against women's lack of rights. Many members were sent to prison, and went on hunger strike to draw attention to their cause.

With the outbreak of World War I in 1914, many women took on men's jobs, proving that they were just as capable as men. In 1918 the vote was given to all British women over 30 (the voting age for men was only 21). Women in the USA were given the right to vote in 1920. In 1928 the voting age for British women was lowered to 21.

▶ Suffragettes in prison who went on hunger strikes were force-fed by doctors.

◀ Many women campaigned peacefully for the right to vote. They held rallies to gain support for their cause.

| 96 land gives men the vote, d in 1907 the st women MPs e elected to the nish parliament. | 1913 British suffragette Emily Davison is killed when she throws herself under the king's horse at the Derby horse race. Norway gives women the vote. | 1917 Russia gives women the right to vote. | 1918 British women over 30 are given the vote. Canadian women are given equal voting rights with men. | 1919 Germany, Austria, Poland, and Czechoslovakia all give women the right to vote. | 1920 Women in the US are given the vote. |

World War I

WORLD WAR I began as a European quarrel, caused by rivalry between nations. It spread to the oceans, to the Middle East, and to Africa. The war cost the lives of more than 8 million soldiers, many killed in awful trench warfare. The war was so frightful that afterwards people said it had been the Great War, "the war to end wars." It was not.

 On the Western Front most of the fighting took place in northern France and Belgium. Mules and horses were used to bring supplies and heavy guns to the front.

BETWEEN 1880 and 1907, the European powers had formed alliances and increased their armies and navies. On one side stood the Allies: Britain, France, Russia, and Japan. On the other were the Central Powers: Germany, Austria-Hungary, Turkey, and Serbia. Italy later joined the Allies. The spark that started

In the trenches soldiers ate and slept while waiting for orders to go into battle. Dug-outs, or underground shelters, offered some protection from enemy shells, but the trenches were usually cold, muddy, and wet.

1914 June 28	1914 July 28–August 3	1914 August 4	1914 August 26	1914 September	1914 November
A Serb, Gavrilo Princip, assassinates Archduke Franz Ferdinand in Sarajevo.	Austria declares war on Serbia. Russia prepares to defend Serbia. Germany declares war on Russia, then on France.	German armies march through Belgium to France. Britain declares war on Germany. World War I begins.	Germany defeats Russian forces at the battle of Tannenberg.	At the battle of the Marne the Allies halt the German advance on Paris.	At the end of the battle of Ypres German forces are prevented from reaching the Channel.

◀ The war in Europe was fought on the Western Front, between France and Germany, and the Eastern Front, from the Baltic toward the Black Sea. There was also fighting in the Middle East, the Italy–Austria border, and in Africa.

...he war was the assassination of ...ustrian Archduke Franz Ferdinand by a ...erb in June 1914. This led to a series of ...obilizations (preparing for war), and on ...ugust 4 German armies invaded ...elgium. This drew Britain, Belgium's ally ...ince 1830, into the war.

World War I was fought mostly on ...and (there was only one big naval ...attle, at Jutland in 1916). Both sides got ...ogged down in trench warfare, their ...rmies unable to advance without ...uge losses. Soldiers had to go "over ...he top" (leave the trench), scramble ...hrough their own barbed-wire ...efenses, then cross open ground ("no-...an's land") to reach the enemy lines. So ...uick and powerful were the machine ...uns and heavy artillery guns that ...oldiers were killed in their thousands. In

the battle of the Somme alone (1916), there were over a million casualties.

By 1917, Russia was so weak that it began peace talks with Germany. For a while Germany had an advantage, but in 1918 the arrival of more than a million US soldiers boosted the Allies, who began to advance. There were food shortages and unrest in Germany, and emperor Wilhelm II abdicated. On November 11, an armistice was signed between Germany and the Allies, ending the war.

WAR PLANES
World War I (1914–1918) was the first war in which airplanes were widely used. They were first used to spy on enemy trenches and troop movements. Later, they were used in aerial combat and in bombing raids.

| ...15 ...pril–May ...ermany uses ...ison gas for ...rst time at ...econd battle ...Ypres. | 1915 May 22 Italy joins the Allies. | 1916 February Start of battle for Verdun, France, lasting for five months. | 1916 July 1 Start of the battle of the Somme, France; ends in November. | 1917 On April 6 the USA joins the war on the Allied side. | 1917 July Third battle of Ypres (Passchendaele). | 1918 March 3 Cease-fire between Russia and Germany. | 1918 November Armistice is signed on November 11 at 11 o'clock. World War I ends. |

The Russian Revolution

IN THE 19TH century, efforts to modernize Russia by freeing the serfs (peasants), building factories, and introducing democracy came to nothing. Czar Alexander II made reforms, but in 1881 he was assassinated. Czar Alexander III undid most of his father's work, and in desperation some Russians turned to revolution.

THE FIRST SERIOUS rebellion broke out in 1905, after troops fired on striking workers in the capital, St Petersburg. The rebellion was soon crushed and the leaders, including Lenin, went into exile. The new czar, Nicholas II, promised the people more civil rights, but the promise was soon broken.

When World War I started, life for most people in Russia went from bad to worse. The railroads no longer carried food, fuel, and supplies to the cities. The economy almost collapsed and people went hungry. In March 1917 riots broke out again. This time the troops joined the rioters. Nicholas abdicated and his advisers resigned.

A temporary government was set up, led by Alexander Kerensky, but unrest continued. The Bolsheviks, led by Lenin, planned a take-over. In November they attacked the Winter Palace in St Petersburg and seized power (an event known as the October Revolution, because Russia used a different calendar at that time). The Bolsheviks

▷ Armed workers led by the Bolsheviks stormed St Petersburg's Winter Palace in 1917, starting the revolution. They were joined by Russian soldiers, tired of fighting the Germans in World War I.

▽ Leon Trotsky (1879–1940), a leader of the Bolshevik revolution, was the most powerful man in Russia after Lenin. When Stalin came to power in 1924, he was exiled and later murdered.

◁ Czar Nicholas II with his wife Alexandra and their five children. After the revolution, they were all imprisoned, and in 1918 they were executed.

LENIN

Vladimir Ilyich Ulyanov (1870–1924) used the name Lenin. He led the Bolsheviks from 1898, but was exiled from 1905 to 1917. On his return the Bolsheviks seized power and he became Russia's new leader.

▶ Many Russians blamed Rasputin (1869–1916) for persuading Czar Nicholas II to ignore the people's complaints. Rasputin, a priest, claimed he had the power to heal the emperor's sick son.

moved the capital to Moscow and made peace with Germany. They broke up large estates and gave the land to the peasants. Workers took control of the factories and the state took control of the banks. In 1918 civil war broke out between the Bolshevik Red Army and anti-Communist

White Russians. This ended in victory for the Bolsheviks in 1921. The following year, the Union of Soviet Socialist Republics was formed. Lenin died in 1924, and was succeeded by Joseph Stalin. Stalin's rule was tyrannical. He had millions of people killed or sent to prison camps, where they died.

1887	1894	1905	1917	1918	1922
Lenin becomes Marxist.	Nicholas II becomes czar.	Some 200,000 people march on the Winter Palace in St Petersburg. Lenin is exiled.	Lenin returns. Nicholas II abdicates and a republican government is formed. Revolutionaries attack the Winter Palace and the government falls.	Russia withdraws from World War I. The imperial family is executed. Civil war between the Red Army (Communists) and White Russians (anti-Communists) lasts until 1920.	The Russian empire is renamed the Union of Soviet Socialist Republics.

Irish Home Rule

A N UPRISING in Ireland in 1916 by nationalists, who wanted "home rule" – an Irish republic independent of Britain – led to decades of argument and violence.

MOST PEOPLE in the north of Ireland, known as Ulster, wanted to stay part of the United Kingdom. Most people in the south wanted an independent Irish republic. In 1916 republicans in Dublin rose in rebellion on Easter Monday. After four days they were forced to surrender.

In 1918, nationalist Sinn

▶ This map shows Ireland after the division in 1921. Three of the nine counties of Ulster became part of the Irish Free State; the other six stayed part of the United Kingdom.

Fein members set up an Irish parliament, the Dail Eireann. This led to war between the military wing of Sinn Fein (later called the Irish Republican Army, or IRA) and the British. In 1921 Michael Collins agreed a deal with the British. The deal made most of Ireland independent, but left out the six counties of Northern Ireland. This led to more fighting. Collins was assassinated.

In 1949 Ireland became a republic. The IRA continued to fight for a united Ireland, an aim fiercely resisted by Unionists in Northern Ireland. In 1998 a ceasefire (the Good Friday agreement) brought hope for a peaceful solution to an ancient dispute.

◀ During the Easter rising of 1916, British soldiers faced Irish Republicans across Dublin barricades. One hundred British soldiers and 450 Irish republicans were killed.

1886–1893	1905	1912	1916	1919	1921	1937	1949
Attempts to give Ireland its own parliament are defeated in London.	Sinn Fein, the Irish nationalist party, is founded.	Third Irish Home Rule bill is introduced in the British parliament, but World War I starts in 1914 before it can be enacted.	Easter Rising in Dublin.	Bitter fighting between Irish republicans and British troops.	Anglo-Irish Treaty leads to a split Ireland and civil war until 1923.	The Irish Free State becomes Eire.	Eire becomes the Republic of Ireland.

The Roaring Twenties

FOR PEOPLE in America and Europe, the 1920s were years of recovery and fun after the horrors of World War I. It was a time of new ideas, jazz music, radio, and "talking pictures" (motion pictures with sound). Women enjoyed greater freedom. So did gangsters, in the lawless years that followed the ban in the USA on alcoholic drinks.

▶ A new dance craze in 1925 was the Charleston. Young people loved it; many older people were disapproving.

illegal drinking clubs or buying "bootleg" alcohol made in backstreet workshops. Gangsters fought to control the illegal trade. Prohibition was ended in 1933.

The 1920s brought a false sense that all was well. Problems left by World War I had not been solved. In Germany the economy had collapsed. In Britain, there was a first-ever General Strike by workers. The bubble burst in October 1929, when millions of people lost their savings in the Stock Market Crash. The party of the "Jazz Age" was over; the Depression was beginning.

N THE "ROARING TWENTIES" society ecame more free and easy. For the first me, women cut their hair short and vore short skirts. The heroes of the ge included the lone flier Charles indbergh and the movie star udolf Valentino.

In 1920, the S government brought in rohibition, a law to ban the haking and selling of alcoholic drinks. 1any people broke the law by visiting

▶ In 1927, US flier Charles Lindbergh became the first person to fly alone across the Atlantic. It took him 33 hours in his plane the "Spirit of St Louis" (left).

The Great Depression

AFTER World War I, the economies of many European countries were in ruins. Defeated Germany had to pay reparations (money as compensation for the war) to Britain and France. German money became worthless. By 1929, the whole world economy seemed to be falling apart. Millions of people lost money, jobs, and homes.

On the Jarrow Crusade (1935) in England, 200 men walked from Jarrow in northern England to London to draw attention to unemployment in their home town.

IN THE USA, whose banks had loaned money to other nations for the war, many people had invested savings in stocks. Buying pushed up prices of company shares beyond their real value. In August 1929 share prices started to fall, and people began to panic. They sold their shares, which made prices fall even faster. Many people lost all their savings in the Stock Market Crash. Banks and businesses closed and many people lost their jobs.

A severe drought in the American Midwest made things even worse. In the Dust Bowl, where fertile topsoil was worn away by over-farming, the drought and wind turned

Soup kitchens serving free food were set up in many cities to feed the hungry. It was estimated that over a fourth of the population of the USA relied on begging, charity handouts, and limited public welfare

1929	1932
In October the New York Stock Exchange on Wall Street crashes after people panic and sell their shares.	At the height of the Depression there are 12,000,000 unemployed people in the USA. Franklin D Roosevelt is elected President.

the fields to dusty deserts. Many farms were abandoned as families headed west to California.

The crisis in the USA affected the world, as money loaned overseas by US banks was called

THE NEW DEAL
Part of President Roosevelt's New Deal in 1933 included a program to create more jobs. Young people were given work in the national forests, and a series of dams were built on the Tennessee river to provide electricity and prevent soil erosion. New welfare and labor laws improved working conditions.

back. Britain and Germany were hit especially hard, and unemployment rose rapidly. Jobless men lined up for handouts of food and clothes. Countries tried to protect their industries by taxing foreign goods. By 1932, when the Depression reached its deepest, world exports of raw materials had fallen by over 70 percent, ruining the economies of poorer countries that depended on selling food and raw materials.

The New York Stock Exchange on Wall Street, October 1929. As share prices fell, many investors rushed to the Exchange to discover that they had lost all their money.

▶ The Depression brought misery for millions of people who lost their jobs. This chart shows how unemployment soared in 1932. It started to fall as economies recovered.

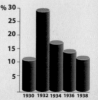

1933
Roosevelt introduces the New Deal to protect people's savings and create jobs. In Germany there are 6,000,000 unemployed.

1935
In Britain 200 men march from Jarrow to London with a petition drawing attention to unemployment.

1936
The Depression ends in Germany as public works and weapons production bring full employment.

1939
About 15 percent of the workforce in the USA is still unemployed.

1941
Full employment returns to the USA as it enters World War II.

The Rise of Fascism

FASCISM is the name of a political movement that grew up after World War I. In the 1920s, Fascist parties promised strong leadership and a war on Communism. They roused people by promising national glory, more jobs, and revenge for past humiliations. The two most dangerous Fascist leaders were Italy's Benito Mussolini and Germany's Adolf Hitler.

◄ Benito Mussolini (1883–1945) at first impressed many Italians with his "modernizing" government. He became a tyrant, however, and led Italy into World War II, with disastrous results. In the end, Mussolini was overthrown and killed by his own people.

ITALY WAS THE FIRST country to have a Fascist government. Benito Mussolini marched his followers into Rome in October 1922 and threatened to overthrow the government. The king asked him to form a new government. Armed Fascists terrorized and killed members of other political groups, and by January 1923 Italy had become a one-party state. Two years later, Mussolini started ruling as dictator and became known as "Il Duce" (The Leader).

Spain's Fascist group, the Falangist party, was founded in 1933. In 1936,

▲ Republican fighters surrender during the Spanish Civil War (1936–1939). In this war, the Fascist leader Franco was helped by Italy and Germany. The Republicans were aided by the USSR and by volunteers from other countries.

1922	1923–1930	1925	1931	1932	1933
Fascists led by Mussolini as prime minister come to power in Italy.	Primo de Rivera rules Spain as dictator.	From this date Mussolini rules Italy as dictator.	Spanish monarchy overthrown as Republican party wins the election.	Sir Oswald Mosley forms the British Union of Fascists.	Nazis led by Adolf Hitler come to power in Germany. In Spain, the Falangist (Fascist) party is created.

General Francisco Franco (1892–1975) led the Falangist (Fascist) party in Spain and won the civil war. Franco kept Spain out of World War II.

Britain's Prime Minister Neville Chamberlain returned from his meeting with Adolf Hitler in 1938 promising peace. But when the Munich Agreement proved worthless, war was inevitable.

Under the leadership of General Franco, the Falangist party overthrew the elected government in Spain. A terrible civil war lasted until 1939, when Franco became dictator of Spain.

In Germany, the Nazi party and its leader Adolf Hitler won power in 1933. Hitler set up a program to create jobs and built up munitions and the armed forces. He banned other political parties, introduced a secret police, and persecuted the Jews. In 1938, Hitler sent tanks into Vienna to persuade the Austrians to agree to a union with Germany. He also threatened to take over the Sudetenland in Czechoslovakia. To try to keep the peace, the Munich Agreement gave the Sudetenland to Germany. The following March, however, Hitler's troops took over the whole of Czechoslovakia and began to threaten Poland.

Adolf Hitler (1889–1945) saluting to a rally of Nazis at Nuremberg in 1938. The Nazis made Germany a police state, jailing or murdering opponents, and controlling radio, films and newspapers.

1934	1935	1936–1939	1937	1938
Hitler gains total power – his rivals are killed on the Night of the Long Knives.	Italy invades Abyssinia (Ethiopia).	Spanish Civil War between Republicans and Nationalists (Falangists). Nationalists win and Franco becomes dictator of Spain.	German aircraft bomb the Spanish town of Guernica in support of the Nationalists.	Hitler unites Germany and Austria. Nazi mobs attack Jews in Germany on "Kristallnacht." Munich Agreement is signed.

Revolution in China

BY 1900, large parts of China were dominated by foreign powers. The Chinese Nationalist party, the Kuomintang, was founded by Sun Yat-sen. He tried to unify China under a democratic government. In 1911 China became a republic and in 1912 the last emperor abdicated.

The Empress Dowager Cixi was mother to one emperor and aunt to another. Acting as regent, she refused to allow change in China, which helped bring about the fall of the Manchu empire.

SUN DIED in 1925. Chiang Kai-shek then became president of China and leader of the Kuomintang. The rival Chinese Communist party first met in Shanghai in 1921. Mao Zedong was an early member.

Throughout the 1920s, warlords in the north of China tried to gain control of the country.

The Long March from Jiangxi in the south to Shaanxi in the north took 568 days. Of the 100,000 who set out, about 80,000 died on the journey. The Communist marchers were pursued by the Kuomintang.

1905	1911	1921	1925	1926	1927	1931
Sun Yat-sen founds the Kuomintang (Chinese Nationalist party).	Collapse of the Manchu empire. Sun Yat-sen becomes president.	Foundation of the Chinese Communist party.	Death of Sun Yat-sen. Chiang Kai-shek succeeds him as leader of China.	With help from Communists, Chiang Kai-shek defeats the northern warlords.	Civil war between the Communists and the Kuomintang. Communists are forced out of Shanghai and into the Jiangxi hills.	Communist set up a riva government in the south

◀ This map shows the route of the Long March (1934–1935). It covered about 6,000 miles (9,700 km). At the end of the march, Mao Zedong said: "It proclaims to the world that the Red Army is an army of heroes."

Jiangxi to wipe them out. To escape, Mao led 100,000 Communists on the "Long March" from Jianqxi in the south to Shaanxi in the north. Mao was then confirmed as leader of the Communists.

To fight them, the Kuomintang and the Communists united in 1926. But in 1927 civil war broke out between the Kuomintang and the Communists. The Communists took refuge in the province of Jiangxi. There, in 1931, they set up a rival government. In 1933 Chiang Kai-shek sent his army to

In 1937 Japan invaded China and the Communists and Nationalists united to fight the Japanese. When World War II ended in 1945, civil war broke out again. This time the Communists waged a successful war against the Kuomintang, who fled to Taiwan. On October 1, 1949, mainland China became the People's Republic of China with Mao as its first president.

▶ Mao Zedong (1893–1976) was born into a peasant family in Hunan province. While fighting in the revolutionary army of 1911 he became interested in politics. In 1923 he joined the Chinese Communist party, and eventually became China's leader.

1933	1934	1935	1937–1945	1938	1939	1946	1949
Chiang Kai-shek attacks the Communists in Jiangxi.	Mao leads Communists on the "Long March."	Mao becomes leader of the Communist party.	The Kuomintang and Communists unite to fight against Japan.	Japan controls most of the east. Mao's Communists control the northwest.	The Soviet army stops the Japanese from advancing farther west in China.	Civil war breaks out again.	The People's Republic of China is proclaimed. Chiang escapes to Taiwan.

World War II

WORLD WAR II began on September 3, 1939, two days after German armies invaded Poland. When Germany's leader, Adolf Hitler, refused to withdraw his troops, Britain and France declared war. The war was fought between the Axis powers (chiefly Germany, Italy, and Japan) and the Allies (who included Britain and its Commonwealth partners, France, the Soviet Union, and the United States).

ON SEPTEMBER 17, the Soviet Union invaded Poland from the east. By the end of 1939, Soviet troops had also invaded Estonia, Latvia, Lithuania, and Finland. In the spring of 1940 German troops invaded Denmark, Norway, Belgium, the Netherlands, and France. Using vast numbers of tanks and bomber planes, they swiftly overwhelmed defenses – a tactic known as Blitzkrieg (German for "lightning war"). Infantry completed the

Winston Churchill (1874–1965) was prime minister of Britain from 1940 to 1945. Here he is making his famous "V for victory" sign.

take-overs. By June 1940, most of Europe had fallen. Britain stood alone. In August and September, Hitler's air force, the Luftwaffe, attacked southeast England and London in daylight raids. Despite having fewer planes, the British air force managed to fight off the German and so prevent an invasion. Even so, many British towns and cities were bombed in the Blitz attacks that followed.

The Battle of Britain raged above southern England from August to October, 1940. RAF planes (right) fought off German planes (left). Over 2,600 aircraft were shot down.

1939 Germany annexes Czechoslovakia. Italy annexes Albania. Italy and Germany form an alliance.	1939 August 23 Germany and the USSR sign a non-aggression pact.	1939 August 25 Britain, France, and Poland form an alliance.	1939 September 1 Germany invades Poland.	1939 September 3 Britain and France declare war on Germany.	1939 September 17 The USSR invades Poland.	1939 December 17 The River Plate naval battle in South America. Germany loses the battleship Graf Spree.

Under German control
Neutral countries

FINLAND
NORWAY
SWEDEN
IRELAND
NETHERLANDS
BRITAIN
DENMARK
RUSSIA
BELGIUM
GERMANY
POLAND
PORTUGAL
FRANCE
CZECHO-
SLOVAKIA
AUSTRIA
HUNGARY
ROMANIA
SPAIN
YUGOSLAVIA
SWITZERLAND
ALBANIA
BULGARIA
TURKEY
ITALY
GREECE
NORTH
AFRICA

◄ By the end of 1941, Germany controlled most of Europe and North Africa and part of Russia. In Europe, only neutral countries and Britain were still free.

forced the British back to the Egyptian border.

Encouraged by his successes, Hitler launched an attack on his former ally, the Soviet Union, in June 1941, invading the vast country with the help of Finland, Hungary, and Romania. By the end of 1941, however, Allied fortunes were about to change as the USA joined the war, following the unprovoked attack on its navy at Pearl Harbor in Hawaii by the Japanese.

In September 1940, Italian troops moved into Egypt, where Britain had part of its army stationed to defend the Suez Canal. By February 1941, the Italians had been defeated, but German troops

◄ Many children from British cities were sent to live with families in the country, away from the bombs. They were evacuees.

1940 March	1940 April–May	1940 June	1940 August–October	1940 November
The USSR takes Finland.	Germany occupies Norway, Denmark, Belgium, and the Netherlands.	Germany occupies France. Allies evacuate from Dunkirk.	Battle of Britain.	Italy tries to invade Greece. Hungary, Romania, and Slovakia join the Axis powers.

THE MODERN WORLD

World at War

THE JAPANESE attack on the US naval base at Pearl Harbor brought the United States, with its industrial and military might, into the war. Before this, many Americans had supported Britain in its fight against Nazi Germany, but had been reluctant to get involved in a European war. Now it was different.

◀ British general Bernard Montgomery (1887–1976) led the Allies to victory over German and Italian forces in the North African desert.

on supply ships. The Allies began to bomb German cities, the British bombing by night while the Americans raided by day. They used ships and planes to hunt enemy submarines (U-boats).

By August 1941 the US forces in the Pacific had defeated the Japanese at the battles of the Coral Sea, Midway, and Guadalcanal. These victories halted the Japanese advance. The US used aircraft carriers against Japanese ships, and from captured island bases sent planes on bombing raids against Japan itself.

MILLIONS OF US TROOPS were soon on their way to fight in Europe and the Pacific, and the US threw its air force and navy into the battles against both Germany and Japan. US guns, tanks, and planes were shipped across the Atlantic Ocean to Britain, still suffering from German air raids and from shortages caused by German submarine attacks

▶ The US naval base at Pearl Harbor in Hawaii was attacked without warning by the Japanese air force on December 7, 1941. Four battleships were destroyed, many more damaged, and 3,300 people killed. This attack brought the USA into the war on the side of the Allies.

1941 February	1941 April	1941 May	1941 December 7	1941 December	1942 February to May	1942 August
Allies capture 113,000 Italian soldiers in North Africa.	Yugoslavia and Greece fall to Germany.	German invasion of USSR begins.	Japan attacks Pearl Harbor. The US declares war on Japan. Italy and Germany declare war on the US.	Japan invades Malaya and Hong Kong.	Singapore, the Dutch East Indies, the Philippines, and Burma fall to Japan.	US victory at Guadalcanal ends Japanese expansion. The siege of Stalingrad begins.

German and Finnish forces besieged the Russian city of Leningrad (now St Petersburg) from 1941 to 1944. About one million people died of cold, hunger, disease, and injury.

In Africa, British and Commonwealth troops won a decisive battle at El Alamein, Egypt, in late 1942. As the British advanced west across the desert, they trapped the enemy between more Allied forces advancing from Algeria and Morocco.

The North African battles were over by May 1943, and the Allies began plans for the invasion of Italy and France.

In Russia, German armies got to within sight of Moscow by November 1941, but were forced back. The Germans were beaten at Stalingrad (now Volgograd) In 1943, and retreated from Russia as the Soviet Red Army moved steadily west. The long-awaited "second front" in western Europe opened on June 6, 1944, when Allied armies landed in Normandy, France.

After bombing raids, rescuers battled fires and pulled out survivors. German planes bombed Britain during the Blitz. Later, Allied bombers destroyed homes and industrial plants in Germany and Japan. An Allied raid on the German city of Dresden in 1945 killed about 80,000 people.

1942 October In North Africa, Allies defeat Axis forces at the battle of El Alamein, Egypt.

1943 February The battle of Stalingrad ends in defeat for the Germans.

1943 May Axis troops in North Africa surrender.

1943 July Allied troops invade Sicily. Mussolini's government is overthrown and Italy declares war on Germany.

Horror and Holocaust

THE WAR in Europe was over by May 1945, and the war in the Pacific by August. As the Allies liberated conquered countries and occupied Germany, they discovered the horrors of the Holocaust – the Nazi plan to round up and exterminate Jews.

Nagasaki (left) and Hiroshima in Japan were flattened in an instant by atomic bombs. Many people died later from radiation.

heartland of German manufacturing and arms production. Meanwhile, Soviet troops were heading toward Berlin. Realizing he was facing defeat, Hitler committed suicide on April 30. Soviet troops captured Berlin two days later. On May 9, Germany officially surrendered.

THE ALLIED INVASION of Europe started on June 6, 1944. By July 2, one million troops had landed in France. In March 1945 Allied troops crossed the river Rhine and in April they reached the Ruhr, the

US B-17 bombers raided targets in Europe and Asia.

The Allies planned to invade Japan in late 1945, but feared heavy losses. On August 6, 1945, an atomic bomb was dropped on the Japanese city of Hiroshima, and three days later a second bomb fell on Nagasaki. The Japanese surrendered, and on August 14 World War II was over.

The Allied war leaders (left to right) Churchill, Roosevelt, and Stalin – the "Big Three" – met to plan the defeat of Germany and Japan.

Almost six years of war had cost 17 million lives and done enormous damage. Many casualties were civilians.

1944	1944 June	1944 July	1944 December	1945 February	1945 March	1945 April
Germans launch V-1 pilotless planes and V-2 rockets against England.	Allied forces land in Normandy, France, to start the liberation of Europe.	German plotters attempt to kill Hitler, but fail.	Start of battle of the Bulge, last German offensive in Europe.	At the Yalta Conference, Allies agree to divide Germany into four zones after the war.	US troops capture Iwo Jima island, in the Pacific.	Adolf Hitler kills himself.

Allied soldiers rescued sick and starved Holocaust survivors from Nazi death camps such as Belsen and Auschwitz. Millions of people had been killed in the camps.

NUREMBERG TRIALS

After World War II, the Allies set up an international military court at Nuremberg in Germany to try the Nazi leaders for war crimes. Twelve were sentenced to death and six were sent to prison. Hermann Goering (above) committed suicide before his sentence could be carried out. Concentration camp commanders were also tried.

The Allies were shocked to learn of the ill-treatment of prisoners-of-war by the Japanese. In Germany, they saw the evidence of the Holocaust – concentration camps in which the Nazis had systematically murdered millions of Jews and other helpless victims. Around six million Jews had been starved, tortured, or killed in gas chambers.

After the war, the USSR controlled most of eastern Europe. Germany was divided. War criminals were tried for crimes against humanity. As reconstruction began, the United Nations was formed to try to prevent future wars.

The Allied invasion of Normandy began on June 6, 1944 (D-Day). About 156,000 troops were landed in the largest seaborne attack ever mounted.

1945 May
Soviet troops enter Berlin. Germany surrenders.

1945 June
US forces capture Okinawa island, close to Japan.

1945 August
Atomic bombs dropped on Hiroshima and Nagasaki. Japan surrenders.

1945 October
The United Nations is formed.

India and Pakistan

AT THE START of the 20th century, India was the largest colonial territory in the world. It included Pakistan and Bangladesh, as well as India, and had been ruled directly from Britain since 1858.

BUT THE PEOPLE of India wanted independence. So in 1917, the Indian National Congress began a campaign for Home Rule. Britain was reluctant to let go. Instead, mainly in gratitude for India's support during World War I, the British government passed the

◀ Mohandas Gandhi (1869–1948), also known as Mahatma ("Great Soul"). Famed for urging non-violence, he was assassinated at a peace rally in Delhi by a Hindu extremist.

▶ Jawaharlal Nehru (left) was India's first prime minister (died 1964). Mohammed Ali Jinnah (right) was the first leader of independent Pakistan.

Government of India Act (1919). This made some reforms, but most power remained with Britain. In the same year, British soldiers in Amritsar opened fire on a crowd protesting against British rule. Almost 400 people were killed. The campaign for Indian independence began to grow.

By 1920, Mohandas K Gandhi had become leader of the Indian National Congress. He launched a policy of non-cooperation with the British and was himself arrested several times. In prison he continued his campaign by going on hunger strike.

In 1930, he led thousands to the coast on a Salt March, in protest against having to buy heavily taxed salt. In 1945, the British government finally agreed to India's independence. The majority of Indians were Hindus, but Mohammed Ali Jinnah now began to

1885	1887	1905	1919	1920	1934	1945
Indian National Congress (INC) founded.	Gandhi goes to London to study law. He works in South Africa from 1893.	Foundation of the Muslim League in India.	Government of India Act passed. Massacre at Amritsar.	Gandhi, now leader of the INC, urges non-cooperation with British.	Mohammed Ali Jinnah becomes president of the Indian Muslim League.	British government agrees to grant independence to India.

◀ This map shows how India was divided. East Pakistan broke away to become Bangladesh in 1971. Burma (now Myanmar) and Ceylon (now Sri Lanka) gained their independence in 1948.

...campaign for a separate state for India's many Muslims, who did not want to live under Hindu rule. On August 14, 1947, two areas to the northeast and northwest of India became the independent country

of Pakistan, with Jinnah as its first governor general. The next day the rest of India gained its independence, led by Jawaharlal Nehru as prime minister. Immediately violence broke out. Millions of people found themselves living in the "wrong" country – Muslims in India and Hindus in Pakistan. Mass migrations began. As people fled, hundreds of thousands of people were killed.

1947
August 14
...ortheast and
...orthwest India
...ecome
...akistan.

1947
August 15
The rest
of India
becomes
independent.

▲ The partition of India was followed by a mass migration of Muslims from India to Pakistan and of Hindus from Pakistan to India. Over one million people were killed as violence flared up between them.

Israel and Palestine

THE ANCIENT homeland of the Jews was the land around Jerusalem. The Jews were later expelled and by the 20th century most Jews lived elsewhere, in Europe, the USA, and Russia. The land, now called Palestine, had for many years been part of the Ottoman empire. The Jews' desire to return led to a long conflict with the people living there.

> Polish-born David Ben Gurion (1886–1973) emigrated to Palestine in 1906. Known as the Father of the Nation, he was Israel's first prime minister.

MOST Palestinians were Arabs. Small numbers of Jews, known as Zionists, began to settle in Palestine in the 1880s. In 1917, Britain declared its support for a Jewish homeland in Palestine. The Ottoman empire was breaking up following Turkey's defeat in World War I. The new League of Nations gave Britain its (mandate) permission to rule Palestine in the short term.

Jews continued to settle in Palestine, especially when in the 1930s the Nazis in Germany began to persecute German Jews. To escape imprisonment or murder, those Jews who could began to leave Germany. Some went to other European countries or to the USA.

< T E Lawrence (1888–1935), known as Lawrence of Arabia, was a British soldier who helped to lead an Arab revolt against the Ottoman empire during World War I. After that war, many Arabs hoped to see a new Arab nation, to include Palestine. This did not happen.

1840	1882	1917	1920	1922	1929	1933	1939
After brief rule by Egypt, Palestine becomes part of the Ottoman empire again.	First Zionist settlement established in Palestine.	The Balfour Declaration supports a Jewish homeland in Palestine.	The Treaty of Sevres ends the Ottoman empire.	Britain is given the mandate to govern Palestine.	First major conflict between Jews and Arabs.	Persecution of the Jews begins in Germany.	Britain agrees to restrict the number of Jew emigrating to Palestine.

Others moved to Palestine. The growing numbers of immigrants led to fighting between Jews and Arabs, and Britain tried to restrict the numbers of settlers allowed in.

After World War II, many more Jews wanted to move to Palestine. Britain took the matter to the United Nations and in 1947 it was decided to split Palestine into two states, one Jewish and the other Arab. Jerusalem would become international, since it was sacred to Jews, Muslims, and Christians. The Jews agreed to this, but the Arabs

Since 1948 Israeli defense forces have been on constant alert against attack. Israel's neighbors became its enemies, refusing to recognize the new Jewish state. In turn, Israel refused to acknowledge Palestinian land claims.

did not. Britain gave up its mandate on May 14, 1948, and, on the same day, the Jewish leader David Ben Gurion announced the founding of the state of Israel. The Arab League (Syria, Lebanon, Iraq, Iran, Jordan, and Egypt) declared war on Israel. Israel quickly defeated them, gaining more land.

The Wailing Wall in Jerusalem is a Jewish place of prayer. After 1948, the Wall was in the part of the city held by Jordan. Israel regained it in 1967 and claimed all Jerusalem as its capital. Finding a future for Jerusalem that satisfies all has proved very difficult.

Golda Meir (1898–1978) was Israel's prime minister from 1969 to 1974. Born in Russia, she lived in the USA as a child and moved to Palestine in 1921.

1947	1948	1949
The United Nations votes to divide Palestine.	On May 14 the state of Israel is founded and the Arab League declares war.	A UN-negotiated cease-fire leaves Israel with the territory given to it in 1947.

The Cold War

THE USA and the Soviet Union emerged from World War II as the world's dominant superpowers. Former allies, they soon became enemies in what was known as the Cold War.

This cartoon shows Soviet leader Nikita Khruschev (on the left) and US president John F Kennedy arm-wrestling on top of nuclear missiles. In 1962 a clash of the two superpowers was avoided only when Soviet ships (above) carrying rockets to Cuba turned back.

THE COLD WAR started when the Soviet Union set up Communist governments in the countries of Eastern Europe liberated by the Red Army. This effectively divided Europe by an "iron curtain." To stop Communism spreading to the West, the US-backed Marshall Plan was set up to give financial aid to countries whose economies had been ruined by the war.

The Berlin Wall was built across the city in 1961 to divide the eastern part from the west, and so prevent people escaping from Communist rule.

After the war Germany was divided between the Allies. The USA, Britain, and France controlled the west of the country, while the east was controlled by the Soviet Union. The capital, Berlin, lay within Soviet-controlled territory, but was also divided. In 1948 the Soviets tried to blockade West Berlin, forcing the Allies to airlift in supplies. In 1949 Germany was divided into West and East.

1947	1948	1949	1950–1953	1953	1955	1956
The US-backed Marshall Plan gives financial aid to European countries.	Blockade of West Berlin for five months by the Soviet Union.	North Atlantic Treaty Organization (NATO) is formed. Communists come to power in mainland China.	The Korean War. North Korea, supported by China, invades South Korea, supported by the USA.	Death of Joseph Stalin.	Warsaw Pact formed among countries of Eastern Europe.	Soviets invade Hungary to preserve Communist rule.

◀ This map shows how Europe was divided after World War II. The NATO alliance (1949) confronted the Warsaw Pact (1955) in the Cold War between democracy and Communism.

withdraw. To prevent a nuclear war from starting, the missiles were removed.

Both sides built up huge stocks of nuclear weapons. This led to another crisis in 1962, when Cuban dictator Fidel Castro allowed the Soviet Union to build missile bases in Cuba, close to the USA. US President John F Kennedy ordered the US Navy to blockade Cuba, and eventually the Soviets agreed to

The two sides in the Cold War spent vast sums on weapons. Although they never fought directly, they did get involved in the Korean War in the 1950s and the Vietnam War in the 1960s and 1970s. They also carried on a spying and propaganda campaign against one another for many years. Any moves toward freedom in Communist Europe were crushed by the Soviet Union.

NATO

The North Atlantic Treaty Organization (whose symbol is shown here) was set up on April 4, 1949, with its headquarters in Brussels, Belgium. It was a military alliance between several Western European countries, Canada, and the United States, against aggression from any outside nation. In 1955, the Soviet Union formed an alliance of Communist states, the Warsaw Pact.

🔼 In 1968, Prague, the Czech capital, was invaded by Soviet tanks. A new Czech government had brought in reforms that were feared by the Soviet Communist leaders.

1958	1960	1961	1962	1963	1964	1968
Fidel Castro comes to power in Cuba and allies Cuba with the Soviet Union.	A split develops between the Soviet Union and China.	The Berlin Wall is built.	Cuban missile crisis.	The USA and the Soviet Union sign a Nuclear Test-Ban Treaty.	The USA becomes involved in the Vietnam War.	Invasion of Czechoslovakia by the Soviet Union to preserve Communist rule.

The Space Race

SCIENTISTS in Germany in the 1940s had developed the first guided missiles, using technology that might make it possible for people to travel in space. This prompted the USA and the Soviet Union to embark on a "space race."

IN 1957 THE Soviet Union launched *Sputnik 1*, the first artificial Earth satellite. It took 96 minutes to orbit the Earth. In the following year the USA launched its first satellite, *Explorer 1*. Both sides spent vast amounts of money on space science.

John F Kennedy (1917–1963) became president of the US in 1960. He promised to send Americans to the Moon by 1970.

The first person to orbit the Earth was Yuri Gagarin of the Soviet Union in 1961. The USA set out to land a man on the Moon by 1970. This ambition was achieved when Neil Armstrong became the first person to walk on the Moon in 1969.

Buzz Aldrin became the second person, after Neil Armstrong, to walk on the Moon, on July 21, 1969. The third crew member, Michael Collins, remained aboard *Apollo 11*, orbiting the Moon.

Yuri Gagarin aboard *Vostok 1* orbited the Earth for 89 minutes on April 12, 1961, at about 186 miles (300 km) from the surface.

1957	1958	1959	1961	1963	1965	1969
The Soviet Union launches the first artificial satellite, *Sputnik 1*. Laika the dog is the first animal in space.	The USA launches its first satellite, *Explorer 1*.	The Soviet space probe *Luna 2* reaches the Moon.	Soviets launch first manned spacecraft, *Vostok 1*. A month later, the USA launches its first manned spacecraft, *Mercury*.	Russian cosmonaut Valentina Tereshkova is the first woman in space.	Russian cosmonaut Alexi Leonov becomes the first person to walk in space.	US astronaut Neil Armstrong is the first person to land on the Moon.

◀ Laika the dog inside *Sputnik 2* was the first living creature to go into space. The spacecraft was unable to return to Earth, so Laika died in space.

During the 1970s, Britain, China, France, India, and Japan all launched small spacecraft. Many of these were satellites, used for weather forecasting and for communications. The USA and the Soviet Union sent craft deeper into space, sending back pictures and scientific information from the planets Mars, Venus, Jupiter, Saturn, Uranus, and Neptune.

Since the 1990s and the easing of the Cold War, US and Russian scientists have worked together on projects such as building the International Space Station.

▶ Cape Canaveral, Florida, is the launch site for many US space missions. Space Shuttle flights began in 1981. Two shuttles have been lost in accidents, in 1986 and 2003.

▾ The *Mir* space station was launched by the Soviet Union in 1986. Astronauts spent up to 437 days on *Mir*, which stayed in orbit until 2001.

Improvements in computer technology made it possible for the US spacecraft *Pathfinder* to land on Mars in 1997. The pictures it sent back were seen by people at home watching television.

◀ *Pathfinder* landed on Mars in 1997 and sent out this small rover named *Sojourner* to examine the planet's surface.

▶ *Sputnik 1*, launched on October 4, 1957, was the first craft to go into space. It traveled at 17,000 mph (28,000 km/h). Its radio bleep was picked up around the world.

1970	1971	1972	1975	1977	1990	1995
A Soviet spacecraft lands on Venus.	A Soviet spacecraft lands on Mars.	The USA makes its last Apollo Moon landing.	Soviet and US spacecraft link up in space.	US *Viking* craft land on Mars.	Hubble space telescope is launched by a US shuttle.	Russia's Valeriy Polyiakov stays in space for 437 days on the Mir space station.

New Africa

FROM the 1950s, most African countries gained independence from colonial rule. They developed their own systems of government and built up new economies. Famine, poverty, and civil wars have caused major hardships.

Kwame Nkrumah (1909–1972) led Ghana, formerly the Gold Coast, to independence in 1957, and was president from 1960 to 1966. He believed in pan-African unity.

THE BORDERS of many countries in the new Africa were as they had been fixed by the European colonizers in the late 1800s. These borders often ignored traditional tribal groupings, and independence was sometimes followed by civil war as peoples within one country tried to set up new states of their own. This happened in the Congo (formerly Belgian) and in Nigeria (formerly British-ruled), where a breakaway state

named itself Biafra. In Ethiopia, which had never been a colony, a revolution overthrew the king, Haile Selassie. In Angola, nationalists fought against the Portuguese, who were reluctant to give up control. And in Rwanda and Burundi, there was fighting between rival ethnic groups, each wanting control of the country. In Uganda, a brutal dictator, Idi Amin, expelled Ugandan

Robert Mugabe became leader of Zimbabwe in 1980. Blacks fought a long struggle to gain power there. Mugabe controversially took land from white farmers to give to his supporters.

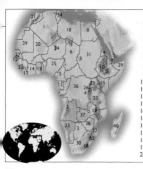

1 Algeria 1962	21 Morocco 1956
2 Angola 1975	22 Mozambique 1975
3 Botswana 1966	23 Namibia 1990
4 Burundi 1962	24 Niger 1960
5 Cameroon 1960	25 Nigeria 1960
6 Chad 1960	26 Rwanda 1962
7 Djibouti 1960	27 Senegal 1960
8 Egypt 1922	28 Sierra Leone 1961
9 Eritrea 1993	29 Somalia 1960
10 Ethiopia	30 South Africa 1931
11 Gabon 1960	31 Sudan 1956
12 Gambia 1965	32 Swaziland 1968
13 Ghana 1957	33 Tanzania 1964
14 Ivory Coast 1960	34 Tunisia 1956
15 Kenya 1963	35 Uganda 1962
16 Lesotho 1966	36 Zaire (Congo) 1960
17 Liberia	37 Zambia 1964
18 Libya 1951	38 Zimbabwe 1900
19 Malawi 1964	39 Mauritania 1960
20 Mali 1960	40 Madagascar 1960

This map shows many of the independent nations of Africa, with the date they achieved nationhood. Only Ethiopia and Liberia were never colonized.

Local rulers, such as these tribal chiefs in Ghana, continued to wield power in many African countries.

Kenneth Kaunda led Zambia (formerly Northern Rhodesia) to independence from Britain in 1964. He served as president until 1991, when he was voted out of power in the country's first multi-party elections.

Asians in the 1970s. Problems also occurred in countries where white settlers wanted to stay in control, as in Algeria, Rhodesia (now Zimbabwe), and South Africa. In South Africa, from 1948 to 1990, the whites-only government used a system known as apartheid to keep blacks out of power. Once apartheid was abolished, free elections were held and in 1994 Nelson Mandela became the first black president of South Africa.

Africa has famine on a massive scale when drought hits areas with poor soil and the crops fail. People caught in the disaster have to rely on aid or face starvation and disease.

1964	1965	1966	1969	1975	1976	1977	1980	1993
Malawi and Zambia independent from Britain.	Gambia independent; whites in Rhodesia declare independence.	Botswana and Lesotho independent from Britain.	War as Biafra seeks independence from Nigeria.	Angola and Mozambique independent from Portugal.	Civil war in Angola.	Djibouti independent from France.	Zimbabwe (Rhodesia) has black-majority government.	Eritrea, part of Ethiopia since 1962, declares itself independent.

Fight for Rights

DURING the second half of the 20th century, people all over the world fought for civil rights. Many were being treated unfairly because of their race, skin color, religion, or gender. Others were being denied the vote, barred from forming free labor unions, or prevented from choosing the political leaders they wanted.

▲ Polish workers protest. *Solidarity* was a labor union started in the shipyards of Gdansk, Poland, in 1980. It campaigned for workers' rights and led to an anti-Communist movement.

THE CIVIL RIGHTS movement came to the fore in the USA in the 1960s. In the southern states, blacks were discriminated against in schools, jobs, transportation, and health care. Protests began in 1955, after Rosa Parks, an African-American, was arrested for refusing to give up her seat to a white man on a bus in Alabama. Non-violent protests were inspired by the words of Civil Rights leader Dr Martin Luther King. He led a march to Washington, DC, in 1963. Over 250,000 people took part, and in 1964 the US government passed a Civil Rights Act that made racial discrimination illegal.

◀ Martin Luther King (1929–1968) was an outstanding speaker. His belief in non-violent resistance to oppression won him the Nobel peace prize in 1964. His most famous speech included the words: "I have a dream." In 1968 King was shot dead in Memphis, Tennessee.

1955	1957	1960	1962	1963	1964	1966
Rosa Parks is arrested in Alabama for refusing to give up her seat on a bus.	In the USA, Martin Luther King brings many civil rights groups together.	South African police fire on anti-apartheid demonstrators at Sharpeville, killing 69.	Nelson Mandela is imprisoned for political activities.	Martin Luther King organizes a march to Washington, DC, asking for equal rights for all.	The Civil Rights Act is passed in the USA to end all discrimination because of race, color, religion, or national origin.	American feminists found the National Organization for Women.

There was a similar struggle in South Africa, where the white minority government's policy of apartheid (separating the races) was oppressive and cruel. After 69 African protesters were shot dead at Sharpeville in 1969, the campaign became more violent. Black leader Nelson Mandela was jailed from 1962 until 1990. After a long international campaign of protest and sanctions against South Africa, Mandela was released from prison and apartheid ended in 1990.

APARTHEID

Apartheid means "apartness." It was a policy used in South Africa from 1948 to 1990 to divide the country into separate areas for whites and blacks. There was segregated education, employment, housing and health care. Most whites had good jobs and lived in comfort; blacks did the hard work and lived in crowded townships.

In Communist countries, people demanded the right to form free labor unions and to vote for whatever kind of government they wanted. Women campaigned for equal pay and job opportunities. New laws in some countries banned sex and age discrimination in employment.

▶ Nelson Mandela (born 1918) was imprisoned in 1962 for his political views, and only released in 1990. In April 1994 he was able to vote for the first time in the country's first free elections. Mandela's party, the African National Congress (ANC), won and he became president.

▲ Black townships in South Africa were disturbed by unrest and violence in the 1980s. Many people were killed and homes set on fire as a tide of protest arose against apartheid.

1971	1980	1985	1986	1989	1993	1995
Swiss women are given the right to vote.	Solidarity, an independent labor union, is set up in Poland (banned until 1989).	Marriage between blacks and whites is made legal in South Africa.	Fighting in black townships in South Africa by civil rights protesters.	In Beijing, China, government troops crush a student demonstration for greater democracy.	Nelson Mandela and F W de Klerk win the Nobel peace prize for their work to end apartheid.	Fourth World Conference on Women, held in Beijing, with women present from 185 countries.

The Vietnam War

VIETNAM, together with Cambodia and Laos, was part of the French colony of Indochina. It was occupied by the Japanese in World War II. During this time the Viet Minh league, led by the Communist Ho Chi Minh, declared Vietnam independent from France.

◄ Ho Chi Minh (1892–1969) led Vietnam's struggle for independence from France. As president of North Vietnam from 1954 he fought for a united Vietnam, achieved after his death.

AFTER the war, France refused to recognize Ho Chi Minh's government and war broke out between the French and the Vietnamese. This war ended in defeat for the French at the battle of Dien Bien Phu in 1954. An international agreement then divided Vietnam into Communist North and non-Communist South.

Almost immediately civil war broke out. From 1959, Communist guerrillas in the South, known as the Viet Cong, were helped by North Vietnam. The USA, anxious to prevent the spread of Communism, sent military aid to the South Vietnamese. The Viet Cong's guerrilla tactics were hard to combat. In an attempt to cut off their supply lines, US planes bombed North Vietnam. Villages in the south and vast areas of forest were sprayed with chemicals to destroy any Viet Cong hiding places. Many civilians were killed.

In 1968, the Viet Cong's Tet offensive in the South convinced most

▶ US soldiers in Vietnam were dropped in by helicopter so that they could make surprise attacks on the Viet Cong guerrilla fighters.

1946	1954	1961	1964	1965	1966
Start of the war between Ho Chi Minh's Vietnamese nationalists and French colonial troops.	Vietnamese Communists defeat the French at Dien Bien Phu. The country is divided into North Vietnam and South Vietnam.	South Vietnamese ask for military advice from the USA to combat Communist Viet Cong guerrillas.	War between North Vietnam (backed by the USSR) and South Vietnam (backed by the USA).	USA sends combat troops to South Vietnam.	Australian troops arrive in Vietnam to fight with US troops. The first anti-war demonstrations take place in the USA.

218

▶ Viet Cong and North Vietnamese soldiers used guerrilla warfare. One tactic was to dig a maze of tunnels. Over 16,000 soldiers lived underground, hiding from US planes.

◀ Most of the war was fought in the jungles of South Vietnam. The Ho Chi Minh trail, from China through Laos into South Vietnam, was the Viet Cong's supply line from the North.

ANTI-WAR DEMONSTRATIONS

The Vietnam War was the first to be widely covered on television. People were able to see events as they happened. As growing numbers of US troops were killed or injured, people took to America's streets in protest. By 1967, the protests had spread beyond the USA. The strength of anti-war feeling helped persuade President Richard Nixon to withdraw from the war.

Americans that the war could not be won. In 1969 the US began to withdraw its troops and a ceasefire was agreed in 1973. Fighting continued until 1975, when North Vietnamese troops took over the South. Vietnam was united.

▼ Most Vietnamese lived by farming, mostly growing rice in the fields around their villages. Many suffered greatly in the war as crops and villages were destroyed.

1967	1968	1969	1971	1973	1975	1976
Peace moves fail. Anti-war demonstrations spread to other countries.	North Vietnamese and Viet Cong launch an attack known as the Tet offensive against the South. Some Americans believe that the war could go on for many years.	The USA withdraws 25,000 of its 540,000 troops. The fighting – and the anti-war protests – continue.	Fighting spreads to Laos.	Ceasefire. US troops withdraw. Vietnamese continue to fight.	Communists take control of South Vietnam.	Vietnam is reunited under a Communist government.

China's New Power

WHEN the Communists, led by Mao Zedong, won power in China, they set out to modernize the country. Their aim was to provide food, schools, hospitals, and work for China's millions. These plans were blown off course in the 1960s by Mao's "Cultural Revolution." Later leaders were less radical, but refused to allow the people more freedom or democracy.

◀ The little red book containing the "thoughts of Chairman Mao" was carried by every Red Guard during the turmoil of the Cultural Revolution in China.

THE COMMUNISTS gave women the same rights as men and shared out land among the peasants. They built new roads, railroads, factories, and power plants. In the "Great Leap Forward," every village was meant to be self-sufficient, growing its own food and producing clothes and tools in small factories. But the policies failed, and after bad harvests and mass starvation, Mao retired.

▶ This poster of a triumphant Mao appeared in 1949, when he first came to power. Civil war had left the country in financial disorder. Mao's initial reforms, called the Five Year Plan, helped to improve China's economy.

在毛澤東的勝利旗幟下前進

Mao returned to power in 1966, determined that China should not lose its revolutionary spirit (as he thought had happened in the USSR). He set in progress the Cultural Revolution, with the aim of overthrowing the old China. All his youthful followers carried his little red

1949
Mao Zedong's Communist party takes power in China.

1953
In the Five Year Plan, peasants are encouraged to set up collective (cooperative) farms.

1958–1960
The Great Leap Forward. It is abandoned when its policies result in widespread famine.

1959
Mao Zedong retires as Chairman of the Chinese Communist party.

1966
Mao sweeps back to power and starts the Cultural Revolution. By 1968 factory productivity is 12 percent lower than it was in 1966.

1973
Rivalry grows between Mao's supporters, known as the "Gang of Four," and Deng Xiaoping over who will succeed Mao.

During the Cultural Revolution, schools and colleges were closed and teachers and students forced to work on the land. Opposition was brutally put down by Red Guards.

Deng Xiaoping (1904–1995) ruled China from 1977 until his death. He reopened contacts with the outside world and encouraged China's economy to grow by setting up privately owned factories.

book for inspiration. Traditional customs and thinking were prohibited. Foreigners and old people were insulted. College professors and teachers were turned out of their jobs to work in the fields. Hospitals and factories, left without doctors and managers, closed.

When Mao died in 1976, his revolution ended. His successor was Deng Xiaoping, who set up trade links with the outside world and encouraged Chinese business. This policy continued under the next leader, Jiang Zemin. China began to prosper again, but the government was still hesitant to allow political freedom and showed little regard for human rights. Student protests in 1989 were brutally crushed.

Tiananmen Square, Beijing, full of students demonstrating for democracy in May 1989. The Chinese government sent in troops and tanks to clear the protesters and many people were killed.

1974	1976	1977	1989	1995
China tests its first nuclear weapons.	Death of Mao. He is briefly succeeded by the Gang of Four, who want to continue the Cultural Revolution.	Deng Xiaoping comes to power. He visits the United States.	Tiananmen Square demonstration by pro-democracy students.	Death of Deng Xiaoping. China's next leader, Jiang Zemin (to 2002), modernizes its economy.

Middle East in Crisis

THE MIDDLE EAST has been a world troublespot since 1948, when an uneasy peace followed the Arab-Israeli war. Israel fought three more wars against its Arab neighbors, and the Palestinians remained without a homeland of their own. Terrorism became a terrible weapon in this conflict, which was bound up with two other issues: the world's thirst for oil, much of which comes from Middle East states, and the rise of Islamic fundamentalism.

◀ Ayatollah Khomeini (1900–1989) was a revolutionary religious leader of Iran. He came to power in 1979 after the Shah of Iran was overthrown. Under Khomeini, Iran became a strictly Muslim state.

ISRAEL'S POPULATION increased during the 1950s as Jews emigrated from Europe, Russia, and the USA. The Palestinian Arabs, pushed into separate communities within Israel, began a campaign for their own state.

Wars were fought in 1956, 1967, and 1973. The first war began after Egypt took control of the Suez Canal. Britain and France invaded Egypt, but later withdrew. Israel also attacked Egypt. In the Six-Day War in 1967, Israel won control of all Jerusalem, the West Bank of the Jordan river, and other territory. It fought off Egyptian and Syrian attacks in the Yom Kippur War of 1973.

☑ Beirut, the capital of Lebanon, was ravaged by fighting that broke out in 1976. Peace returned to the historic city in the mid-1990s.

1956	1964	1967	1973	1976	1979	1980–1988
Egypt takes control of the Suez Canal.	Formation of the Palestinian Liberation Organization (PLO).	Six-Day War, between Israel and Egypt, Jordan, and Syria, is won by Israel.	The Yom Kippur War. Israel fights Egypt and Syria.	Fighting breaks out in Lebanon.	Peace treaty between Israel and Egypt. Shah of Iran is overthrown and Islamic republican government set up.	Iran-Iraq War.

The USA has tried to mediate in the Middle East, though many Arabs see America as Israel's ally. In 1993, President Bill Clinton (center) welcomed a deal between Israeli Prime Minister Yitzhak Rabin (left) and Yasser Arafat, leader of the Palestinians, to establish Palestinian self-rule. Rabin was assassinated in 1995.

Israel also became involved in the civil war in Lebanon, where many Palestinians lived in refugee camps. By the 1990s, Israel had signed peace agreements with Egypt, Jordan, and Syria, and the Palestinians had attained limited self-government. Yet terrorist attacks by extremist groups opposed

Saddam Hussein (born 1938) ruled oil-rich Iraq from 1979 to 2003. A brutal dictator, he took his people into three wars: against Iran in 1980–88, and against US-led forces in 1991 and 2003.

to new Israeli settlements, and even Israel's very existence, continued.

In 1979 the Shah of Iran was overthrown and an Islamic regime took over. Iran went to war with Iraq in 1980. Neither side won a costly conflict. In 1990 Iraq tried to take over its tiny neighbour Kuwait, but was defeated in the brief Gulf War by a UN force led by the USA. Iraq's ruler Saddam Hussein was finally deposed in 2003, when US-led forces invaded Iraq.

1982	1987	1990–1991	1993	1994	1995	2003
Israel invades Lebanon.	Fighting between Palestinians and Israeli troops in the West Bank and Gaza Strip.	In the Gulf War, Iraq invades Kuwait, but is repulsed by UN troops.	Israeli and Palestinian leaders hold talks in the USA.	Israel and Jordan sign a peace agreement.	Israel signs an agreement to extend self-rule to the Palestinians.	Short war in Iraq removes Saddam Hussein. Middle East peace hopes flicker.

Asian Industry

AFTER World War II, Asia made a spectacular economic recovery. Japan, Singapore, South Korea, Malaysia, and Taiwan all became "tiger economies," with rising living standards and modern factories. These produce goods that are sold all over the world.

▶ Tokyo is the center of the Japanese business world. With the port of Yokohama and the industrial area of Kawasaki, it is one of the world's largest cities.

Japan was reluctant to play a big part in world affairs, other than in trade. It had given up its large military forces at the end of World War II, and no Japanese troops took part in any of the post-war conflicts, such as the Korean and Vietnam wars. South Korea emerged from its war with its Communist neighbor, North Korea, to undergo an economic transformation similar to Japan's. It too had a well-trained and

JAPAN, whose factories had been bombed during World War II by the Allies, was aided by the USA in the 1940s and 1950s. New factories, with the latest machinery, began turning out cars, radios, office equipment, and gadgets for the home. In the 1980s, the factories began using automated robots to make electronic and other goods, and Japan became the world's biggest maker of cars and trucks.

▶ Hong Kong, whose name means "good harbor," is a major center for banking, finance, and industry in China.

1949
Chinese Nationalists set up a republic on the island of Taiwan, which though not recognized by the United Nations, builds a thriving economy.

1953
Korean War ends. South Korea grows rapidly as an industrial nation.

1960s
Japan starts selling cars on the world market.

1965
India and Pakistan go to war over the disputed territory of Kashmir, which remains a problem unsolved.

1970s
Taiwan starts to develop high-technology industries.

1975
Vietnam War ends. Vietnam emerges from isolation to become an active trading nation. Japan launches the first VHS (Video Home System) on to the market.

In India many women and children are employed making shoes and clothes for export.

ASIA MODERNIZES

Much of Europe's industrial heartland was destroyed in World War II. Asian countries, without a background of old, heavy industries, were able to build new factories for new industries, such as electronics. Some Asian countries developed heavy industries, such as shipbuilding and steel production, again with modern equipment and cheap labor.

...rganized work force, and invested ...oney in new machinery and ...omputers. North Korea, under ...ommunist rule, lagged far behind the ...outh in terms of wealth.

Singapore and Hong Kong, both ...mall, grew rich on trade and banking. ...ong Kong was under British rule until ...997, when by agreement it was ...eturned to China. It retained its special ...atus as a trading area for China, which ...n the 1990s relaxed its restrictions on ...rivate businesses. Vietnam has also ...urned to a "free market" economy. ...dia, Malaysia, Indonesia, and the ...hilippines have prospered from ...dustries employing many people who

are paid low wages to make shoes and clothes, or assemble electronic equipment for export. India, still mainly an agricultural country, has expanded its industrial production by over six times since 1950. The biggest employers are the clothing and textile industries.

In the 1980s, automated robots became ...idely used in Japan for making cars and ...omputers. The Japanese were among the ...rst to use modern assembly methods.

...76	1970	1980s	1984	1995	1997
...om this date, Japan ...s a balance of ...ade surplus, which ...eans its exports are ...ore valuable than ...s imports.	Vietnam and China fight a short war. Compact disks are co-developed by a Dutch and a Japanese company.	Japan becomes a world leader in automobile manufacture.	India's Prime Minister Indira Gandhi is assassinated. She is succeeded by her son Rajiv, who is himself murdered in 1991.	By this date, over half of China's industrial output is from privately owned businesses.	Britain returns Hong Kong to Chinese control.

226

The Cold War Ends

THE COLD WAR, a time of suspicion, spies, and super-missiles, began to look less dangerous in the 1970s. The United States and the Soviet Union found they could agree on some things, such as cutting their arms bills, and signed agreements. The pressure on the Soviet leader was intense; his Communist empire was cracking apart.

◪ Many symbols of Communism were destroyed after the Soviet Union broke up. Statues of past leaders such as Lenin were pulled down and used as scrap metal. The Communists had dealt similarly with symbols of czarist rule in 1917.

⌃ The Berlin Wall was demolished in 1989 after the collapse of Communism in East Germany. It had divided the city since 1961. People took pieces as souvenirs.

IN 1972 the USA and USSR signed the first SALT (missile disarmament) agreement. By 1980 the Russians had become involved in a long and costly war in Afghanistan, and their economy was in a bad way. In 1985, a new leader, Mikhail Gorbachev, set about introducing reforms. He also sought friendship with the West. The US president was Ronald Reagan, elected in 1980 on an anti-Communist stand. He was ready to spend billions of dollars on a defensive missile shield in space. But in 1987 Reagan and his

▶ McDonald's first restaurant in Moscow. Gorbachev began opening up Russia to Western enterprise. Long queues for new Western fast-food soon built up.

1967
The USA, Britain, and the Soviet Union sign a treaty banning the use of nuclear weapons in outer space.

1969
US President Lyndon B Johnson starts the Strategic Arms Limitation Talks.

1972
The first SALT agreement is signed by US President Richard Nixon and Leonid Brezhnev of the Soviet Union.

1979
Second SALT agreement is signed by US President Carter and Brezhnev. Soviet troops invade Afghanistan. Margaret Thatcher becomes British prime minister.

EUROPEAN UNION

The European Union (formerly the European Economic Community) was founded in 1957, when it had six members: France, West Germany, Italy, Belgium, the Netherlands and Luxembourg. One of its main aims was to encourage free trade between member countries. By 2002 it had 15 members, most of whom were using the same money (euros). New members eager to join in 2004 included former Communist countries such as Poland and Hungary.

▶ Czech crowds demonstrate in Prague in 1989. Throughout that year, people across Eastern Europe began to demand democracy and an end to repression.

British ally, Margaret Thatcher, signed an important agreement with the USSR to ban medium-range nuclear missiles.

Gorbachev's reforms in the Soviet Union led to demands for free elections in Eastern Europe. By the end of 1989, Communism had collapsed in Poland, Hungary, East Germany, Czechoslovakia, and Romania. In 1990, East and West Germany were reunited and free elections were held in Bulgaria. In August 1991 an attempted coup in the Soviet Union led to the downfall of Gorbachev's government. Boris Yeltsin took over until 1999, when he was succeeded by Vladimir Putin. The Soviet Union broke up, and with its collapse, the Cold War was over. There was just one superpower in the world, the United States of America.

▶ Long-time Communist Mikhail Gorbachev (on the left) and Ronald Reagan (on the right) got on well despite Reagan's hatred of Communism. For the first time in 40 years, there were real smiles between US and Soviet leaders.

1981	1985	1989	1990	1991
Ronald Reagan becomes US President. He increases military spending.	Mikhail Gorbachev comes to power in the Soviet Union and starts to make reforms.	Free elections are held in Poland. Communism collapses in Hungary, East Germany, Czechoslovakia, and Romania. The Berlin Wall is demolished.	East and West Germany are reunited. Free elections are held in Bulgaria.	A multiparty government is set up in Albania. The Soviet Union is abolished and replaced by 15 independent nations.

One World

THE 20TH CENTURY brought startling changes in the speed at which information moved around the world. Countries came together in new groupings, some with their own parliaments and laws, like the European Union. Multinational corporations, doing business in many countries, became richer than all but a few countries.

THESE CHANGES made people more aware of global events. They feel they are citizens not just of a country, but of a planet – and a small planet, with limited resources. Local ways of life are rapidly vanishing, replaced by a "mono-culture." In many countries (though not all), people wear Western-style clothes instead of traditional dress, eat the same fast foods, and watch the same TV shows, beamed to them by satellite TV.

The world's wealth is not distributed equally. Many people go hungry and have no clean water.

> Recycling helps conserve the Earth's resources. Paper, glass, metal, and some plastics can all be reused again and again. Too much garbage is burned in incinerators or buried in landfill sites.

1962
Rachel Carson's book *Silent Spring* alerts people to the dangers of pollution.

1971
Founding of Greenpeace, the international organization concerned with protecting the environment.

1972
Government concern for the environment starts when the US bans DDT, a powerful pesticide.

1976
US scientists voice fears about damage to the ozone layer in the atmosphere.

1985
In New Zealand, French agents blow up the Greenpeace ship *Rainbow Warrior*, which is protesting against nuclear testing in the Pacific. "Live Aid" concerts in Britain and the USA raise money for Ethiopia's famine victims.

FAMINE IN AFRICA

TV pictures of people starving in Africa frequently shock the world. Money donated to charities to help provide food and medicine tackles the problem in the short term. But long-term projects are essential to prevent future famines.

Rich countries use too big a share of the Earth's resources to support high living standards.

During the 1970s, pressure groups such as Greenpeace began to campaign on environmental issues. There is much that can be done to safeguard resources for future generations, such as stopping the dumping of nuclear waste, protecting endangered wildlife, saving what remains of tropical rainforests, recycling more, and turning to alternative energy sources (such as as wind, wave, and solar power) before we burn up all the Earth's fossil fuels (coal, oil, and gas).

Governments meet at international conferences to discuss environmental problems and set targets, but in the end the answers lie with us all.

THE UNITED NATIONS

The United Nations Organization came into operation after World War II, on October 24, 1945. Taking over from the failed League of Nations, its aim was to keep world peace and to solve international problems by cooperation rather than fighting. This is reflected in its symbol, which shows a map of the world surrounded by olive branches.

▶ Burning fossil fuels releases carbon dioxide into the atmosphere, where it dissolves in rainwater, making acid rain that can destroy trees and kill fish.

1986
An explosion and fire at the nuclear power plant at Chernobyl, Ukraine (then part of the Soviet Union), releases large amounts of radioactivity.

1987
Scientists discover a hole in the ozone layer above the Antarctic.

1992
All nations send representatives to the first Earth summit in Rio de Janeiro, Brazil, organized by the UN to discuss the future of the planet.

1998
UN environment summit at Kyoto, Japan, targets a 5 percent cut in carbon dioxide emissions by 2012. 178 countries (but not the USA) agree.

2000
122 governments agree to stop using a number of dangerous chemicals in paints and pesticides.

21st Century World

WHEN THE 21st century began, people looked forward to a new millennium (the next 1,000 years). No one could say what kind of new world would take shape. Would computers take over more jobs from people? Scientists have made amazing advances in understanding how the human body works by identifying genes. Could science create new plants or even animals? The events of September 11, 2001, made the world seem more dangerous. Yet there was also hope, for a peaceful, fairer world for all.

▶ Using the Internet, people can communicate and exchange information around the globe, through a network of computers, telephone lines, and satellites.

THE 20TH CENTURY saw two terrible world wars and many civil wars. It closed with NATO bombing Yugoslavia. Later the Yugoslav leader Slobodan Milosevic was put on trial for war crimes – the first time that a head of state had been brought to court in this way. Regional conflicts were caused by ethnic or religious quarrels, or by the desire of one group to break away from a country.

The danger hardest to fight came from terrorists. The world's strongest nation, the United States, was attacked in 2001 by terrorists belonging to the Al-Qaeda organization, who struck at the heart of New York City and Washington, DC. American forces, with support from other nations, attacked Afghanistan, thought to be the hiding place of the terrorist leader Osama Bin Laden.

◀ In modern wars, air power and hi-tech weapons may be used alongside the guns and rocket launchers of local fighters, as in Afghanistan in 2001.

1986	1998	1999	1999	2000	2000	2000
First US patent on a genetically engineered plant – a variety of corn.	A cease-fire is agreed in Northern Ireland. A new power-sharing assembly is set up.	Vladimir Putin becomes leader of Russia.	By this year the Commonwealth of Nations has 54 members – 33 of them are republics.	Hispanic Americans are the largest minority group in the USA.	Data from the US *Global Surveyor* suggests that Mars may have water – vital for any future manned exploration.	The US presidential election ends in a legal row over ballots. George W Bush wins.

The United Nations relies on debate and agreement before taking action against a nation. It sent weapons inspectors into Iraq to seek out "weapons of mass destruction" (nuclear, chemical, and germ weapons). UN members disagreed about whether war against Iraq, or any "rogue state," was justified.

The Middle East continues to be a troublespot in the 21st century. Political disagreements can sometimes be settled in one meeting between leaders with vision and a realization that compromise is usually needed. Other problems take effort from many people. Hopes for the

SECRETS OF
THE GENE
The study of the DNA molecule (right) opened the door to genetic engineering — changing living things by altering their genetic makup.

21st century would be to reduce the gap between the richest nations and the poorest, to fight ignorance and disease, to combat the menace of illegal drugs, and to protect the Earth's natural resources.

The world is rich enough to support even today's population of over 6 billion. But never before in human history has it seemed so small and under such pressure. Humans may visit Mars in the next 100 years, but there is no nearby planet like Earth to move to. *Homo sapiens* has to live in, and conserve, the world our prehistoric ancestors first explored.

We must keep a balance between development which too often means recklessly cutting down rainforests) and conservation, preserving the Earth's natural riches for all to share.

New York City's World Trade Center towers fell to horrifying terrorist attacks in 2001.

	10,000–2000 BC	2000–1000 BC	1000–500 BC	500–200 BC	200 BC–AD
POLITICS	c. 3500 BC Sumerians set up city-states in Mesopotamia	c. 1800 BC Babylon begins to build new empire in Mesopotamia	c. 1000–960 BC David rules united kingdom of Judah and Israel	479–431 BC Athens dominates ancient Greece	147–146 BC Roman[s] and conquer Greece
	c. 3100 BC King Menes unites Upper and Lower Egypt	c. 1600–1100 BC The Mycenaeans dominate ancient Greece	883–859 BC Ashurnasirpal II rules kingdom of Assyria in Mesopotamia	336–323 BC Alexander the Great of Macedonia rules Greece, Persia, and Egypt	49–44 BC Julius Cae[sar] rules Rome as dictat[or]
	c. 2500 BC Indus Valley civilization in ancient India is at its height	c. 1200 BC Beginning of Olmec rule in western Mexico	753 BC Traditional date of the foundation of the city of Rome	221 BC Qin Shi Huangdi unites China, calls himself the First Emperor	27 BC Octavian becom[es] Rome's first emperor[,] taking the title Augu[stus]
EXPLORATION	c. 3000 BC Phoenician ships are sailing around the Mediterranean Sea	c. 1492 BC Egyptians travel to the Land of Punt (possibly Ethiopia)	c. 650 BC Greek sailors discover the Strait of Gibraltar	c. 470 BC Carthaginian navigator Hanno founds settlement in West Africa	138–125 BC Chang [Qian] of China explores ce[ntral] Asia and India
	c. 2300 BC Egyptian explorer Harkhuf sails south along the river Nile	c. 1001 BC People from Southeast Asia begin colonizing Polynesia	c. 600 BC Phoenicians sail into Atlantic and may have sailed round Africa	449–444 BC Greek historian Herodotus explores the Near East	120 BC Eudoxus of C[yzicus] travels from Egypt to [India]
			c. 515 BC Greek geographer Scylax explores the river Indus	c. 330 BC Pytheas of Marseille sails around the British Isles	55–54 BC Roman ge[neral] Julius Caesar twice i[nvades] Britain
TECHNOLOGY	c. 4000 BC Boats on the river Nile are the first to use sails	c. 2000 BC Tobacco is grown in Mexico and South America	c. 1000 BC Phoenicians introduce purple dye made from murex snails	c. 500 BC Indian surgeon Susrata performs eye operations for cataracts	c. 200 BC Gear whee[ls] invented
	c. 3500 BC Sumerians in Mesopotamia invent writing and the wheel	c. 2000 BC Babylonians began counting in 60s – hence 360° in a circle	876 BC First known use of a symbol for zero on an inscription in India	c. 500 BC Steel is made in India	c. 110 BC The Chine[se] invent the horse col[lar] which is still in use
	c. 3000 BC Egyptians build irrigation system to water their fields	c. 1450 BC Ancient Greeks begin using shadow clocks	c. 700 BC Assyrians begin using water clocks	406 BC Dionysius of Syracuse, Greece, makes the first war catapult	
ARTS	c. 2800 BC Building begins at Stonehenge in England	c. 1500 BC Tapestries are made in Egypt, China, and Babylonia	At this period: Music flourishes in Babylonia, Greece, and Israel	c. 450–387 BC Greek playwright Aristophanes is at work	c. 140 BC The *Venus* is carved in Greece
	c. 2600 BC Work begins on the Great Pyramid in Egypt	1339 BC In Egypt, king Tutankhamen is buried with hoard of treasure	c. 950 BC Solomon's temple is built in Jerusalem	447–438 BC Greeks build the Parthenon temple in Athens	c. 112 BC Pharisees [sect] develops in Palestin[e]
	c. 2000 BC In Sumeria the *Epic of Gilgamesh* is written down	c. 1100 BC First Chinese dictionary is compiled	c. 850 BC Chavin people of Peru make many clay pots and sculptures	351 BC Tomb of Mausolus, one of the Seven Wonders of the World, is built	47 BC The great libr[ary at] Alexandria, Egypt, i[s] destroyed by fire
RELIGION	c. 3000 BC During this period: Sumerians worship mother-goddess Tammuz	c. 2000 BC Babylonians begin worship of the god Marduk	700s BC The Hebrew prophet Isaiah is active	c. 400 BC The first five books of the Bible reach their final form	168 BC Antiochus IV [of] Syria persecutes the [Jews] and sacks Jerusalem
	c. 3000 BC During this period: Egyptians worship their pharaoh as a god-king	c. 1500 BC Probable date of origin of the Hindu religion	c. 563 BC Birth of the Buddha (Siddhartha Gautama in Nepal)	260 BC Emperor Ashoka Maurya makes Buddhism India's state religion	c. 165 BC The Book [of] Daniel in the Old Testament is writte[n]
		c. 1364–1347 BC New religion based on worship of one god, Aten, in Egypt	c. 551 BC Birth of the Chinese philosopher Confucius (Kong Qiu)	c. 255 BC Probable version of the Old Testament is compiled	4 BC Probable date [of] Jesus of Nazareth
DAILY LIFE	c. 8000 BC Farming first practiced in Near East and in Southeast Asia	c. 1500 BC First glass vessels used in Egypt and Mesopotamia	c. 950 BC Poppies are grown in Egypt	430–423 BC Plague breaks out in Athens	c. 170 BC Rome has [its first] paved streets
	c. 5000 BC Aboriginal Australians begin using boomerangs	c. 1450 BC Explosion of Thera volcano in Mediterranean wipes out Cretan civilization	c. 900 BC Noble Egyptians and Assyrians begin wearing wigs	c. 250 BC Parchment is first made in Pergamum (now Bergama, Turkey)	46 BC Romans adop[t the] Julian Calendar an[d the] idea of leap years
	During this period: copper is first used in Asia and North America		776 BC The first Olympic Games are held in Greece	214 BC The building of the Great Wall of China is started	c. 50 BC Basic Hind[u] medical book, the *Ayurveda*, is compil[ed]

	AD 0–600	AD 600–700	AD 700–800	AD 800–900	AD 900–1000
POLITICS	00s Kingdom of Axum ...s to power in what is ...y Ethiopia 350–550 The Gupta ...pire dominates India 476 Collapse of Western ...nan empire; Byzantine ...pire survives in the East	c. 600 Huari empire begins to develop in Peru AD 655–698 Arabs dominate North Africa and spread Islam AD 687 Pepin of Herstal becomes leader of the Franks in Gaul	AD 732 Charles Martel of France defeats Muslims at battle of Poitiers AD 786 Harun al-Rashid becomes Caliph of Baghdad AD 800 Frankish king Charlemagne is crowned Emperor of the West	AD 800s Ife kingdom rises to power in Nigeria AD 802 Khmer empire is founded in Cambodia AD 878 Alfred the Great defeats Vikings and divides England with them	AD 926 Welsh, Picts, and Scots submit to King Athelstan of England AD 956 Otto I of Germany is crowned as Holy Roman emperor AD 968 Toltecs in Mexico build their capital city, Tula
EXPLORATION	14–37 Hippalus of ...me sails from the Red ...to the Indus river D 50 Greek scientist ...lemy publishes *Guide to ...graphy* 399 Chinese monk Fa-...en begins journey to ...ia, Sri Lanka, and Java	AD 629–645 Chinese monk Hsian-Tang goes to India to obtain Buddhist texts AD 698 Willibrord of Utrecht (Netherlands) discovers Heligoland	AD 787 First Viking raid on Britain c. AD 800 Vikings colonize Shetland Islands, Orkneys, Hebrides, and Faeroes	c. AD 850 Arab merchant Soleiman sails to Melaka, now in Malaysia c. AD 860 Irish saint Brendan of Clonfert is said to have sailed to America and back	c. AD 982 Viking Erik the Red explores Greenland coast c. AD 986 Viking Bjarni Herjolfson lands in North America c. AD 1000 Viking Leif Eriksson sails to Vinland, North America
TECHNOLOGY	D 100 Scientist Hero of ...xandria makes the first ...m engine D 150 The Chinese ...ke the first paper 271 Chinese invent the ...t form of compass; it ...nts south	c. AD 600 Earliest known windmills are built in Persia (now Iran) c. AD 650 Greek fire, which burns in water, is invented in Egypt c. AD 670 Hindu works on mathematics are translated into Arabic	c. AD 725 Native Americans build Casa Grande fort, Arizona AD 765 Japanese print first pictorial books AD 782 In England, Offa's Dyke (a barrier against the Welsh) is started	c. AD 850 Earliest reference in China to gunpowder	c. AD 940 Astronomers in China produce a star map c. AD 960 French priest Gerbert introduces Arabic numerals to Europe AD 984 Canal locks are invented in China
ARTS	164 The oldest Maya ...numents are built 386 Ambrose, bishop of ...an, introduces hymn ...ging 478 First Shinto shrines ...cted in Japan	AD 650 Art of weaving develops in Byzantium AD 650 Neumes, early form of music notation, are developed AD 700 Rock-cut temples are begun at Ellora, India	c. AD 750 Wind organs begin to replace water (hydraulic) organs	c. AD 850 Building of Great Zimbabwe, now in modern Zimbabwe	AD 942 Arabs introduce trumpets and kettledrums into Europe AD 961 Emperor Li Yu of China establishes an academy of painting at Nanking
RELIGION	30 Probable date of the ...cifixion of Jesus of ...zareth 45 St Paul begins his ...sion to the Gentiles 313 Roman Emperor ...nstantine decrees ...eration of Christians	AD 622 Arab prophet Muhammad flees from Mecca to Medina AD 632 Abu Bakr, the first Caliph, begins to spread Islam through Arabia c. AD 680 St Wilfrid converts people of Sussex to Christianity	AD 730 Venerable Bede works on his *History of the English Church* AD 782 Alcuin of York goes to Aachen to teach in Charlemagne's school	AD 845 Persecution of Buddhists in China is rife AD 879 The oldest mosque in Cairo, Ibn Tulun, is built	AD 959 In England, St Dunstan becomes Archbishop of Canterbury AD 963 First monastery is established at Mount Athos, Greece AD 966 The Poles are converted to Christianity
DAILY LIFE	79 Vesuvius erupts, ...stroys Pompeii and ...rculaneum 200 The Chinese ...ent porcelain 300 Maya of Central ...erica invent a calendar		AD 750 Hops are first used to make beer in Bavaria, Germany AD 789 Charlemagne introduces his foot as a unit of measurement	AD 812 China issues the earliest paper money AD 851 The crossbow first comes into use in France AD 870 Calibrated candles are used in England to measure time	AD 942 Weaving of linen and wool is established in Flanders (Belgium) AD 962 Hospice is established at St Bernard's Pass, Switzerland AD 1000 The Danegeld (a tax to buy off Viking raiders) levied in England

	1000–1050	1050–1100	1100–1150	1150–1200	1200–1250
POLITICS	**1016** Canute II of Denmark becomes King of England **1040** Macbeth murders Duncan of Scotland and becomes king **1042** Saxon Edward the Confessor becomes King of England	**1066** Harold II becomes King of England; he defeats an invasion from Norway, but is killed at the battle of Hastings and William of Normandy becomes king **1076** Pope Gregory VII excommunicates German emperor Henry IV	**1120** Heir of Henry I of England is drowned in the *White Ship* disaster **1135** Henry I dies; his nephew Stephen takes the throne; he is challenged by Henry's daughter Matilda and civil war breaks out	**1154** Henry Plantagenet becomes King of England as Henry II **1155** Pope Adrian IV "gives" Ireland to Henry II of England **1187** Muslim leader Saladin captures Jerusalem	**1206** Tribal chief Temuji is proclaimed Genghis Khan, ruler of Mongolia **1215** King John of Engla is forced to agree to Magna Carta **1228** Emperor Frederick of Germany leads the Si Crusade to Palestine
EXPLORATION	**1004–1013** Vikings try unsuccessfully to settle in Vinland, North America	**1096–1099** Members of the First Crusade travel to Turkey and Palestine	*c.* **1150** Rabbi Benjamin of Tudela, Spain, travels to Mesopotamia and Iran	*c.* **1154** Al-Idrisi's map muddles the Nile and the Niger rivers **1183–1187** Ibn Jubayr, a Spanish Moor, travels to Mecca, Baghdad, and Damascus	**1245–1247** Franciscan fr John of Pian del Carpin visits Mongolia
TECHNOLOGY	**1035** Spinning wheels are in use in China *c.* **1050** Arabs introduce the decimal system into Spain *c.* **1050** Chinese begin printing books from movable type	**1066** Halley's Comet is seen, and is feared in Europe to portend evil **1100** Italians find out how to distill brandy from wine	**1107** Chinese use multi-color printing for paper money **1129** Flying buttresses are first used in building churches in Europe **1142–1154** Books on algebra and optics are translated from Arabic	**1150** The Chinese make the first rockets **1189** First European paper mill is built in Hérault, France	**1202** Italian Leonardo Fibonacci introduces 0 (zero) to Europe **1221** Chinese use bombs containing shrapnel
ARTS	*c.* **1050** Polyphonic (many voiced) singing is introduced in the Christian Church	**1067** Monte Cassino Monastery, Italy, is rebuilt **1078** Work begins to build the Tower of London	**1110** Earliest known miracle play is performed in England **1147** Geoffrey of Monmouth writes his *History of Britain*	**1151** Golden age of Buddhist art in Burma (now Myanmar) **1174** Bell tower of Pisa, Italy, is built and at once begins to lean	*c.* **1220** Italian poets develop the form of the sonnet **1225** *Sumer is icumin in* is the earliest known Engli round song
RELIGION	**1012** Persecution of heretics begins in Germany **1030** Norway is converted to Christianity **1042** Edward the Confessor begins to build Westminster Abbey	**1084** Carthusian order of monks is founded **1098** First Cistercian monastery is founded at Cîteaux, France	**1119** Military Order of Knights Templars is founded **1123** First Lateran Council in Rome forbids priests to marry	**1154** Adrian IV becomes the only English pope (Nicholas Breakspear) **1155** Carmelite Order of monks is founded in Palestine **1170** Archbishop Thomas à Becket is murdered in Canterbury Cathedral	**1215** Spanish priest Dominic founds the Dominican Order **1229** The Inquisition in Toulouse, France, forbid laymen to read the Bible **1233** Pope Gregory IX as the Dominicans to carry out the Inquisition
DAILY LIFE	*c.* **1009** Persians introduce 7-day week to China, which had 10-day weeks	**1086** *Domesday Book* is first complete survey of England **1094** Gondolas come into use in Venice	**1124** Scotland has its first coins **1133** St Bartholomew's Hospital, London, founded **1133** St Bartholomew's Fair begins in London (closed 1855)	**1151** Game of chess is introduced into England **1189** Silver florins are first minted at Florence, Italy	**1230** Returning Crusade bring disease of leprosy Europe **1233** Coal mining at Newcastle, England, beg **1244** First competition fo the Dunmow Flitch for married couples is held

50–1300	1300–1350	1350–1400	1400–1450	1450–1500	
dward I becomes / England	1301 Edward I of England creates his son Prince of Wales	1363 Mongol ruler Tamerlane begins the conquest of Asia	1413 Henry V becomes King of England and claims large areas of France	1453 Hundred Years' War ends	**POLITICS**
ublai Khan, or of China, tries to er Japan, but fails	1306 Robert Bruce is crowned King of Scotland	1368 Ming dynasty in China ousts the Mongol Yuan dynasty	1428–1430 Joan of Arc leads the French armies against England	1453 Turks capture Constantinople; end of the Byzantine empire	
largaret, the Maid way, becomes of Scotland, aged she dies in 1290	1337 Hundred Years' War between England and France begins	1375 Truce halts Hundred Years' War (until 1378)	1438 Inca rule begins in Peru	1455 Wars of the Roses break out in England; end with accession of Henry VII (Tudor) in 1485	
254 Guillaume de quis, a French avels to Mongolia	1325–1349 Moroccan explorer Ibn Battuta visits Mecca, India, and China	c. 1352 Ibn Battuta explores African empires of Songhai and Mali	1420 João Zarco of Portugal discovers Madeira	1488 Bartolomeu Dias rounds Cape of Good Hope, at the tip of Africa	**EXPLORATION**
295 Venetian Marco Polo spends s at the court of Khan in China		1391 Venetian brothers Niccolo and Antonio Zeno set off to Iceland and the Faeroe Islands		1492 Christopher Columbus explores the Caribbean	
				1498 Vasco da Gama makes the first sea voyage to India	
nglish scientist Bacon proposes e of spectacles	c. 1310 First mechanical clocks are made in Europe	c. 1380 Cast iron becomes generally used in Europe	1408 The Dutch use a windmill for pumping water	1454 Gutenberg produces the first printed Bible	**TECHNOLOGY**
Cable bridges are ver deep valleys in des	1327 Grand Canal in China, begun AD 70, is completed	1391 Geoffrey Chaucer of England writes on how to make and use an astrolabe	c. 1440 Johannes Gutenberg of Germany begins printing with type	1476 William Caxton prints the first book in English	
lorence, Italy, bans e of Arabic als	1336 University of Paris insists that students study mathematics	c. 1400 Ethiopians start making a drink from wild coffee		1480 Italian artist Leonardo da Vinci designs a parachute	
Persian poet Saadi The Fruit Garden	1325 Aztecs of Mexico build their capital city, Tenochtitlan	1369 Geoffrey Chaucer writes The Book of the Duchesse	1414 German monk Thomas à Kempis writes The Imitation of Christ	1463 French poet François Villon sentenced to death for brawling, but escapes	**ARTS**
rench composer de la Halle writes opera Le Jeu de et de Marion	1341 Italian poet Petrarch is crowned as poet laureate in Rome	1375 First appearance of Robin Hood in English legends	1426 Netherlands becomes the center of music in Europe	1473 Sheet music printed from wood blocks is produced in Germany	
	1348 Italian poet Giovanni Boccaccio begins writing the Decameron (to 1353)	1387–1400 Chaucer writes The Canterbury Tales	1444 Cosimo de' Medici founds a library in Florence, Italy		
Order of Augustine its, or Austin Friars, ded	1309 Pope Clement V moves his office from Rome to Avignon, France	1377 Gregory XI returns the papacy to Rome	1415 Bohemian reformer Jan Hus is burned at the stake for heresy	1453 St Sophia Basilica, Constantinople, becomes a mosque	**RELIGION**
1271 Quarrels keep papacy vacant until ry X is elected	1322 Pope John XXII bans the singing of counterpoint in churches	1378 Gregory dies: Great Schism begins when two popes are elected, one in Rome, one in France	1417 End of the Great Schism: Martin V is elected pope in Rome	1484 Papal bull is issued against witchcraft and sorcery	
Popes Gregory X, ent V and Adrian V turn; John XXI ds them	1349 Persecution of Jews breaks out in Germany			1492 Roderigo Borgia becomes pope as Alexander VI	
In London, 278 Jews anged for clipping	1332 Bubonic plague is first heard of in India	1360 France issues its first francs	1416 Dutch fishermen begin using drift nets	1467 Scots parliament bans football and golf	**DAILY LIFE**
Legend of the Pied of Hamelin begins; be founded on fact	1347–1351 The Black Death (bubonic plague) kills 75 million Europeans		1433 Holy Roman emperors adopt the double-eagle as an emblem	1485 Yeomen of the Guard formed in England	
	1348 Edward III of England founds the Order of the Garter	1373 English merchants are made to pay tunnage and poundage taxes	c. 1450 Mocha in southern Arabia (now in Yemen) begins exporting coffee	1489 The symbols + and – come into general use	

	1500–1520	1520–1540	1540–1560	1560–1580	1580–1600
POLITICS	**1509** Henry VIII becomes King of England, marries Catherine of Aragon **1517** Ottoman Turks conquer Egypt **1519** Charles I of Spain becomes Holy Roman emperor, uniting Austria and Spain	**1531** Protestants in the Holy Roman empire form a defensive alliance **1533** Henry VIII divorces his wife and marries Anne Boleyn **1536** England and Wales are united by the Act of Union	**1541** Ottoman Turks conquer Hungary **1553** Mary I, a Roman Catholic, becomes Queen of England **1558** Elizabeth I, a Protestant, succeeds Mary as Queen of England	**1562** Huguenots (French Protestants) begin emigrating to England **1567** Mary, Queen of Scots, abdicates after her husband's murder **1571** Christian fleet defeats a Turkish fleet at battle of Lepanto	**1581–1582** Livonian Poles allow Livonia a Russian access to se **1587** Mary, Queen o Scots, imprisoned in England, is execute **1588** The Spanish A an attempt to invad England, fails
EXPLORATION	**1502–1508** Ludovico de Varthema is the first Christian to visit Mecca **1519–1521** Hernando Cortés conquers Aztec empire in Mexico **1519–1522** Sebastian del Cano is the first captain to sail around the world	**1527–1536** Cabeza de Vaca explores southern North America **1531–1532** Francisco Pizarro explores Peru and conquers the Incas **1535** Jacques Cartier explores the St Lawrence River for France	**1541** Spanish soldier Hernando de Soto discovers the Mississippi **1553–1554** Richard Chancellor opens up trade between England and Moscow, which he reaches by way of the White Sea	**1577–1580** Francis Drake of England sails around the world	**1584** Sir Walter Rale begins colonization Virginia **1596–1597** Dutch navigator Willem Ba dies trying to find th Northeast Passage
TECHNOLOGY	**1502** Peter Henlein of Germany makes the first pocket watch **1507** The name America is used on maps for the first time **1520** First turkeys are imported to Europe from America	**1523** Anthony Fitzherbert writes the first English manual on agriculture **1528** Michelangelo designs fortifications for the city of Florence, Italy **1530** Swiss physician Paracelsus writes book on medicine	**1543** Nicolas Copernicus declares that the Earth revolves around the Sun **1551** Leonard Digges invents the theodolite, used for surveying **1557** Julius Scaliger of Italy discovers the metal platinum	**1569** Gerhardus Mercator invents his projection for maps **1570** The camera obscura, or pinhole camera, is invented **1573** Danish astronomer Tycho Brahe proves that stars are more distant than the Moon	**1589** William Lee in England invents a k machine **1592** Galileo of Italy invents a primitive thermometer **1600** William Gilber England proposes th Earth is a giant mag
ARTS	**1503** Leonardo da Vinci paints the *Mona Lisa* **1508–1512** Michelangelo paints the ceiling of the Sistine Chapel, Rome **1513** Niccolo Machiavelli writes *The Prince* on the theory of government	**1532** François Rabelais of France writes the comic book *Pantagruel* **1538** The first five-part madrigals are published	**1543** Benvenuto Cellini makes golden salt cellars for the King of France **1545** First ever book fair is held in Leipzig, Germany **1548** Building of the Pitti Palace, Florence, begins	**1570** Andrea Palladio writes influential work on architecture **1572** Luis de Camões of Portugal writes his epic poem *Os Lusíadas* **1576** First theater in England opens in London	**1587** Christopher M of England writes pl *Tamburlaine the Grea* **1590–1594** William Shakespeare of Eng begins writing his pl
RELIGION	**1507** Church begins selling indulgences to pay for St Peter's Basilica, Rome **1517** Martin Luther begins the Reformation in Europe **1519** Ulrich Zwingli reforms the Church in Switzerland	**1526** Sweden converts to Protestantism **1531** English Church breaks from Rome, with the monarch as its head **1534** Ignatius Loyola of Spain founds the Jesuit order	**1545** Council of Trent begins the Counter Reformation **1549** Jesuit missions are sent to Brazil and Japan **1555** In England, persecution of Protestants begins; many are burned	**1560** Scotland breaks with the Roman Catholic Church **1570** Pope Pius V excommunicates Queen Elizabeth of England **1572** Massacre of St Bartholomew; French Protestants are killed	**1590–1592** Three po die in a period of th months **1593** Attendance in on Sundays is made compulsory in Engl
DAILY LIFE	**1504** First shillings are minted in England **1517** The first coffee is imported into Europe **1519** Hernando Cortés reintroduces horses to North America	**1525** Hops are introduced to England from France **1528** Severe outbreak of bubonic plague hits England **1531** Halley's Comet returns, causing great alarm	**1547** Fire destroys Moscow **1550** People begin playing billiards in Italy **1555** Tobacco is imported to Spain from America	**1560** Madrid becomes the capital of Spain **1565** The first potatoes arrive in Spain from America **1568** Bottled beer is first produced in London	**1582** Most Roman C countries adopt new Gregorian calendar **1596** Tomatoes are introduced into Eur from America **1596** Sir John Harin of England invents t water closet (lavator

600–1620	1620–1640	1640–1660	1660–1680	1680–1700	
ames VI of Scotland es King of England es I, uniting crowns	1624 Cardinal Richelieu becomes all-powerful in France	1642 Civil War breaks out in England between King Charles I and Parliament	1662 England sells its last French possession, Dunkirk, to France	1686 France annexes the island of Madagascar	**POLITICS**
French Estates al (parliament) ded until 1789	1629 Charles I of England quarrels with Parliament, rules without it until 1640	1649 Charles I is beheaded and England becomes a republic under Cromwell	1664 England seizes New Netherland (now New York) from the Dutch	1688–1689 Peaceful revolution in England drives the Catholic James II off the throne; Protestants William III and Mary II are offered the throne	
1648 Thirty Years' ngulfs most of e	1637 Manchu rulers of China turn Korea into a vassal state	1660 England's monarchy is restored under Charles II	1665–1674 England is at war with the Dutch Republic		
Samuel de plain of France res Nova Scotia coast	1613 Pedro Paez of Spain discovers source of the Blue Nile in Ethiopia	1642 Abel Tasman of the Netherlands discovers New Zealand and Tasmania	1673 Jacques Marquette and Louis Joliet of France explore the Mississippi	1686 William Dampier of England explores northern coast of Australia	**EXPLORATION**
Luis Vaez de Torres vers strait between alia and New Guinea	1627 Thomas Herbert of England explores Persia (now Iran)	1650 Franciscan missionaries explore the upper river Amazon	1679 Louis de Hennepin and René Cavalier of France reach the Niagara Falls	1689 Louis de Lahontain of France reaches the Great Salt Lake in Utah	
Pilgrim Fathers sail to ica in Mayflower and Plymouth Colony	1637–1639 Pedro Teixeira of Portugal explores the river Amazon	1651 Dutch pioneers begin to settle at the Cape of Good Hope			
Hans Lippershey of etherlands invents icroscope	1622 William Oughtred, English mathematician, invents the slide-rule	1642 Blaise Pascal of France designs an adding machine	1665 Isaac Newton of England develops calculus	1682 Edmund Halley of England observes comet now named after him	**TECHNOLOGY**
With a telescope o of Italy discovers r's moons	1624 Flemish chemist Jan van Helmont invents the word "gas"	1642 Evangelista Torricelli of Italy invents the barometer	1675 Greenwich Royal Observatory is founded in England	1684 Robert Hooke of England invents the heliograph	
Galileo agrees with eory that the Earth around the Sun	1637 Pierre Fermat and René Descartes of France develop analytic geometry	1650 Otto von Guericke of Germany invents an air pump	1679 Denis Papin of France invents the pressure cooker	1698 Thomas Savery of England invents the first steam pump	
Miguel de Cervantes ain writes the first of Don Quixote	1623 The First Folio prints most of Shakespeare's plays	1642 Rembrandt van Rijn of the Netherlands paints The Night Watch	1662 Work begins on Louis XIV's Palace of Versailles in France	1688 Aphra Behn is the first professional woman writer in English	**ARTS**
Composer Claudio everdi is working in ua, Italy	1624 Frans Hals of the Netherlands paints The Laughing Cavalier	1652 Vienna opens its first opera house	1667 The colonnaded square of St Peter's, Rome, is completed	1692 Henry Purcell of England composes opera The Fairy Queen	
Royal mosque at an, Persia (Iran) is	1633 John Milton of England writes poems L'Allegro and Il Penseroso	1660 Samuel Pepys, English civil servant, begins his diary	1677 John Dryden is England's leading poet		
James I of England s down on Roman olics and Puritans	1633 The Catholic Church forces Galileo to say Sun revolves around Earth	1645 Presbyterianism is made England's official religion	1662 England forbids Nonconformist priests to preach	1684 Increase Mather becomes a leading preacher in Massachusetts	**RELIGION**
The Authorized on of the Bible is shed in Britain	1634 First Oberammergau Passion Play is put on as thanks for avoiding the plague	1648 George Fox founds the Society of Friends (Quakers)	1678–1684 John Bunyan of England writes The Pilgrim's Progress	1692 At witch trials in Salem, Massachusetts, 19 people are hanged	
Protestants in nia are oppressed	1637 Japan bans Christian missionaries	1650 Archbishop James Ussher of Ireland says the Creation was in 4004 BC		1699 Roman Catholic priests face life in jail in England	
Table forks come into England and France	1625 England has its first fire engines and hackney coaches	1650 England has its first coffee house (in Oxford) and starts drinking tea	1665 Plague ravages London, killing 68,596 people	1683 Wild boars become extinct in Britain	**DAILY LIFE**
The first China tea is rted into Europe by utch	1626 The Dutch buy Manhattan Island from Native Americans for $24	1654 Paris has its first mail boxes	1666 Fire destroys most of London and ends the plague there	1692 Lloyd's Coffee House, London, becomes marine insurance office	
First black slaves are oyed in Virginia	1630 The card game cribbage is invented	1658 Sweden's state bank issues the first banknotes in Europe	1677 Ice cream becomes popular in Paris	1697 Fire destroys most of the Palace of Whitehall, London	

	1700–1720	1720–1740	1740–1760	1760–1780	1780–1800
POLITICS	**1702** Anne, daughter of James II, succeeds to the English throne **1707** England and Scotland are united as Great Britain **1715** Jacobite (Stuart) rebellion in Britain against new king, George I, fails	**1721** Robert Walpole is Britain's first prime minister (to 1742) **1727–1728** War between Britain and Spain over Gibraltar	**1745–1746** Second Jacobite rebellion, led by Bonnie Prince Charlie, fails **1756** Seven Years' War begins in Europe **1760** George III becomes British king (to 1820)	**1763** Seven Years' War ends: Britain gains French lands in India and America **1775–1783** American War of Independence from Britain **1776** The 13 American Colonies declare independence from Britain	**1789** The French Revolution begins **1789** George Washin is elected US presid **1800** Napoleon Bon assumes power in Fr
EXPLORATION	**1708** Alexander Selkirk, the original "Robinson Crusoe," is rescued from an island off the coast of Chile **1719** Bernard de la Harpe of France explores North American rivers	**1722** Jacob Roggeveen of the Netherlands discovers Easter Island and Samoa **1736** Anders Celsius leads French expedition to Lapland **1740** George Anson of Britain begins round-the-world voyage (to 1744)	**1741** Vitus Bering explores Alaskan coast for Russia **1748** American Pioneers cross the Cumberland Gap in the Appalachian Mts.	**1766** Louis de Bougainville of France discovers Tahiti and New Guinea **1768–1771** James Cook of Britain makes his first round-the-world voyage	**1790** George Vanco (British) explores n west coast of Americ **1793** Alexander Ma (British) explores northwest Canada **1795** In Africa, Scot explorer Mungo Par travels along river N
TECHNOLOGY	**1707** Johann Böttger of Germany discovers how to make hard porcelain **1709** Abraham Darby of England begins using coke to smelt iron **1714** Gabriel Fahrenheit of Germany makes a mercury thermometer	**1733** John Kay of Britain invents the flying shuttle **1735** John Harrison of Britain builds first accurate chronometer **1737** Georg Brandt of Sweden discovers cobalt	**1742** Anders Celsius of Sweden invents the centigrade thermometer **1751** Carl Linnaeus of Sweden publishes his landmark book on botany **1752** American Benjamin Franklin invents the lightning conductor	**1769** James Watt of Scotland invents the steam condenser **1769** Nicolas Cugnot of France builds first steam road carriage **1773** First cast iron bridge built at Coalbrookdale, England	**1783** Montgolfier bi of France make first balloon ascent **1792** Claude Chapp France invents the mechanical semaph **1793** Benjamin of United States invent cotton gin
ARTS	**1709** Bartolommeo Cristofori of Italy invents the piano **1710** Building of St Paul's Cathedral in London is completed **1719** Daniel Defoe writes first part of the story of *Robinson Crusoe*	**1721** J S Bach of Germany composes the *Brandenburg Concertos* **1735** Imperial ballet school in St Petersburg, Russia, opens **1737** England begins censorship of plays	**1741** German George Frederick Handel composes *Messiah* in England **1747** Samuel Johnson of Britain begins work on his dictionary **1751–1772** French scholars compile the *Encyclopédie*	**1768** The Royal Academy of Arts is founded in London **1773** Johann von Goethe of Germany writes first version of *Faust* **1778** In Milan, Italy, La Scala Opera House opens	**1786** In Scotland Ro Burns publishes his book of poems **1790** In Austria, Mo composes the opera *Fan Tutte* **1793** Building of the Capitol in Washingto C, begins
RELIGION	**1716** Chinese emperor bans the teaching of Christianity **1719** Dunkards, German Baptist Brethren, settle in Pennsylvania	**1730** John and Charles Wesley establish the Methodist movement **1734** The Koran is translated into English **1737** Alexander Cruden of Britain compiles his *Concordance to the Bible*	**1759** Jesuits are expelled from Portugal and its colonies	**1766** Catherine the Great of Russia grants her people freedom of worship **1767** Jesuits are expelled from Spain **1776** Mystic Ann Lee forms the first Shaker colony in America	**1781** Religious toler proclaimed in Austr **1785** State of Virgin passes a statute of re freedom **1790** Jews in Americ granted civil libertie
DAILY LIFE	**1711** South Sea Company takes over £9 million of Britain's National Debt **1712** The last execution of a witch in England takes place **1720** South Sea Company crashes; thousands of people are ruined	**1722** Thomas Guy, British bookseller, helps found Guy's Hospital, London **1725** New York City gets its first newspaper, the *New York Gazette* **1727** Brazil sets up its first coffee plantation	**1744** First official cricket match in Britain (Kent versus All England) **1752** Britain adopts the Gregorian calendar, dropping 11 days **1755** Earthquake kills 30,000 people in Lisbon	**1768** Publication of the *Encyclopaedia Britannica* in weekly parts begins **1770** Paris has its first public restaurant **1779** First running of the Derby horse race at Epsom, England	**1787** United States a the Stars and Stripes **1792** Denmark aboli the slave trade **1792** Scot William Murdoch is first pers light his home with g

1800–1820	1820–1840	1840–1860	1860–1880	1880–1900	
1 Act of Union unites ...at Britain and Ireland	1821 Simón Bolívar liberates Venezuela from Spain	1845 The United States annexes Texas	1861–1865 American Civil War: 11 states secede from the Union	1881 President James Garfield of the USA is assassinated	**POLITICS**
3 USA buys Louisiana ...n France	1822 Brazil becomes independent of Portugal	1848 Year of Revolutions: Austria, France, Germany, Italy, and Hungary	1865 President Abraham Lincoln is assassinated; Civil War ends	1883 The scramble for European colonies in Africa starts	
4 Napoleon becomes ...peror of France and ...lly defeated in 1815	1837 Queen Victoria comes to the British throne, aged 18	1853–1856 The Crimean War: Britain, France, and Turkey against Russia	1867 The United States buys Alaska from Russia for $7,200,000	1899 The Boer War in South Africa starts (to 1902)	
2–1806 Lewis and Clark ...edition crosses North ...rica from east to west	1829 Charles Sturt finds the Murray River in Australia	1852–1856 David Livingstone (British) explores the Zambesi River	1871 Henry Stanley is sent to look for Livingstone and finds him at Ujiji	1882 Adolphus Greely (USA) explores Greenland and the Arctic	**EXPLORATION**
2 William Moorcroft ...itish) explores Tibet	1831 James Clark Ross of Britain reaches the North Magnetic Pole	1854 Richard Burton (British) explores East Africa, including Ethiopia	1872 HMS *Challenger* begins a world survey of the oceans	1888–1892 Emin Pasha of Germany explores central Africa	
2–1825 Denham Dixon ...other Britons cross the ...ara	1840–1841 Edward Eyre crosses the Nullarbor Plain of Australia	1858 John Speke and Richard Burton discover Lake Tanganyika	1879 Nils Nordenskiöld of Sweden sails through the Northeast Passage	1893 Fritjof Nansen of Norway tries to reach the North Pole, but fails	
4 George Stephenson ...itish) builds first ...ccessful steam locomotive	1825 First passenger railroad opens in northern England	1844 Artist Samuel Morse of the USA demonstrates the use of the Morse Code	1873 Joseph Glidden of the USA invents barbed wire	1885 Karl Benz of Germany builds the first motor-car	**TECHNOLOGY**
5 Humphry Davy ...itish) invents the ...ers' safety lamp	1827 Joseph Niépce of France takes the world's first photograph	1847 James Simpson of Britain uses chloroform as an anesthetic	1876 Alexander Graham Bell (British/American) invents the telephone	1895 Guglielmo Marconi of Italy invents wireless telegraphy	
6 Réné Laennec of ...nce invents the ...hoscope	1834 Cyrus McCormick of the United States invents a reaping machine	1860 Christopher Scholes of the USA invents a practical typewriter	1879 Electric lamp bulbs are invented	1900 Graf von Zeppelin (Germany) invents the rigid airship	
1 Joseph Haydn of ...stria composes oratorio ...Seasons	1822 Royal Academy of Music is founded in London	1843 Richard Wagner of Germany writes opera *The Flying Dutchman*	1868 Louisa M Alcott writes *Little Women*	1883 Royal College of Music in London founded	**ARTS**
3 Franz Schubert of ...stria writes his first ...phony	1835 Hans Christian Andersen publishes his first fairy tales in Denmark	1846 Adolphe Sax of Belgium invents the saxophone	1874 Impressionist movement in painting starts in Paris	1884 Mark Twain writes *Huckleberry Finn*	
4 Walter Scott writes ...first novel, *Waverley*		1860 George Eliot (Mary Anne Evans) of Britain writes *The Mill on the Floss*	1875 Gilbert and Sullivan produce their first light opera, *Trial by Jury*	1895 Promenade Concerts begin in London	
4 British and Foreign ...le Society is formed in ...adon	1826 Jesuits are allowed to return to France	1846 Mormons in the USA begin migrating to the Great Salt Lake, Utah	1865 William Booth founds the Salvation Army in Britain	1890 James Frazer of Britain writes *The Golden Bough: A Study in Magic and Religion*	**RELIGION**
8 Napoleon abolishes ...Inquisition in Italy and ...in	1827 John Nelson Darby founds the Plymouth Brethren	1854 Pope Pius IX proclaims Immaculate Conception as dogma	1871 Charles Russell founds the Jehovah's Witnesses		
2 Restrictions on ...nconformists in ...gland are relaxed	1830 Joseph Smith founds the Church of Latter-Day Saints (Mormons)		1879 Mary Baker Eddy founds the Christian Science Church	1896 Theodor Herzl of Austria proposes a Jewish state in Palestine	
7 Britain ends the slave ...de	1829 First Oxford and Cambridge Boat Race on river Thames in Britain	1844 First co-operative society is formed in Rochdale, England	1864 Louis Pasteur of France invents pasteurization	1887 Victoria celebrates her Golden Jubilee as Britain's queen	**DAILY LIFE**
5 Tambora Volcano in ...onesia erupts: 50,000 ...ple are killed	1834 Fire destroys Britain's Houses of Parliament	1851 The Great Exhibition is held in Hyde Park, London	1868 The first Trades Union Congress meets in Britain	1900 The Labour Party is founded in Britain	
9 Freedom of the press ...uaranteed in France	1840 Penny Postage and adhesive stamps are introduced in Britain	1855 Britain abolishes stamp duty on newspapers	1874 Walter Wingfield invents Sphairistiké – now called lawn tennis		

	1900–1910	1910–1920	1920–1930	1930–1940	1940–1950
POLITICS	1901 Edward VII succeeds Victoria as British monarch 1902 The Boer War ends 1904–1905 Russo-Japanese War; Japan wins	1911 China becomes a republic after 2,000 years under emperors 1914–1918 World War I: nearly 10 million soldiers die 1917 October Revolution in Russia: Lenin and the Bolsheviks seize power	1922 Benito Mussolini forms a Fascist government in Italy 1924 Joseph Stalin becomes ruler of the Soviet Union 1924 Britain has its first Labour government	1933 The Nazi leader Adolf Hitler becomes dictator of Germany 1936–1939 Spanish Civil War 1939 World War II begins as Germany and the Soviet Union invade Poland	1941 The US enters World War II, following Japan[...] attack on Pearl Harbo[...] 1945 World War II en[...] with German and Japa[...] surrender 1945–1951 Labour ret[...] to power in Britain; m[...] industries nationalized
EXPLORATION	1901–1903 Erich von Drygalski of Germany explores Antarctica 1907–1909 Ernest Shackleton of Britain nearly reaches the South Pole 1909 Robert Peary of the USA reaches the North Pole	1911 Roald Amundsen of Norway leads first party to reach the South Pole 1912 Briton Robert Falcon Scott also reaches the South Pole, but perishes 1919 Alcock and Brown make first non-stop flight across the Atlantic	1926 Richard Byrd and Floyd Bennett of the USA fly over the North Pole 1926 Umberto Nobile of Norway makes airship flight over North Pole 1929 Richard Byrd flies over the South Pole	1931 First submarine ventures under the Arctic Ocean ice 1932 Auguste Piccard ascends 17 miles (28km) in a stratospheric balloon	1946–1947 Operation Highjump maps coast[...] Antarctica from the ai[...] 1947 Thor Heyerdahl [...] Norway sails the raft *[...] Tiki* across the Pacific [...] Peru to the Tuamoto[...] Islands
TECHNOLOGY	1903 In the USA, the Wright Brothers make the first powered flights 1907 Louis Lumière of France develops color photography 1909 Louis Blériot of France flies across the English Channel	1917 Ernest Rutherford of Britain splits the atom 1919 First mass spectrograph machine is built 1920 First public broadcasting station in Britain opens	1922 Insulin is first given to diabetics 1925 John Logie Baird invents a primitive form of television 1928 Alexander Fleming accidentally discovers penicillin	1935 Radar is developed for use in detecting aircraft 1937 Frank Whittle builds the first jet aero engine 1940 Howard Florey develops penicillin as a working antibiotic	1942 Magnetic record[...] tape is invented 1946 ENIAC, first full[...] electronic digital computer, is built 1948 Peter Goldmar[...] invents the long-playi[...] record
ARTS	1901 Ragtime music becomes popular in America 1905 First regular cinema opens in Pittsburgh, Pennsylvania 1909 Sergei Diaghilev's Ballets Russes starts performing in Paris	1914 Charlie Chaplin creates his film character in *The Tramp* 1916 Artists and poets start the Dadaist movement in Switzerland 1917 The Original Dixieland Jazz Band is formed in New York	1926 A A Milne writes *Winnie the Pooh* 1927 Theremin, the first electronic musical instrument, is invented	1935 American George Gershwin writes *Porgy and Bess* 1937 First full-length cartoon film, *Snow White and the Seven Dwarfs* 1938 Radio play *War of the Worlds* causes panic in the United States	1947 *The Diary of Ann[...] Frank* is published 1949 George Orwell v[...] the satire *Nineteen Eig[...] Four* 1950 United Nations building in New York is completed
RELIGION	1904 Germany partly lifts its ban on Jesuits 1909 First Jewish kibbutz is founded in Palestine	1912 Church of Scotland issues a revised prayer book 1917 Balfour Declaration: Britain backs homeland for Jews in Palestine 1920 Joan of Arc is canonized (declared to be a saint)	1924 Mahatma Gandhi fasts in protest at religious feuding in India 1929 Presbyterian Churches in Scotland unite	1932 Methodist Churches in Britain reunite (split since 1797) 1933 All Protestant Churches in Germany unite 1937 Protestant parson Martin Niemöller is interned by Hitler	1946 Pope Pius XII cr[...] 32 new cardinals 1947 The Dead Sea Sc[...] are discovered in cave[...] Qumran, Jordan 1948 The World Coun[...] Churches is establishe[...]
DAILY LIFE	1902 Eruption of Mt Pelée in Martinique kills 38,000 people 1903 The first teddy bears are made in Germany 1906 An earthquake destroys most of San Francisco; 3,000 people die	1912 Liner *Titanic* sinks on her maiden voyage; more than 1,500 people drowned 1918 British women over the age of 30 gain the vote 1918 First airmail service is established in the United States	1920 Women in the USA gain the vote 1929 Wall Street crash: biggest world economic crisis begins 1930 Youth Hostels Association founded	1932–1934 Pontine Marshes in Italy are drained 1934 Dionne Quintuplets are born in Canada 1936 King Edward VIII abdicates to marry divorcee Wallis Simpson	1941–1949 Clothes rationing in force in Britain 1945 Bebop form of ja[...] comes into fashion 1947 First microwave [...] go on sale

1950–1960	1960–1970	1970–1980	1980–1990	1990–2000s	
Egypt's ruler Gamel ...er seizes Suez Canal	1961 Communists build the Berlin Wall	1974 US President Nixon resigns over Watergate scandal	1982 Argentina's invasion of the Falkland Islands fails	1991 Collapse of the Soviet Union: republics become independent	**POLITICS**
Seventeen African ...nies gain ...pendence from ...opean powers	1963 US President John F Kennedy is assassinated	1979 Margaret Thatcher becomes Britain's first woman prime minister	1989 Communist rule ends in East Germany; Berlin Wall is demolished	1991 Breakup of Yugoslavia: civil war leads to NATO involvement	
	1965–1973 The Vietnam War	1980 Marshal Tito, leader of Yugoslavia since 1953, dies		1997 Scots vote for a national parliament and Welsh for an assembly	
	1967 Six-Day War between Israel and Arab nations				
...–1958 Vivien Fuchs of ...ain makes first crossing ...ntarctica	1961 Yuri Gagarin of the Soviet Union makes the first manned space flight	1971 Space probes orbit Mars and send back photographs	1981 The first space shuttle, *Columbia*, orbits the Earth	1993 Two Britons complete the first foot crossing of Antarctica	**EXPLORATION**
...US nuclear ...arine *Nautilus* travels ...er the North Polar ice	1968 US space craft *Apollo 8* first orbits the Moon	1979–1989 Space probe *Voyager 2* flies past and photographs Jupiter, Saturn, Uranus, and Neptune	1982 Soviet space probes land on Venus and send back color pictures	1997 US robot, controlled from Earth, explores surface of Mars	
...The Bathyscaphe ...e descends 35,800 feet (...10 m) into the ...ana Trench	1969 Neil Armstrong of the USA is the first person to walk on the Moon		1984 Two US astronauts fly in space untethered to their spacecraft	2000 *Global Surveyor* finds evidence of water on Mars	
Heart-lung machine ...vented	1967 Christiaan Barnard (S. African) performs first human heart transplant	1972 *Apollo 17* crew make last manned visit to the Moon	1984 The first Apple Macintosh microcomputer goes on sale	1993 Astronauts repair the Hubble Space Telescope (launched 1990)	**TECHNOLOGY**
Albert Sabin invents ...vaccine against polio	1963 Theory of continental drift is proved by two British geophysicists	1978 Louise Brown, the first "test tube baby," is born	1986 The Dutch complete their flood protection scheme after 33 years	1994 Channel Tunnel is completed, linking Britain and France	
...Soviet Union ...ches the first Earth ...ites, *Sputnik 1* and *2*	1969 First flight of the supersonic airliner *Concorde*	1980 Smallpox is eradicated world wide	1988 Undersea tunnel linking Honshu and Hokkaido, Japan, opens	2001 Mapping of human genetic code nears completion	
...s Rock and Roll ...ops	1965 Op Art, based on optical illusions, becomes popular	1971 *Fiddler on the Roof* closes after record New York run of 3,242 performances	1983 Symphony written by Mozart aged nine is discovered	1993 Missing treasure from Troy found in 1873 is rediscovered in Russia	**ARTS**
John Osborne's *Look ...n Anger* is staged in ...on	1966 New Metropolitan Opera House opens in New York City		1985 Live Aid rock concert raises $60 million for African famine relief	2001 *Harry Potter* and *Lord of the Rings* are worldwide favorites in books and movies	
New buildings ...leted in Brasilia, ...al of Brazil	1968 Four Soviet writers are jailed for "dissidence"	1980 Former Beatle John Lennon is murdered in New York	1986 Wole Soyinka is the first black African to win the Nobel Prize for Literature		
John XXIII becomes ...	1968 In Northern Ireland, Catholics and Protestants clash over civil rights	1978 Deaths of Pope Paul VI and his successor Pope John Paul I; succeeded by Pope John Paul II, a Pole and first non-Italian pope for 456 years	1981 John Paul II becomes the first pope to visit Britain	1992 Ten women become Anglican priests in Australia	**RELIGION**
...Supreme Religious ...r for World Jewry is ...d in Jerusalem	1969 Pope Paul VI removes 200 saints from the liturgical calendar		1986 Desmond Tutu becomes the first black archbishop of Cape Town	1996–2001 Strict Islamic law is imposed in Afghanistan before removal of Taliban regime	
...Swedish Lutheran ...h admits women ...ers	1970 Jewish and Roman Catholic leaders confer in Rome		1990 First Anglican women priests are ordained in Northern Ireland		
Mount Everest is ...ed for the first time	1966 Miniskirts come into fashion	1976 Earthquakes shake China, Guatemala, Indonesia, Italy, the Philippines and Turkey: 780,000 people die	1982 Disease kills 20 million elm trees in Britain	1997 Hong Kong is returned to China	**DAILY LIFE**
Roger Bannister ...h) runs the mile in ...four minutes	1967 Francis Chichester completes single-handed voyage around the world	1987 World stock market crash on Black Monday	2001 USA declares "war on terrorism" after attacks on New York City and Washington, DC		
First life peerages are ...d in Britain	1970 Storms and floods kill 500,000 people in East Pakistan (Bangladesh)	1978–1979 Union troubles close London's *The Times* newspaper for nearly a year	1989 World ban on ivory trading is imposed	2002 Euro is currency of European Union	

IMPORTANT BATTLES OF HISTORY

Marathon (490 BC) The armies of Athens crushed an attempt by Persia to conquer Greece

Salamis (480 BC) Greek ships defeated a larger Persian fleet and thwarted an invasion

Syracuse (414–413 BC) During a long war between the city states of Athens and Sparta the Athenians besieged Syracuse but lost power after a heavy defeat

Gaugamela (331 BC) Alexander the Great of Macedonia defeated the Persians and conquered the Persian Empire

Metaurus (207 BC) A Roman army defeated a Carthaginian attempt to invade Italy

Actium (30 BC) A Roman fleet destroyed the Egyptian fleet of Mark Antony and Cleopatra, ending Egypt's threat to Rome

Teutoburg Forest (AD 9) German tribes led by Arminius ambushed and destroyed three Roman legions

Châlons (451) Roman legions and their Visigoth allies defeated the Huns, led by Attila

Poitiers (732) The Franks led by Charles Martel defeated a Muslim attempt to conquer western Europe

Hastings (1066) Duke William of Normandy defeated the Saxons under King Harold II and conquered England

Crécy (1346) Edward III of England defeated Philip VI of France, using archers to shoot his opponents

Agincourt (1415) Henry V of England defeated a much larger French army and captured Normandy

Orléans (1429) The French under Joan of Arc raised the siege of Orléans and began liberating France from England

Constantinople (1453) Ottoman Turks captured the city and ended the Byzantine (Eastern Roman) Empire

Lepanto (1571) A Christian fleet defeated a Turkish fleet in the Mediterranean and halted Muslim designs on Europe

Spanish Armada (1588) England's navy fought off a Spanish attempt to invade and conquer

Naseby (1645) Parliamentary forces defeated Charles I during the English Civil War

Blenheim (1704) During the War of the Spanish Succession, British and Austrian forces stopped a French and Bavarian attempt to capture Vienna

Poltava (1709) Peter the Great of Russia fought off an invasion by Charles XII of Sweden

Plassey (1757) An Anglo-Indian army defeated the Nawab of Bengal, beginning Britain's domination of India

Quebec (1759) British troops under James Wolfe defeated the French and secured Canada for Britain

Bunker Hill (1775) In the American War of Independence, British troops drove the Americans from hills near Boston, Mass.

In the same war:

Brandywine Creek (1777) British troops forced American forces to retreat

Saratoga (1777) American troops surrounded a British army and forced it to surrender

Savannah (1778) Britain captured the port of Savannah from the Americans and gained control of Georgia

King's Mountain (1780) Americans surrounded and captured part of a British army

Yorktown (1781) A British army surrendered to a larger American force, ending the American War of Independence

---

The Nile (1798) British defeat the French in Abu Kir Bay, ending Napoleon's attempt to conquer Egypt

Trafalgar (1805) A British fleet defeated a Franco-Spanish fleet, ending Napoleon's hopes of invading England

Austerlitz (1805) Napoleon of France defeated a combined force of Austrian and Russian soldiers

Leipzig (1813) Austrian, Prussian, Russian, and Swedish armies defeated Napoleon I, leading to his abdication the following year

Waterloo (1815) A British, Belgian, and Dutch army supported by the Prussians defeated Napoleon I, ending his brief return to power in France

Fort Sumter (1861) In the opening battle of the **American Civil War**, Confederate forces captured this fort in the harbor of Charleston, South Carolina.

In the same war:

Merrimack and Monitor (1862) This Civil War battle was the first between two ironclad warships

Gettysburg (1863) Union forces defeated the Confederates, marking a turning point in the American Civil War

Vicksburg (1863) After a long siege Union forces captured this key city on the Mississippi River

Chickamauga (1863) At this town in Georgia the Confederates won their last major battle

Chattanooga (1863) A few weeks after Chickamauga Union forces won a decisive victory over the Confederates

Sedan (1870) Germany defeated France in key battle of Franco-Prussian War

Tsushima (1905) A Japanese fleet overwhelmed a Russian one, ending the Russo-Japanese War

World War I (1914–1918)

Tannenberg (1914) At the start of World War I two Russian armies invaded East Prussia, but a German army under Paul von Hindenburg crushed them

Marne (1914) The French and British halted a German invasion of France at the start of World War I

Ypres (1914–1915) A series of German attacks on this Belgian town were beaten back with heavy losses on each side in two fierce battles

Verdun (1916) French forces under Philippe Pétain fought off a German attempt to take this strong point

Jutland (1916) This was the major naval battle of World War I; neither Germans nor British won

Brusilov Offensive (1916) A Russian attack led by General Alexei Brusilov nearly knocked Germany's Austrian allies out of the war

Somme (1916) A British and French attack was beaten back by German machine-gunners; total casualties for both sides were more than 1 million

3rd Ypres (1917) British and Canadian troops attacked to drive the Germans back, fighting in heavy rain and mud

Passchendaele (1917) This village was the furthest advance of 3rd Ypres; casualties of both sides totalled 500,000

4th Ypres (1918) was part of a general German offensive, which died down after heavy fighting

Marne (1918) French, US, and British forces halted the last German attack of World War I

World War II (1939–1945)

Britain (1940–1941) In World War II, German attempt to eliminate Britain's air force failed

The Atlantic (1940–1944) Germany narrowly lost the submarine war against Allied shipping

Pearl Harbor (1941) In a surprise air attack Japan knocked out the United States fleet at Hawaii

Coral Sea (1942) In the first all-air naval battle, Americans thwarted a Japanese attack on New Guinea

Stalingrad (1942–1943) The German siege of Stalingrad (now Volgograd, Russia) ended with the surrender of a German army of 100,000 men

El Alamein (1942) The British Eighth Army finally drove German and Italian forces out of Egypt

Midway (1942) An American fleet defeated a Japanese attempt to capture Midway Island

Normandy (1944) American and British troops landed in occupied France to begin the defeat of Germany; the largest ever seaborne attack

Leyte Gulf (1944) In the biggest naval battle of World War II, an American fleet thwarted a Japanese attempt to hold on to the Philippines

Ardennes Bulge (1944–1945) A final German attempt to counter the Allied invasion failed

Hiroshima/Nagasaki (1945) Two US atomic bombs on these Japanese cities ended World War II

Inchon (1950) US forces defeated North Koreans during the Korean War

Dien Bien Phu (1954) Vietnamese defeated French in Indo-China

Falklands (1982) A British seaborne assault recaptured the Falkland Islands following an Argentine invasion

Desert Storm (1991) A UN force including American, British and Arab units ended Iraq's invasion of Kuwait

CHINESE DYNASTIES

Hsia Dynasty	c. 2000–1500 BC
Shang or Yin Dynasty	c. 1766–1027 BC
Zhou Dynasty	1027–256 BC
Qin Dynasty	221–206 BC
Former Han Dynasty	202 BC–AD 9
Xin Dynasty	AD 9–22
Later Han Dynasty	25–260
Three Kingdoms	221–265

Six Dynasties:

Western Chin	265–316
Eastern Chin	317–420
Liu Sung	420–479
Southern Ch'i	429–502
Liang	502–557
Southern Ch'en	557–587

Tatar Partition:

Bei Wei Dynasty	486–554
Northern Ch'i Dynasty	550–557
Northern Chou Dynasty	557–581
Sui Dynasty	581–618
T'ang Dynasty	618–906

Partition (rulers were mostly non-Chinese):

Hou Liang Dynasty	907–936
Hou T'ang Dynasty	923–936
Hou Chin Dynasty	936–948
Hou Han Dynasty	946–950
Hou Chou Dynasty	951–960
Northern Song Dynasty	960–1126
Southern Song Dynasty	1127–1279
Yuan (Mongol) Dynasty	1279–1368

Ming Dynasty	1368–1644
Qing (Manchu) Dynasty	1644–1912

ROMAN EMPERORS

Augustus	27 BC–AD14
Tiberius	14–37
Caligula	37–41
Claudius	41–54
Nero	54–68
Galba	68–69
Otho	69
Vitellius	69
Vespasian	69–79
Titus	79–81
Domitian	81–96
Nerva	96–98
Trajan	98–117
Hadrian	117–138
Antoninus Pius	138–161
Marcus Aurelius	161–180
Lucius Verus	161–169
Commodus	180–192
Pertinax	193
Didius Julian	193
Septimius Severus	193–211
Caracalla (jointly with Geta)	211–217
Geta	211–212
Macrinus	217–218
Elagabalus	218–222
Alexander Severus	222–235
Maximin	235–238
Gordian I	238
Gordian II	238
Pupienus	238
Balbinus	238
Gordian III	238–244
Philip "Arabs"	244–249
Decius	249–251
Hostilian	251
Gallus	251–253
Aemilian	253
Valerian	253–259
Gallienus	259–268
Claudius II	268–270
Quintillus	270
Aurelian	270–275
Tacitus	275–276
Florian	276
Probus	276–282
Carus	282–283
Numerian	283–284
Carinus	283–285
Diocletian (in the east)	284–305
Maximian (in the west)	286–305
Constantius I (in the west)	305–306
Galerius (in the east)	305–311
Severus	306–307
Maximian (again)	306–308
Maxentius (in the west)	306–312
Maximinus Daia	308–313
Licinius (in the east)	311–324
Constantine I, the Great	311–337
Constantine II	337–340
Constantius II	337–361
Constans	337–350
Julian the Apostate	361–363
Jovian	363–364
Valentian I (in the west)	364–375
Valens (in the east)	364–378
Gratian (in the west)	375–383
Valentinian II (in the west)	375–392
Theodosius the Great	379–395
Maximus	383–388
Eugenius	393–394
Arcadius (in the east)	395–408
Honorius (in the west)	395–423
Constantius III	421
Johannes	423–425
Theodosius II (in the east)	408–450
Valentinian (in the west)	425–455
Marcian (in the east)	450–457

Petronius (in the west)	455
Avitus (in the west)	455–456
Majorian (in the west)	457–461
Leo I (in the east)	457–474
Severus (in the west)	461–465
Anthemius (in the west)	467–473
Olybrius (in the west)	472
Glycerius (in the west)	473
Julius Nepos (in the west)	473–475
Leo II (in the east)	473–474
Zeno (in the east)	474–491
Romulus Augustulus (in the west)	475–476

Some emperors overlapped because they were set up by one army or another, and were then deposed, or murdered by their own troops; from 282 there were often two emperors, one ruling the west from Rome, the other ruling from Constantinople (formerly Byzantium). There were no Roman emperors after 476.

EASTERN ROMAN (BYZANTINE) EMPERORS

(The Eastern Roman Empire outlasted that of Rome; it is often called the Byzantine Empire from the old name for Constantinople, its capital – now Istanbul.)

Zeno	474–491
Anastasius I	491–518
Justin I	518–527
Justinian the Great	527–565
Tiberius II	578–582
Maurice	582–602
Phocas	602–610
Heraclius I	610–641
Constantine III	641
Heracleon	641
Constans II	641–668
Constantine IV	668–685
Justinian II	685–695
Leontius	695–698
Tiberius III	698–705
Justinian II (restored)	705–711
Philippicus	711–713
Anastasius II	713–715
Theodosius III	715–717
Leo III	717–741
Constantine V	741–775
Leo IV	775–780
Irene (empress)	797–802
Nicephorus I	802–811
Stauracius	811
Michael I	811–813
Leo V	813–820
Michael II	820–829
Theophilus I	829–842
Michael III	842–867
Basil I	867–886
Leo VI, the Wise	886–912
Alexander II	912–913
Constantine VII	912–959
Romanus I	920–944
Romanus II	944–963
Basil II (a minor until 976)	963–1025
Nicephorus II	963–969
John I	969–976
Constantine VIII	1025–1028
Zoë (empress)	1028–1050
Romanus III (husband of Zoë)	1028–1034
Michael IV (husband of Zoë)	1034–1041
Michael V (usurper)	1041–1042
Constantine IX (husband of Zoë)	1042–1055
Theodora (empress)	1042–1055
Michael VI	1056–1057
Isaac I	1057–1059
Constantine X	1059–1067
Romanus IV	1068–1071
Michael VII	1071–1078
Nicephorus III	1078–1081
Alexius I	1081–1118
John II	1118–1143
Manuel I	1143–1180
Alexius II	1180–1183
Andronicus I	1183–1185

Alexius III	1195–1203
Isaac II (restored)	1203–1204
Alexius IV	1203–1204
Alexius V	1204

Latin (Crusader) Emperors

Baldwin I	1204–1205
Henry	1205–1216
Peter of Courtenay	1216–1217
Yolande (Peter's wife, regent)	1217–1219
Robert of Courtenay	1219–1228
Baldwin II	1228–1261
John of Brienne (co-emperor)	1231–1237

The Palaeologus family

Michael VIII	1261–1282
Andronicus II	1282–1320
Michael IX (co-emperor)	1295–1320
Andronicus III	1328–1341
John V (a minor)	1341–1347
John VI	1347–1354
John V (restored)	1355–1376
Andronicus IV	1376–1379
John V (restored)	1379–1391
John VII	1390
Manuel II	1391–1448
Constantine XI	1448–1453

The Ottoman Turks captured Constantinople in 1453, ending the Byzantine empire.

NOTABLE POPES

(Up to 2003, 246 men have held the office of Pope, the supreme head of the Roman Catholic Church; these have been among the most influential.)

St Peter (the Apostle)	33–c. 67
St Clement I (wrote an epistle to the Church)	c. 88–c. 97
St Leo I (asserted papal supremacy)	440–461
St Gregory I (sent missionaries to England)	590–604
St Leo IX (split with the Eastern Church)	1049–1054
Nicholas II (decreed that only cardinals could elect popes)	1059–1061
St Gregory VII (quarrelled with Emperor Henry IV of Germany)	1073–1085
Adrian IV (only English pope; "gave" Ireland to Henry II of England)	1154–1159
Innocent III (influenced European politics)	1198–1216
Boniface VIII (decreed that all human beings should submit to papal authority)	1294–1303
Alexander VI (member of the ruthless Borgia family; fathered many children)	1492–1503
Paul III (summoned the Council of Trent)	1534–1549
Gregory XIII (reformed the calendar)	1572–1585
Benedict XIV (encouraged education)	1740–1758
Pius IX (longest reign; called himself a "prisoner" after Italian unification)	1846–1878
Pius XII (led humanitarian work in World War II)	1939–1958
John XXIII (led a revival of religious life)	1958–1963
Paul VI (carried on the work of John XXIII)	1963–1978
John Paul II	1978–

PRIME MINISTERS OF AUSTRALIA

Name and Party	Held office
Edmund Barton (Protectionist)	1901–1903
Alfred Deakin (Protectionist)	1903–1904
John C Watson (Labor)1904	
George H Reid (Free trade)	1904–1905
Alfred Deakin (Protectionist)	1905–1908
Andrew Fisher (Labor)	1908–1909
Alfred Deakin (Fusion)	1909–1910
Andrew Fisher (Labor)	1910–1913
Joseph Cook (Liberal)	1913–1914
Andrew Fisher (Labor)	1914–1915
William H Hughes (Labor)	1915–1917
William H Hughes (Nationalist)	1917–1923
Stanley M Bruce (Nationalist)	1923–1929
James Scullin (Labor)	1929–1932
Joseph A Lyons (United)	1932–1939
Earle Page (Country)	1939
Robert G Menzies (United)	1939–1941
Arthur Fadden (Country)	1941
Francis M Forde (Labor)	1945
Ben Chifley (Labor)	1945–1949
Robert G Menzies (Liberal)	1949–1966
Harold E Holt (Liberal)	1966–1967
John McEwen (Country)	1967–1968
John G Gorton (Liberal)	1968–1971
William McMahon (Liberal)	1971–1972
Gough Whitlam (Labor)	1972–1975
Malcolm Fraser (Liberal)	1975–1983
Robert Hawke (Labor)	1983–1991
Paul Keating (Labor)	1991–1996
John Howard	1996–
(Liberal-National coalition)	

20TH CENTURY BRITISH PRIME MINISTERS

Marquess of Salisbury (Conservative)	1895–1902
Arthur Balfour (Conservative)	1902–1905
Sir Henry Campbell-Bannerman (Liberal)	1905–1908
Herbert Asquith (Liberal)	1908–1915
Herbert Asquith (Coalition)	1915–1916
David Lloyd-George (Coalition)	1916–1922
Andrew Bonar-Law (Conservative)	1922–1923
Stanley Baldwin (Conservative)	1923–1924
James Ramsay MacDonald (Labour)	1924
Stanley Baldwin (Conservative)	1924–1929
James Ramsay MacDonald (Labour)	1929–1931
James Ramsay MacDonald (Coalition)	1931–1935
Stanley Baldwin (Coalition)	1935–1937
Neville Chamberlain (Conservative)	1937–1940
Winston S Churchill (Coalition)	1940–1945
Winston S Churchill (Conservative)	1945
Clement Attlee (Labour)	1945–1951
Sir Winston S Churchill (Conservative)	1951–1955
Sir Anthony Eden (Conservative)	1955–1957
Harold Macmillan (Conservative)	1957–1963
Sir Alec Douglas-Home (Conservative)	1963–1964
Harold Wilson (Labour)	1964–1970
Edward Heath (Conservative)	1970–1974
Harold Wilson (Labour)	1974–1976
James Callaghan (Labour)	1976–1979
Margaret Thatcher (Conservative)	1979–1990
John Major (Conservative)	1990–1997
Tony Blair (Labour)	1997–

CANADIAN PRIME MINISTERS

Sir John MacDonald (Conservative)	1867–1873
Alexander Mackenzie (Liberal)	1873–1878
Sir John MacDonald (Conservative)	1878–1891
Sir John Abbott (Conservative)	1819–1892
Sir John Thompson (Conservative)	1892–1894
Sir Mackenzie Bowell (Conservative)	1894–1896
Sir Charles Tupper (Conservative)	1896
Sir Wilfred Laurier (Liberal)	1896–1911
Sir Robert L Borden (Conservative)	1911–1917
Sir Robert L Borden (Unionist)	1917–1920
Arthur Meighen (Unionist)	1920–1921
W L Mackenzie King (Liberal)	1921–1926
Arthur Meighen (Conservative)	1926
W L Mackenzie King (Liberal)	1926–1930
Richard B Bennett (Conservative)	1930–1935
W L Mackenzie King (Liberal)	1935–1948
Louis S St Laurent (Liberal)	1948–1957
John C Diefenbaker (Progressive Conservative)	1957–1963
Lester B Pearson (Liberal)	1963–1968
Pierre E Trudeau (Liberal)	1968–1979
Charles J Clark (Progressive Conservative)	1979–1980
Pierre E Trudeau (Liberal)	1980–1984
John E Turner (Liberal)	1984
Brian Mulroney (Progressive Conservative)	1984–1994
Kim Campbell (Progressive Conservative)	1994
Jean Chrétien (Liberal)	1994–

PRESIDENTS OF FRANCE SINCE 1947

Fourth Republic

Vincent Auriol (Socialist)	1947–1953
René Coty (Socialist)	1953–1958

Fifth Republic

Charles de Gaulle (Gaullist)	1959–1969
Georges Pompidou (Gaullist)	1969–1974
Valéry Giscard d'Estaing (Independent Republican)	1974–1981
François Mitterrand (Socialist)	1981–1995
Jacques Chirac (Gaullist)	1995–

CHANCELLORS OF GERMANY SINCE 1949

(West Germany to 1990, united Germany from then)

Konrad Adenauer (Christian Democratic Union)	1949–1963
Ludwig Erhard (Christian Democratic Union)	1963–1966
Kurt Kiesinger (Christian Democratic Union)	1966–1969
Willy Brandt (Social Democrat)	1969–1974
Helmut Schmidt (Social Democrat)	1974–1982
Helmut Kohl (Christian Democratic Union)	1982–1998
Gerhard Schröder (Social Democrat)	1998–

PRIME MINISTERS OF INDIA SINCE 1950

Jawaharlal Nehru (Congress)	1950–1964
Lal Bahardur Shashtri (Congress)	1964–1966
Indira Gandhi (Congress)	1966–1977
Morarji Desai (Janata)	1977–1979
Indira Gandhi (Congress-I)	1979–1984
Rajiv Gandhi (Congress)	1984–1991
Narasimha Rao (Congress)	1991–1996
Atal Bihari Vajpayee (BJP)	1996
Deve Gowda	1996
(United Front Coalition)	
Inder Kumar Gujral (UFC)	1996–1998
Atal Bihari Vajpayee (BJP)	1998–

PRIME MINISTERS OF NEW ZEALAND

Richard Seddon (Liberal)	1893–1906
William Hall-Jones (Liberal)	1906
Sir Joseph Ward (Liberal)	1906–1912
Thomas Mackenzie	1912
William F Massey (Reform)	1912–1925
Francis Bell (Reform)	1925
Gordon Coates (Reform)	1925–1928
Sir Joseph Ward (United)	1928–1930
George Forbes (United)	1930–1935
Michael J Savage (Labour)	1935–1940
Peter Fraser (Labour)	1940–1949
Sidney J Holland (National)	1949–1957
Keith Holyoake (National)	1957
Walter Nash (Labour)	1957–1960
Keith Holyoake (National)	1960–1972
Sir John Marshall (National)	1972
Norman Kirk (Labour)	1972–1974
Wallace Rowling (Labour)	1974–1975
Robert Muldoon (National)	1975–1984
David Lange (Labour)	1984–1989
Geoffrey Palmer (Labour)	1989–1990
Michael K Moore (Labour)	1990
James Bolger (National)	1990–1996
James Bolger (Coalition)	1996–1997
Jennifer Shipley (Coalition)	1997–1999
Helen Clark (Coalition)	1999–

SOUTH AFRICAN LEADERS

(Prime Ministers up to 1994, thereafter Presidents)

Louis Botha (South African Party)	1910–1919
Jan Smuts (South African Party)	1919–1924
James Hertzog (Pact Coalition)	1924–1939
Jan Smuts (United Party)	1939–1948
Daniel Malan (National)	1948–1954
J G Strijdom (National)	1954–1958
D H Verwoerd (National)	1958–1966
B J Vorster (National)	1966–1978
P W Botha (National)	1978–1989
F W de Klerk (National)	1989–1994
Nelson Mandela	1994–1999
Thabo Mbeki	1999–

PRESIDENTS OF THE UNITED STATES

George Washington (no party)	1789–1797
John Adams (Federalist)	1797–1801
Thomas Jefferson (Democratic-Republican)	1801–1809
James Madison (Democratic-Republican)	1809–1817
James Monroe (Democratic-Republican)	1817–1825
John Quincy Adams (Democratic-Republican)	1825–1829
Andrew Jackson (Democrat)	1829–1837
Martin Van Buren (Democrat)	1837–1841
William H Harrison (Whig)	1841
John Tyler (Whig)	1841–1845
James K Polk (Democrat)	1845–1849
Zachary Taylor (Whig)	1849–1850
Millard Fillmore (Whig)	1850–1853
Franklin Pierce (Democrat)	1853–1857
James Buchanan (Democrat)	1857–1861
Abraham Lincoln (Republican) *	1861–1865
Andrew Johnson (National Union)	1865–1869
Ulysses S Grant (Republican)	1869–1877
Rutherford B Hayes (Republican)	1877–1881
James A Garfield (Republican) *	1881
Chester A Arthur (Republican)	1881–1885
Grover Cleveland (Democrat)	1885–1889
Benjamin Harrison (Republican)	1889–1893
Grover Cleveland (Democrat)	1893–1897
William McKinley (Republican) *	1897–1901
Theodore Roosevelt (Republican)	1901–1909
William H Taft (Republican)	1909–1913
Woodrow Wilson (Democrat)	1913–1921
Warren G Harding (Republican)	1921–1923
Calvin Coolidge (Republican)	1923–1929
Herbert C Hoover (Republican)	1929–1933
Franklin D Roosevelt (Democrat)	1933–1945
Harry S Truman (Democrat)	1945–1953
Dwight D Eisenhower (Republican)	1953–1961
John F Kennedy (Democrat)*	1961–1963
Lyndon B Johnson (Democrat)	1963–1969
Richard M Nixon (Republican)	1969–1974
Gerald R Ford (Republican)	1974–1977
Jimmy Carter (Democrat)	1977–1981
Ronald Reagan (Republican)	1981–1989
George Bush (Republican)	1989–1994
William Clinton (Democrat)	1994–2001
George W Bush (Republican)	2001–
* Assassinated	

SECRETARIES-GENERAL OF THE UN

Trygve Lie (Norway)	1946–1953
Dag Hammarskjöld (Sweden)	1953–1961
U Thant (Burma)	1961–1971
Kurt Waldheim (Austria)	1972–1982
Javier Pérez de Cuéllar (Peru)	1982–1991
Boutros Boutros-Ghali (Egypt)	1991–1997
Kofi Annan (Ghana)	1997–

BELGIAN MONARCHS

Leopold I	1831–1865
Leopold II	1865–1907
Albert I	1909–1934
Leopold III	1934–1951
Baudouin	1951–1993
Albert II	1993–

BRITISH RULERS

RULERS OF ENGLAND

Saxons

Egbert	827–839
Ethelwulf	839–858
Ethelbald	858–860
Ethelbert	860–866
Ethelred I	866–871
Alfred the Great	871–899
Edward the Elder	899–924
Athelstan	924–939
Edmund	939–946
Edred	946–955
Edwy	955–959
Edgar	959–975
Edward the Martyr	975–978
Ethelred II (the "Unready")	978–1016
Edmund Ironside	1016

Danes

Canute	1016–1035
Harold I (Harefoot)	1035–1040
Hardicanute	1040–1042

Saxons

Edward the Confessor	1042–1066
Harold II	1066

House of Normandy

William I (the Conqueror)	1066–1087
William II (Rufus)	1087–1100
Henry I (Beauclerk)	1100–1135
Stephen	1135–1154

House of Plantagenet

Henry II	1154–1189
Richard I (Coeur-de-Lion)	1189–1199
John (Lackland)	1199–1216
Henry III	1216–1272
Edward I	1272–1307
(The Hammer of the Scots)	
Edward II	1307–1327
Edward III	1327–1377
Richard II	1377–1399

House of Lancaster

Henry IV	1399–1413
Henry V	1413–1422
Henry VI	1422–1461

House of York

Edward IV	1461–1483
Edward V	1483
Richard III	1483–1485

House of Tudor

Henry VII	1485–1509
Henry VIII	1509–1547
Edward VI	1547–1553
Jane	1553
Mary I	1553–1558
Elizabeth I	1558–1603

RULERS OF SCOTLAND

Malcolm I	1005–1034
Duncan I	1034–1040
Macbeth	1040–1057
Malcolm III (Canmore)	1057–1093
Donald Bane	1093–1094
Duncan II	1094
Donald Bane	1094–1097
Edgar	1097–1107
Alexander I	1107–1124
David I	1124–1153
Malcolm IV	1153–1165
William (the Lion)	1165–1214
Alexander II	1214–1249
Alexander III	1249–1286
Margaret	1286–1290
(the Maid of Norway)	
Interregnum	1290–1292
John Balliol	1292–1296
Interregnum	1296–1306
Robert I (Bruce)	1306–1329
David II	1329–1371

House of Stuart

Robert II	1371–1390
Robert III	1390–1406
James I	1406–1437
James II	1437–1460
James III	1460–1488
James IV	1488–1513
James V	1513–1542
Mary, Queen of Scots	1542–1567
James VI	1567–1625

RULERS OF GREAT BRITAIN

House of Stuart

James I and VI	1603–1625
Charles I	1625–1649

Commonwealth

Oliver Cromwell	1649–1653
(chairman, Council of State)	
Oliver Cromwell (Lord Protector)	1653–1658
Richard Cromwell	1658–1659
(Lord Protector)	

House of Stuart

Charles II	1660–1685
James II	1685–1688
William III (joint ruler with Mary)	1689–1702
Mary II	1689–1694
Anne	1702–1714

House of Hanover

George I	1714–1727
George II	1727–1760
George III	1760–1820
George IV	1820–1830
(Prince Regent 1811–1820)	
William IV	1830–1837
Victoria	1837–1901

House of Saxe-Coburg-Gotha

Edward VII	1901–1910

House of Windsor

George V	1910–1936
Edward VIII	1936
George VI	1936–1952
Elizabeth II	1952–

DANISH MONARCHS SINCE 1808

Frederik VI	1808–1839
Christian VIII	1839–1848
Frederik VII	1848–1863
Christian IX	1863–1906
Frederik VIII	1906–1912
Christian X	1912–1947
Frederik IX	1947–1972
Margrethe II	1972–

FRENCH KINGS SINCE 987

(Before this date the kings of France were rulers of various lands, and some of them were German emperors.)

Hugh Capet	987–996
Robert II	996–1031
Henri I	1031–1060
Philippe I	1060–1108
Louis VI (the Fat)	1108–1137
Louis VII (the Young)	1137–1180
Philippe II	1180–1223
Louis VIII	1223–1226
Louis IX (St Louis)	1226–1270
Philippe III (the Bold)	1270–1285
Philippe IV (the Fair)	1285–1314
Louis X	1314–1316
Jean I	1316
Philippe V	1316–1322
Charles IV	1322–1328
Philippe VI	1328–1350
Jean II	1350–1364
Charles V	1364–1380
Charles VI	1380–1422
Charles VII	1422–1461
Louis XI	1461–1483
Charles VIII	1483–1498
Louis XII	1498–1515
François I	1515–1547
Henri II	1547–1559
François II	1559–1560
Charles IX	1560–1574
Henri III	1574–1589
Henri IV	1589–1610
Louis XIII	1610–1643
Louis XIV	1643–1715
Louis XV	1715–1774
Louis XVI	1774–1792
The First Republic	1792–1804
Napoleon I (Emperor)	1804–1814
Louis XVIII	1814–1824
Charles X	1824–1830
Louis Philippe	1830–1848
The Second Republic	1848–1852
Napoleon III (Emperor)	1852–1870
The Third Republic	1870–1940
(Vichy Régime)	1940–1945
The Fourth Republic	1944–1958
The Fifth Republic	1958–

MONARCHS OF THE NETHERLANDS

Willem I	1815–1840
Willem II	1840–1849
Willem III	1849–1890
Wilhelmina	1890–1948
Juliana	1948–1980
Beatrix	1980–

Kingdom of the Netherlands became independent in 1815

NORWEGIAN MONARCHS SINCE 1905

Haakon VII	1905–1951
Olav V	1951–1991
Harald V	1991–

Danish kings ruled Norway from 1450, and Swedish kings from 1814

SPANISH RULERS SINCE 1874

Alfonso XII	1874–1885
Maria Cristina	1885–1886
Alfonso XIII	1886–1931
Republic	1931–1947
Francisco Franco, Caudillo and Chief of State	1936–1975
Juan Carlos	1975–

SWEDISH RULERS SINCE 1818

Carl XIV Johan (Jean-Baptiste Bernadotte)	1818–1844
Oscar I	1844–1859
Carl XV	1859–1872
Oscar II	1872–1907
Gustav V	1907–1973
Carl XVI Gustav	1973–

Index

Page numbers in **bold** refer to main entries.

Acknowledgments

The publishers wish to thank the following for supplying photographs for this book:

Page 9 (TL) Bridgeman Art Library; 11 (CR) (AFF/AFS Amsterdam, the Netherlands, (BR) Mary Evans Picture Library; 13 (BR) Rex Features; 17 (BR) The Stock Market; 19 (BR) AKG London; 20 (TR) Novosti; 24-25 (C) The Stock Market; 27 (BL) The Stock Market; 28 (CL) Dover Publication; 31 (CL) AKG London; 32-33 (C) ET Archive; 34 (BR) AKG London; 36 (BL) AKG London; 38 (TL) AKG London, 38 (CB) ET Archive; 43 (TL) ET Archive; 49 (TL) Dover Publications; 50-51 (CT) AKG London; 51 (C) MacQuitty International Collection; 52 (BL) ET Archive 53 (BR) Skyscan Photo Library; 54 (BL) AKG London; 56-57 (CB) Dover Publications; 60 (BL) Robert Harding Picture Library; 64 (TR) ET Archive; 67 (B) ETArchive; 68-69 (C) Rex Features; 70 (B) ET Archive; 73 (CR) AKG London; 74-75 (C) ET Archive; 75 (BR) AKG London; 82-83 (C) Bridgeman Art Library; 91 (CT) AKG London; 98-99 (C) ET Archive; 106-107 (C) Mary Evans Picture Libary; 107 (CB) ET Archive; 111 (BL) AKG London; 114-115 (CB) AKG London; 115 (CB) AKG London; 117 (CR) Robert Harding Picture Library; 118 (CL) AKG London; 118-119 (BC) ET Archive; 120 (CR) AKG London; 121 (BR) ET Archive; 122-123 (TC) AKG London; 127 (C) Bridgeman Art Library; 132 (BL) AKG London; 133 (TR) AKG London; 148 (C) ET Archive; 149 (BR) ET Archive; 150 (BR) ET Archive; 154-155 (CB) AKG London; 155 (CR) AKG London; 160-161 (C) ET Archive; 164 (B) AKG London; 165 (B) AKG London; 170 (TL) ILN, (BL) ET Archive; 170-171 (C) ET Archive; 171 (CB) ILN; 172 (TR) ILN; 173 (C) ILN; 177 (C) ILN; 177 (C) ILN; 179 (TC) AKG London; 180 (TL) ILN; 182 (BL) ILN; 183 (TR) ILN; 186 (TR) ILN; 187 (C) ILN; 188-189 (C) ILN; 189 (CL) ILN; 188-189 (B) ILN; 189 (C) ILN; 190-191 (C) ILN; 191 (CR) ILN; 194-195 (C) Corbis; 196 (TL), (CL) ILN; 197 (CR) ILN; 199 (CL) ILN; 201 (C) ILN; 202 (BL) ET Archive, (TR) ILN; 205 (TC), (CR) ILN; 206 (CL), (CR) ILN; 206-207 (CT) ILN; 207 (CR) ILN; 208 (TR) ILN; 207 (CR) ILN; 210-211 (C) Rex Features; 211 (BC) ILN, (BR) Rex Features; 213 (BR) The Stock Market; 214 (BL) Rex Features; 215 (BR) Rex Features; 217 (CR) Rex Features, (CL) Panos Pictures; 219 (CL), (CR) Rex Features; 220 (BL) ET Archive; 220-221 (BC) Panos Pictures; 222-223 (CB) Panos Pictures; 223 (TL) Rex Features; 225 (C) Panos Pictures; 227 (C), (BR) Rex Features, (BL) Panos Pictures; 228 (CL) The Stock Market, (TL) Panos Pictures; 228-229 (C) Rex Features.

All other photographs from Miles Kelly Archives.